THE USBORNE NATURE TRAIL BOOK

CONTENTS

Birdwatching	**3**
Trees and leaves	**34**
Wild flowers	**66**
Garden wildlife	**98**
Insect watching	**130**
Ponds and streams	**162**
Index	**192**

Malcolm Hart, Ingrid Selberg, Margaret Stephens,
Su Swallow, Sue Tarsky, Ruth Thomson

Consultant editors: Peter Holden, Sally Heathcote, Chris Humphries, Alfred Leutscher BSc, Jean Mellanby,
E. H. M. Harris, Michael Chinery, Denis Owen, Alwyne Wheeler, Anthony Wootton
Additional advice from Peter Holden, Chris Humphries and Alfred Leutscher

Designed by Amanda Barlow, Sally Burrough, Nick Eddison, Niki Overy, Diane Thistlethwaite, Robert Walster
Design revision by Non Figg, Julia Rheam, Diane Thistlewaite, Robert Walster and Kathy Ward

Edited by Bridget Gibbs, Helen Gilks, Sue Jacquemier, Ingrid Selberg
Editorial revision by Rachael Swann

If you are walking along a seashore, rambling in the countryside or sitting in a city garden, you can always find birds. This section of the book will help you to identify them and give you lots of information about their habits.

When you go bird spotting take this book with you and turn to the pages which deal with the kind of place you are visiting, such as a wood or pond. Pages 28-31 will give you extra help by showing you the size of certain birds.

Bluetit

The birds on these pages are not drawn to scale

Nuthatch

Chaffinch

BIRDWATCHING

Contents

How to be a birdwatcher   4
What to look for   6
Clues and tracks   8
Making a bird garden   10
Making a nesting box   12
The nesting season   14

Places to look for birds
Ponds and inland waterways   16
Woodlands and forests   18
Towns and cities   20

Sea coasts   22
Moors and mountains   24
Migrating birds   26

Identifying birds by size
Sparrow-sized and
  Blackbird-sized birds   28
Crow-sized and
  Mallard-sized birds   30
Large water birds   31
Birds in flight   32

Siskin

Stonechat

How to be a birdwatcher

The most important thing to have when you go birdwatching is a notebook. If you try and keep all the facts in your head, you will probably forget some of the important ones.

Make sure any notes you make are clear and readable. The picture on the right shows how to set your notebook out. Try to draw the birds you see. Even a bad drawing is better than no drawing at all.

Notes on shape, size, colour and flight pattern will be important later, if you need to identify a bird.

A birdwatcher has to take notes quickly. Use a spiralbound notebook, like the one here. It has a stiff back to help you write easily. File your notes away in date order when you get home or write them up into a neat book. When you are out, put your notebook in a plastic bag to keep it dry.

Look carefully for the shape and obvious marks first. The male Reed Bunting here has a sparrow-like body and beak, a dark head, white collar and white outer tail feathers. It also has a dark throat and dark flecks on its side.

Male Reed Bunting

Black head
White collar
Grey-white underneath
Also F carrying grass (for * ?)
Flight Pattern

2nd August 1991
Weather - Sunny
Clare Park
M Reed Bunting
Dark Brown streaked back

Make sure you have all the details of place, date, time of day and weather entered in your notebook.

Bird shorthand

M = MALE
F = FEMALE
JUV = JUVENILE (YOUNG BIRD NOT IN ADULT FEATHERS)
* = NEST
C10 = ABOUT TEN (WHEN TALKING ABOUT NUMBERS OF BIRDS)

Use these signs instead of writing out the words. It will save you time. Always take two pens or pencils with you.

How to stalk birds

In the countryside there is plenty of opportunity to see many types of birds. When you go birdwatching camouflage your shape by standing in front of or behind a tree or bush. Keep the sun behind you, so you are in shadow. If there is no cover, crawl closer using your elbows and feet. Don't wear clothes that rustle when you move. Never move quickly in the open.

Green Woodpecker
Willow Warbler
Woodcock

What to wear

Travel as light as possible. Remember to wear dull colours.

Hat or hood.

Anorak or warm coat.

Wellingtons if wet. Trainers at all other times.

Notebook and pencils.

Buying binoculars

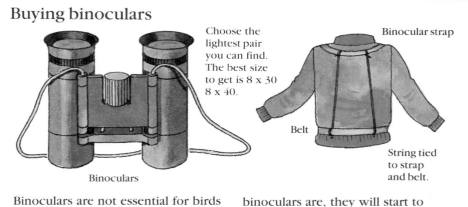

Choose the lightest pair you can find. The best size to get is 8 x 30 8 x 40.

Binocular strap

Belt

String tied to strap and belt.

Binoculars

Binoculars are not essential for birds in the garden or park. But if you want some, go shopping with a person who knows about binoculars. However light your binoculars are, they will start to feel heavy after a while. To take the weight off your neck, you can tie some string onto the strap as shown here.

Quick field sketches

1 Two circles for head and body.

2 Add beak, neck, tail and legs.

3 Add details of feathers.

The best way to make notes on the birds you see is to draw quick sketches of them. Begin by drawing two circles - one for the body and one for the head.

Notice the size and position of the head and body before you start. Add the tail, beak, legs and then add details of feathers if you have time. Do not draw what you do not see. Practise by drawing the birds you can see from your window or sit on a bench in the park and draw the birds there.

Remember to use your ears as well as your eyes. Birdsong is very important when you go birdwatching. It is often the first clue to tell you that a bird is near. The Jay, pictured here, has a very raucous call . Other sounds can give you clues too. You will often hear a Green Woodpecker drilling a hole in a tree before you see it.

You will not get far loaded with heavy equipment and you will be unable to move easily and quietly. If birds can see your shape silhouetted against the sky, they will fly off.

Chaffinch

Nuthatch

Jay

Chaffinch

What to look for

These pages tell you what to look for when you want to identify a bird.

When you see a bird for the first time, there are several questions you should ask. What size is it? Has it any obvious marks, such as the Reed Bunting's black head and white outer tail feathers? How does it fly and feed? How does it behave? Where is it? What colour is it?

Sometimes differences in colour can be confusing. There are some examples of this on the page opposite.

This is a female Sparrowhawk chasing a male Reed Bunting. The labels give examples of the kind of thing to note down when you see a bird.

Rounded wings with slight "fingers".

Hooked beak

Long tail with dark bars.

Yellow legs

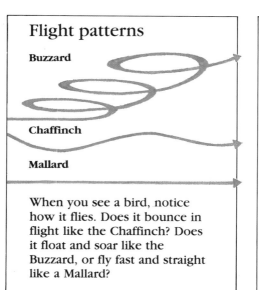

Black head

White collar

White outer tail feathers.

Flight patterns

Buzzard

Chaffinch

Mallard

When you see a bird, notice how it flies. Does it bounce in flight like the Chaffinch? Does it float and soar like the Buzzard, or fly fast and straight like a Mallard?

Shapes in flight

Tern

Heron

Crow

Goose

Magpie

Curlew

Woodpecker

What sort of shapes does a bird make when it is flying? Are the neck and tail long or short?

Has it got short rounded wings or long narrow ones? Do its feet stick out behind its tail?

Sex differences

Male

Female

Blackbirds

The males of some birds, such as the Blackbird, have different coloured feathers and beaks from the females.

Colour changes

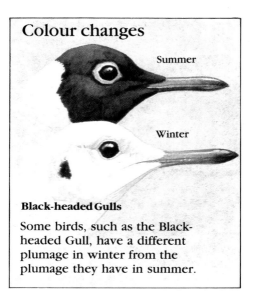

Summer

Winter

Black-headed Gulls

Some birds, such as the Black-headed Gull, have a different plumage in winter from the plumage they have in summer.

Age differences

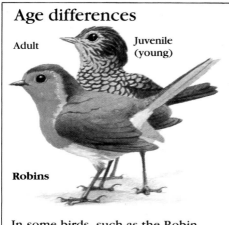

Adult

Juvenile (young)

Robins

In some birds, such as the Robin, the young look very different from their parents.

Looking at beaks

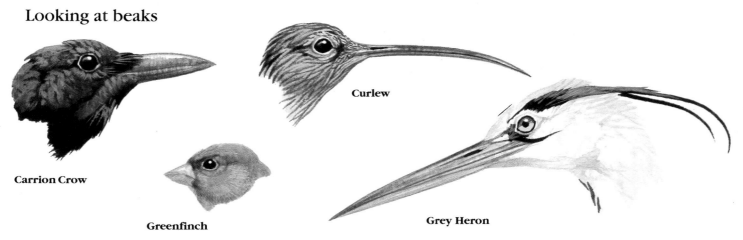

Carrion Crow

Greenfinch

Curlew

Grey Heron

Beaks can give you clues to what a bird eats. The Carrion Crow's beak is an all-purpose tool. The Greenfinch's beak is more suited to eating seeds.

The Curlew uses its long beak to probe for food in mud. The Grey Heron's beak is even longer and is used to catch fish, frogs and insects.

One way to identify a bird is from its song. Go out with someone who knows birdsong well, or borrow records of birdsong from your library

Watch what birds are doing

Grey Wagtail

Treecreeper

Turnstone

The Grey Wagtail often patrols in mud or short grass. It wags its tail up and down. Sometimes it makes a dash after an insect.

The Treecreeper creeps up the trunk of a tree, picking out insects from cracks in the bark with its thin, curved bill.

The Turnstone walks along the beach turning over seaweed and stones, looking for small creatures, such as shellfish, to eat.

Clues and tracks

Sometimes you may not be able to see all the birds that live in an area. Even if you don't see them, special clues can tell you they are present. Some of these clues are easy to spot, such as feathers and the remains of meals.

You may not be able to identify the feathers you find straight away. But later you may see a dead bird, or a bird in a book, that has feathers like the ones you have collected. Remember that most birds have feathers of many different sizes and colours.

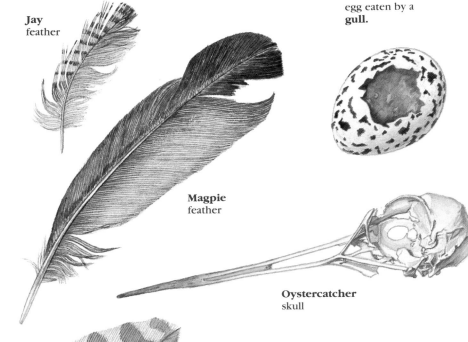

Jay
feather

Magpie
feather

Sandwich Tern
egg eaten by a
gull.

Oystercatcher
skull

Jackdaw
pellet

Sparrowhawk
pellet

Pine cone
nibbled by
a **squirrel.**

Curlew
feather

Hazelnut pecked at
by a **Great Tit.**

Hazelnut pecked at
by a **Woodpecker.**

Always make sure you have something to keep the objects in that you collect. Label everything carefully with lots of detail - the more information the better. Always wash your hands after touching things you have collected.

When you find the remains of nuts and pinecones that have been nibbled, remember that it may not have been a bird. Squirrels and mice eat these as well. So, be careful when you identify the nibbler.

Collecting feathers and wings

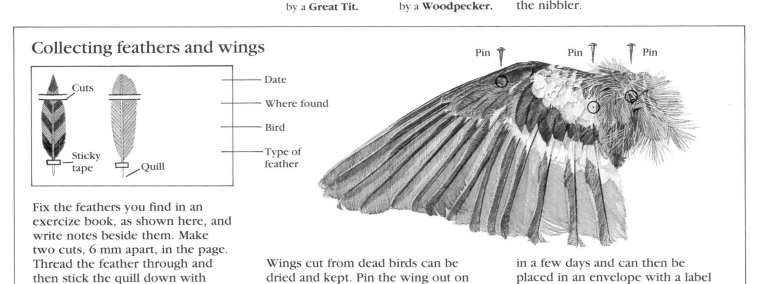

Cuts

Sticky
tape

Quill

Date

Where found

Bird

Type of
feather

Pin   Pin   Pin

Fix the feathers you find in an exercize book, as shown here, and write notes beside them. Make two cuts, 6 mm apart, in the page. Thread the feather through and then stick the quill down with sticky tape.

Wings cut from dead birds can be dried and kept. Pin the wing out on a piece of stiff board. It should dry

in a few days and can then be placed in an envelope with a label and some mothballs.

Pinecones

Squirrel　　**Crossbill**　　**Woodpecker**

Here are three examples of pinecones that have been nibbled by birds or animals. They break open the cones in different ways as they search for seeds to eat.

Nuts

Nuthatch (Hazelnut)　　**Hawfinch** (Cherry)

Woodmouse (Hazelnut)　　**Great Tit** (Walnut)

Animals all have their own ways of opening nuts. Mice chew neat little holes, while some birds leave jagged holes and others split the nuts in half.

The Song Thrush's anvil

Snail shell

Broken shells

Anvil

Song Thrushes use a stone like an anvil to break open snail shells. Look for the anvil - it will be surrounded by the remains of the bird's meal.

Owl pellets

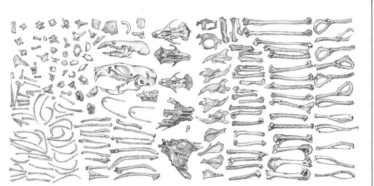

Contents of one owl pellet.

Owls swallow small animals and birds whole, and then cough up the fur, feathers and bones as a pellet. You can find these beneath trees or posts where the owl rests. Pull a pellet apart and sort out the bones. The easiest bones to identify are the skulls of animals the owl has eaten.

Other pellets

Black-headed Gull

Carrion Crow

Heron

Many other birds cough up pellets. But it is harder to identify what is inside them, as most birds do not eat large animals.

Footprint casts

Water

Plaster of Paris

Bird footprint

Ring of cardboard.

Put the cardboard around the footprint. Mix the plaster in the cup and pour it into the ring. Let it harden for 15 minutes. Take the cast and its cardboard home.

Pour in plaster mixed with water.

To make plaster casts you will need water, plaster of Paris, a plastic cup or glass and a strip of cardboard bent into a ring, and fastened with a paperclip.

Paint when plaster cast is set.

Wash off any dirt. Leave the cast for a few more days to dry thoroughly and then carefully remove it from the cardboard. Paint the footprint and then varnish it.

Making a bird garden

On these pages you can see many of the birds that visit gardens or window sills for food. Different kinds of food attract different birds. Put out bones, suet, cheese, oats, peanuts, currants and bits of bacon rind. Scatter some food in the open though for birds that prefer to eat on the ground. A good way of attracting birds is by building a bird bath and a bird table for your garden.

Putting out food

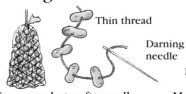

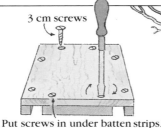

Thin thread

Darning needle

Matchstick

Yogurt pot

Melt the fat in a warm oven.

Supermarkets often sell vegetables in nets. Fill one of these with unsalted peanuts, or thread peanuts in their shells on thread or thin string, and hang them up in the garden.

Make a feeding bell with a yogurt pot. Fill the pot with breadcrumbs, currants, cooked potato and oatmeal. Ask an adult to help you melt some fat.

Let it cool and then pour it on the mixture. Wait until it hardens and then pull some thread through it as shown in the picture. Hang it upside down with the thread.

Make a bird table

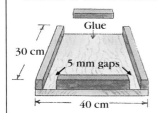

Glue

30 cm

5 mm gaps

40 cm

3 cm screws

Put screws in under batten strips.

Gaps let rain water drain off.

You will need a piece of outdoor quality plywood about 40 cm x 30 cm and four strips of batten about 30 cm long. Glue the battens to the plywood as shown above.

When the glue has dried, turn the table over and put in two screws on every side, as shown above. Protect your table with a wood preservative and screw it to a wooden box.

To make a hanging table, put four screw-eyes into the sides and use string to hang it from a branch, as shown above. Clean the table regularly with disinfectant.

Make a bird bath

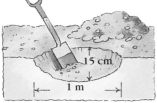

15 cm

1 m

Make sure the polythene has no holes.

Choose a place not too close to the feeding area you have set up. Dig a hole with sloping sides, about 15 cm deep and 1 m wide. Dig from the middle out.

Line the hole with strong polythene (a dustbin liner will do). Weight the polythene down with stones and sprinkle gravel or sand over the lining.

Put a few stones and a short branch in the middle to make a perch. Fill the bath with water. Keep it full and make sure it is free from ice in winter.

Feeding chart

Make a chart of the kinds of food you see different birds eating. Which birds like nuts best? Tick the boxes each time you see a bird eat something.

	CHEESE	BACON	NUTS
BLUE TIT	✓	|||	||||
ROBIN			
STARLING			
BLACK-BIRD			

Soon you will know which foods are popular and can make sure they are always in the garden.

Key to birds
1   Greenfinch
2   House Sparrow
3   Blue Tit
4   Robin
5   Coal Tit
6   Starling
7   Chaffinch
8   Blackbird
9   Mistle Thrush
10   Goldfinch
11   Song Thrush
12   Dunnock
13   Bullfinch

7

8 Female

10

10

7 Male

Plants that birds like to eat

Ivy

Shepherd's Purse

Thistle

Wild grasses

Rowan

Groundsel

Elder

Hawthorn

Cotoneaster

All these plants are good bird food. If you have a garden, try to let a little patch grow wild. Weeds, such as Groundsel, have seeds that birds like to eat. Trees and bushes, such as Rowan, have lots of good berries in the autumn. Some birds like over-ripe apples and sultanas. Dig over a patch of earth, so you make it easier for some birds to find worms and insects.

9

9

1

2 Male

4

3

3

5

2 Female
2 Male

1

3

3

12

6

1

7 Female

8 Male

4

7 Male

13 Male

2 Female

13 Female

11

12

6

Making a nesting box

Encourage birds to visit your garden in spring by building a nesting box. If the entrance hole is small then a Blue Tit will probably nest there. If the hole is larger then you may find a House Sparrow using it.

Other birds, such as Great Tits, Starlings, Tree Sparrows and Wrens, sometimes use nesting boxes. Try not to go close up to the box if birds are nesting there, as you will frighten them away. You can always watch them from indoors.

Side removed to show how box is made.

To make your nesting box you will need some plywood that is 12 mm thick with an overall length of 900 mm and width of 254 mm.

How to cut the wood

A Back	B Front	C Base	Waste

| 241 D Side 102 254 | 254 E Side 102 241 | Top F | G H | Waste |

J Main support

Battens

First cut the pieces in these sizes

A 254 mm x 127 mm
B 241 mm x 127 mm
C 127 mm x 127 mm
D See diagram
E See diagram
F 152 mm x 127 mm
G 102 mm x 25 mm
H 102 mm x 25 mm
J 510 mm x 25 mm

Drill the entrance hole with a hand drill about 50 mm from the top of the front section. The hole should be 25 mm wide.

50 mm
25 mm

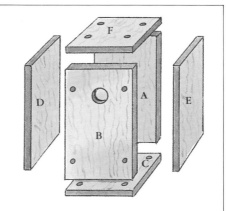

First arrange all the pieces to make sure that they fit together properly. Then drill holes for all the screws.

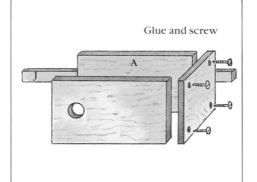

Glue and screw

Fix the main support onto the back with two screws. Glue and screw the bottom onto the back and then the front.

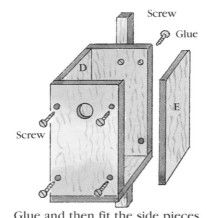

Screw
Glue
Screw

Glue and then fit the side pieces into place. Screw them on if they fit properly. If they don't, check the measurements carefully.

Where to put the box

Your completed nesting box should be fixed to a tree trunk or to a wall that is covered with a climbing plant, such as ivy. If there is no climbing plant, a bare wall or tree trunk will do. The entrance hole should not face south or west as the heat from direct sunlight might kill the young birds. Fix it about 2 m or more above the ground, well away from cats. Every winter, take it down and empty out the old nest. Disinfect the box and give it a new coat of wood preservative before replacing it.

2 m

Box must face north or east.

Other types of box

Special nesting boxes can be bought for House Martins. You can fix them under the edge of the roof.

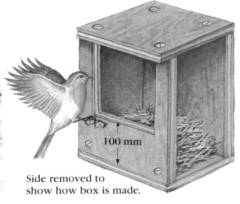

Side removed to show how box is made.

100 mm

An open-fronted box is good for other birds. Make it like the first box, but cut an opening as shown in the picture above.

Keeping a record

Try to make a note of what happens in your nesting box. If a bird nests in the box there will be many details to record throughout the spring and summer.

You may even see some birds visiting the box in winter. They use boxes to sleep in. The notes below tell you the sort of thing to record.

1 Date of first visit.
2 Number of birds visiting.
3 Date bird first enters box.
4 Date birds bring nest material.
5 Type of nest material.
6 Date birds first bring food.
7 Type of food.
8 Date young leave nest.

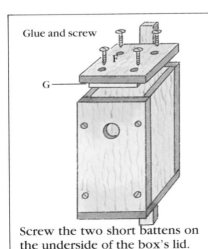

Glue and screw

F

G

Screw the two short battens on the underside of the box's lid. Make sure the removable lid fits tightly and securely.

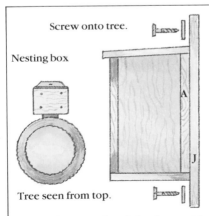

Screw onto tree.

Nesting box

A

J

Tree seen from top.

Paint the outside of the box with wood preservative and let it dry. Screw or nail it on to a tree (see above).

BLACKBIRD
First visit Feb 22nd
2 birds
First entered box
23rd Feb.
Nesting material
March 1st.

The nesting season

The nesting season is a time of great activity for all birds. First they must find a mate and then start looking for a place to build a nest and feed. The spot they choose becomes their territory. Next they lay their eggs and rear their young.

With all this going on it is not difficult to find out where some birds are building a nest or feeding their young. A bird carrying something in its beak, such as worms or grass, is the most common sign. On these pages you will find some more clues to help you.

A parent Song Thrush arrives at the nest. The young birds beg for food with wide open mouths. The parent puts food into their mouths and then flies off on another food-hunting expedition.

Food chart

Make a food chart to record which birds you see carrying food to their young, and record the type of food.

	WORMS	SNAILS	INSECTS
BLACK-BIRD			
ROBIN			
SONG THRUSH			

Remember - it is against the law to disturb breeding birds or their nests and eggs. Always watch from a distance.

Spotting nesting birds

Rook

Nightingale

Droppings

Stonechat

In the spring, you will often see birds carrying nest material in their beaks. Rooks break off large twigs to make their nests.

Look out and listen for a bird singing in the same place every day during spring and summer, such as the Nightingale. It is probably breeding.

You may see adult birds carrying droppings away from the nest in their beaks. They do this to keep the nest clean for their young.

Nest materials

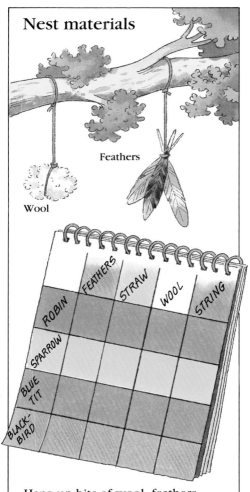

Feathers

Wool

	FEATHERS	STRAW	WOOL	STRING
ROBIN				
SPARROW				
BLUE TIT				
BLACK-BIRD				

Hang up bits of wool, feathers, straw and string from a tree. Make a note of what different materials birds collect to use for their nests.

Where birds nest

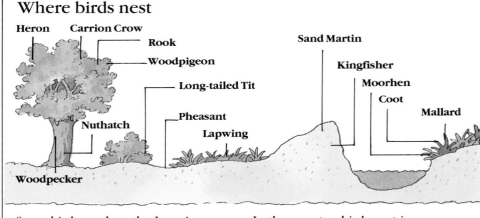

Heron Carrion Crow Rook Woodpigeon Long-tailed Tit Nuthatch Pheasant Lapwing Woodpecker Sand Martin Kingfisher Moorhen Coot Mallard

Some birds, such as the Lapwing, make hardly any nest at all. They lay their eggs in a shallow hollow in the ground.

In the country, birds nest in many different places. They use trees and hedges, the shelter of steep banks and holes in trees.

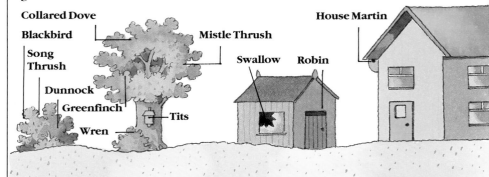

Collared Dove Blackbird Song Thrush Dunnock Greenfinch Wren Mistle Thrush Tits Swallow Robin House Martin

Many birds nest in gardens, but only in sheltered places safe from cats and dogs. They use thick bushes, trees, ivy-covered walls and sheds,

as well as nesting boxes. Other birds, such as the House Martin, build under the roof, and Barn Owls can nest on a ledge in an old barn.

Ponds and inland waterways

Ducks are the birds you are most likely to see on a pond. They have quite long necks, webbed feet and wide, flat bills. They are all good swimmers. Most ducks feed on water plants in the pond.

Ducks can be divided into three kinds. There are diving ducks, such as the Tufted Duck, and dabblers, such as the Mallard. The most rare are the fish-eating ducks called sawbills.

In spring and summer, you will often see ducklings trailing behind their parents on the water's surface, or even hitching a piggy-back ride.

Swimming

Shoveler Coot Moorhen

Webbed feet are best for swimming. The web opens to push hard against the water. When the foot comes back. the web closes so that the foot does not drag through the water.

Coots and Moorhens spend more time on land. Coots' feet are partly webbed. Moorhens have hardly any webbing. Their heads jerk backwards and forwards when the birds swim.

New ducklings are taken to the water by their mother. The ducklings fall in and can swim straight away.

Male and female Mallards have a blue flash on each wing called a speculum.

Great Crested Grebes are fish eaters. The male and female both look after their chicks, carrying them on their backs.

Female Mallard

Male Mallard

Long, flat bills are useful to sift food.

How water birds feed

Swallow catching insects over the water.

Pintail up-ending.

Kingfisher diving for fish.

Wigeon grazing on land.

Moorhen feeding in reeds by the water.

Grey Heron fishing on the edge of the pond.

Mallard dabbling on the surface.

Mute Swan fishing with head and neck under water.

Tufted Duck diving.

Watch how different kinds of birds feed on your local pond. Which birds up-end the most? Which dabble the most? Which dive the most? Why is it do you think that some kinds feed differently from others?

Taking off and landing

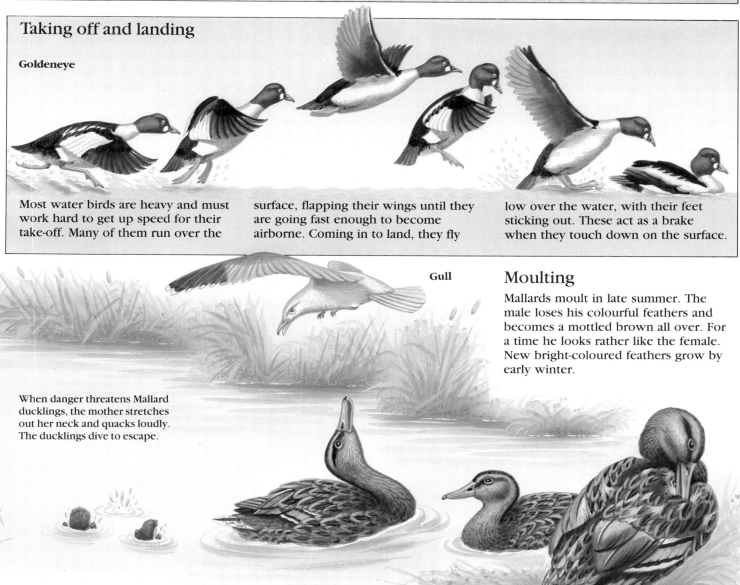

Goldeneye

Most water birds are heavy and must work hard to get up speed for their take-off. Many of them run over the surface, flapping their wings until they are going fast enough to become airborne. Coming in to land, they fly low over the water, with their feet sticking out. These act as a brake when they touch down on the surface.

Gull

Moulting

Mallards moult in late summer. The male loses his colourful feathers and becomes a mottled brown all over. For a time he looks rather like the female. New bright-coloured feathers grow by early winter.

When danger threatens Mallard ducklings, the mother stretches out her neck and quacks loudly. The ducklings dive to escape.

Woodlands and forests

Woodlands and forests are good places to spot birds, but you will see them more easily in places that are not too dark. Woods with open spaces are lighter and have more plants and insects for birds to eat.

Woods with broad-leaved trees, such as oak and beech, contain many more birds than old pine forests, which can be very dark. But old pine forests can have special birds, such as Capercaillies, that can be found nowhere else.

The **Nightingale** (16.5 cm) can often be heard singing in woods and forests, but is rarely seen. It builds its nest among trees and bushes close to the ground.

The sizes given are beak-to-tail measurements.

If it is windy, watch out for falling branches in the woods. Try not to stand or sit near trees which have nests in them. You might frighten away the parent birds.

The **Goldcrest** (9 cm) is the smallest European bird. It is often found in coniferous or mixed woods all year round.

The **Coal Tit** (11.5 cm) is the same size as a Blue Tit. It nests in coniferous forests.

The **Chaffinch** (15 cm) is a common bird, often found in broad-leaved woodlands and coniferous woods. In winter it prefers to live in open land.

The **Chiffchaff** (11 cm) is smaller than a sparrow and visits Europe from Africa during the summer. It is often found in broad-leaved woods and in young pine plantations.

The food of woodland birds

The Tawny Owl feeds on small animals. Its eyesight and hearing are very good.

In autumn, Jays collect acorns. They bury many of them and then dig them up when they need food.

Many birds, such as the Garden Warbler here, feed on caterpillars.

Special beaks

Some birds, such as the Hawfinch and the Crossbill, have special beaks for eating seeds.

The Pied Fly Catcher swoops down on insects from a look-out branch.

Jay

Hawfinch   Crossbill

The **Black Woodpecker** (46 cm) is the largest European woodpecker. It is found mainly in coniferous forests in many parts of Europe, but not in Britain.

Holes in trees

Mud plastered by Nuthatch.

Hole used by a Nuthatch.

Hole used by a woodpecker.

Woodpecker holes

4 cm	4.5 cm	6.5 cm	10 cm
Lesser Spotted	Great Spotted	Green	Black

The different kinds of woodpecker all make nesting holes in trees. These are sometimes used by other birds, such as the Nuthatch, or even bats and dormice.

The **Nuthatch** (14 cm) feeds on nuts from hazel, beech and oak trees.

The **Green Woodpecker** (32 cm) is the same size as a pigeon. It is frequently seen on the ground, feeding on ants, and is usually found in broad-leaved woodlands.

The **Woodcock** (34 cm) is found in broad-leaved woodlands where its plumage blends in perfectly with the dead leaves on the ground. It has a long, thin beak.

The **Lesser Spotted Woodpecker** (14.5 cm) is the smallest European woodpecker. It is found in broad-leaved woods. The male bird has a bright red crown.

Woodlands at night

There are many different kinds of owl living in woods. They range in size from the small Pygmy Owl, which is only 16.5 cm high, to the

These three owls are all drawn to the same scale.

much bigger Eagle Owl, which can be as large as 71 cm.

These four owls are all drawn to the same scale.

The Nightjar sleeps during the day, so is rarely seen. Its song can be heard after dark in summer.

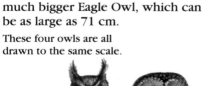

Nightjar

Pygmy Owl   **Scops Owl**   **Little Owl**

Little Owl   **Long-eared Owl**   **Tawny Owl**   **Eagle Owl**

Towns and cities

Bird spotting in towns and cities can be just as rewarding as in the countryside. In densely built up areas, you may only see Pigeons, Starlings and House Sparrows. Where there are gardens and parks you will find many other kinds of birds.

Some of these birds are quite used to people and can be very tame. You may even be able to get quite close to them and tempt them to feed from your hand. The pictures here show some of the most common birds in towns and cities.

The **Kestrel** is a town as well as a country bird. The town Kestrel usually feeds on sparrows, and nests high up on the tops of buildings.

Cliff birds that live in towns

Black Redstart

Black Redstarts once nested on sea-cliffs and rocks. Now you are more likely to find them in towns. They make their nests on buildings.

The **Long-tailed Tit** is a hedge bird that can often be seen in parks and gardens. In autumn and winter, family groups of about a dozen gather together.

The **Black-headed Gull** is one of the commonest town gulls. You will often see large numbers of them near reservoirs and gravel pits and in large grassy areas.

You will sometimes hear the warbling song of the **Skylark** as it flies above parks and wasteland. In winter, you may see flocks around gravel pits and reservoirs.

You will never see a **Swift** on the ground or on a wire. It feeds and even sleeps on the wing. At dusk, Swifts circle high above the roof-tops.

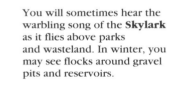

1
Towns and cities are surprisingly good places to look for birds. Birds need food and a place to rest and sleep. Most gardens (3) and parks (2) have

2
some trees and bushes where birds can nest and sleep without being disturbed by people. Many birds find perching places on buildings (5). Gulls fly out to

3
sleep at gravel pits (1) or reservoirs (4). Everywhere people spill or leave food which birds can eat. On the edge of town, birds find lots of food at sewage

Rock Dove

Pigeons

The town Pigeon is a relation of the Rock Dove, which nests on sea-cliffs. The town Pigeon is now much more common than the Rock Dove and is often very tame. It feeds on bread and any other scraps it finds in parks or in the streets, and can be a nuisance in city centres.

Starling

Starlings are one of the most common city birds. They are usually found in huge, noisy flocks.

House Martins build their mud nests under the roofs of many town houses.

White patch only on House Martin.

Swallows look rather like House Martins, but have longer tail feathers. You can often see them catching flies over rivers, gravel pits and reservoirs.

Carrion Crows are quite common in parks and gardens.

Magpies are large black and white birds and are common in parks and gardens. They use twigs to build their nests in tress and tall hedges.

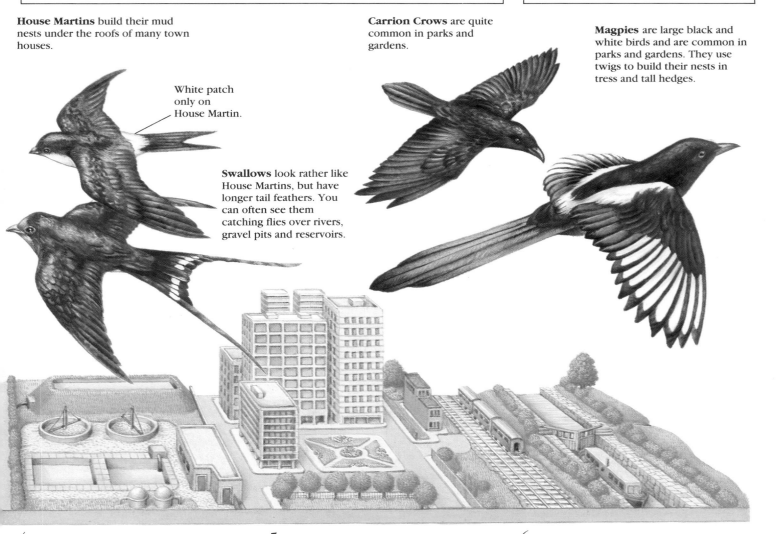

4
works (4) and rubbish dumps (1). Railway sidings and canals (6), where food supplies are unloaded and often spilt, are also good feeding spots for

5
birds, and have fewer people to disturb them. Many birds eat the seeds of weeds growing on waste ground and building sites. In winter, when there is

6
little food in the countryside, many birds fly to the towns and cities. There many people put out food specially for the birds.

Sea coasts

The coast is always a good place to spot birds. In summer, many birds fly from Africa and the Antarctic to breed on European coasts. In winter, small wading birds, such as the Knot, come from the north to feed and wait for spring.

Most of the cliff-nesting birds spend the winter far out at sea. Every year many birds lose their eggs and babies because people tread on the nests or stop the parent birds from feeding the young by frightening them away.

Nesting places

In winter, cliffs are almost deserted, but during the breeding season, they are like large bird cities. The whole cliff is used for nesting. Each type of bird has its favourite spot for nesting.

Waders' beaks

Birds can find much food on the beach. The shape of a wading bird's beak depends on the sort of food it eats. You can try to find out what the birds are eating by digging up the sand and looking for the food in it.

Avocet sifts for food.

Curlew probes deeply.

Dunlin picks food on and under the surface.

Oystercatcher feeds on shellfish.

The **Brent Goose** is a rare winter visitor from Greenland and northern Russia where it breeds. It feeds on a plant called Eelgrass, which grows only on mudflats.

Brent Goose

Knot
(summer plumage)

In winter, large flocks of **Knots** fly south from their northern breeding grounds. They feed on sandy or muddy shores. In winter, their plumage is grey.

The **Common Tern** breeds on salt marshes, shingle or sandy shores. It builds its nest in a hollow in the ground.

Shelduck

The **Shelduck** is one of the most common large birds you will see on a salt marsh. Sometimes it builds its nest in an old rabbit burrow.

Salt marsh

Common tern

Sandy shore

Shingle beach

Fish-eaters' beaks

Fish-eating birds do not all have the same kind of beak. The shape of the beak depends on the size and type of fish that the bird eats.

Common Tern

Razorbill

Gannet

The **Fulmar** is a large bird that spends most of its time out at sea. It looks rather like a gull, but holds its wings straighter and stiffer when it is flying.

Fulmar

The **Shag** is smaller than the Cormorant and does not have the Cormorant's white face. In the breeding season, it grows a little curly crest.

The **Cormorant's** feathers are not waterproof, so you will often see it standing on a rock or post holding out its wings to dry.

Gannets make their nests on cliff tops. Gannets nest in large numbers and build their untidy nests about one metre apart from each other.

Gannet

The **Razorbill** lays its one egg in a crack in the cliff or under a rock. The nest is sometimes a few pieces of seaweed, but often there is no proper nest at all.

The **Guillemot** makes no nest. It lays a single pear-shaped egg on a rock ledge. The shape of the egg stops it rolling off. They nest in large numbers.

Cormorant

Puffins use their bills for digging nesting burrows in the cliff top soil. They clear away the soil with their feet.

Puffin

Razorbill

Guillemot

Shag

Cliffs

Moors and mountains

Many of the birds that live on moors and on mountains are well known because they are game-birds, such as Grouse. There are also large and powerful birds of prey, such as the Golden Eagle or Buzzard. You will see fewer birds in these places than at the coast or in woods because there is less food for them to eat. The smaller birds eat bilberries, young shoots of heather and seeds from mosses and grasses. The large birds of prey feed mainly on small birds and other animals.

Every year people get lost on moors and mountains. Make sure it is not you. Never go on your own and always tell someone where you are going. Keep to paths and wear warm clothes.

The birds and mammals on these pages are not drawn to scale.

The **Golden Eagle** is the largest bird that is found on moors and mountains. It is very rare in most parts of Europe.

The **Buzzard** is one of the most common of the large birds of prey. It is similar to the Golden Eagle, but is smaller and stubbier.

The **Short-eared Owl** nests on the ground. It often hunts in the daytime and feeds on small animals, such as voles and lemmings.

The **Meadow Pipit** is the most common small bird that you see on moorland. It feeds on insects.

These two birds look different, but are in fact very closely related. The **Red Grouse** is only found in Britain and the **Willow Grouse** only in Europe. The Willow Grouse is shown here in part of its winter plumage.

Red Grouse

Willow Grouse

Lemming

Changing colour with the seasons

Ptarmigan in summer

Ptarmigan in winter

The Ptarmigan can hide from its enemies because it always looks the same colour as the countryside. In summer, its coat is mainly brown. In winter it turns white. It lives in the mountains of northern Europe.

Shrikes

Shrikes (also known as Butcher Birds) have a habit of pinning insects, mice, lizards and even small birds onto branches or barbed wire. These food "stores" come in handy when fresh food is scarce. The Red-backed Shrike is a rare summer visitor. The Great Grey Shrike breeds in northern Europe and flies south in the winter. They can be seen in hedges, bushes, trees and on wires.

Red-backed Shrike

Great Grey Shrike

Beetle

The **Black Grouse** lives on the borders of moorland. The male (blackcock) has curved tail feathers.

The **Raven** is the largest of the Crow family. It is as big as the Buzzard. The Raven flies slowly but powerfully, and sometimes tumbles through the air.

The **Golden Plover** usually breeds on moors and hills. It lays its four eggs in a nest on the ground.

The **Wheatear** builds its nest in holes in walls and in old rabbit burrows.

The **Dipper** lives by mountain streams. It feeds on insects it catches under water.

The **Ring Ouzel** is a relative of the Blackbird and lives in remote mountain valleys and on moors.

Short-tailed vole

Migrating birds

Every year millions of birds move from one part of the world to another. This is called migration. Many birds come to Europe from southern Africa in April and May. During the southern African winter, which falls in June, July and August, there is not enough food for birds, such as Swallows.

Swallows fly north to breed in Europe where there is enough food. In late August and September they fly south where the summer is just starting. Again, the reason for this migration is to find good supplies of food.

Keep a record of migrant birds. Note down the first and last dates you see them. Also keep a record of the weather in spring and autumn. Does this have an affect on the dates when birds arrive or leave?

The Swallow

1 Swallows spend the winter months in southern Africa, but in March huge flocks start to move northwards to Europe. They come here to breed.

2 There is very little water in the desert, so the Swallows fly across it without stopping. They live off the food and water which they have stored as fat under their skin.

3 One of the most dangerous parts of the journey is crossing the Mediterranean Sea. Many Swallows take the shortest route, across the Straits of Gibraltar.

4 By the end of May most Swallows have arrived and built their nests. In late summer they get ready for the long journey back to southern Africa.

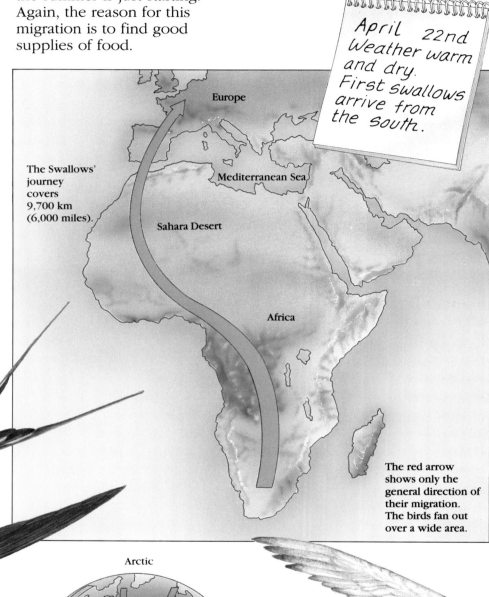

April 22nd
Weather warm and dry.
First swallows arrive from the south.

The Swallows' journey covers 9,700 km (6,000 miles).

Europe

Mediterranean Sea

Sahara Desert

Africa

Arctic

The red arrow shows only the general direction of their migration. The birds fan out over a wide area.

Arctic Tern

Some birds fly even longer distances than the Swallow. One of these is the Arctic Tern. It breeds in the Arctic and then flies south, all the way to the southern tip of South America and southern Africa. During the journey it stays mostly out at sea. These birds nest in large flocks, called terneries. The Arctic Tern shown here is in its summer colour. In autumn, the forehead is white and the bill and legs are blackish.

In some places in Europe, flocks of birds, such as White Storks, can be spotted waiting by the coast for good weather, so they can continue their migration across the sea.

The Redwing is a member of the Thrush family and looks like the Song Thrush but has pink on its sides. It is a winter visitor to Europe, coming from the north and travelling in large flocks.

The Hoopoe, with its parrot-like crest and floppy flight, does not seem capable of flying far, but every autumn it flies to Africa from Europe and makes a return journey in spring.

White Stork

Redwing

Summer visitors
The Blackcap and the Willow Warbler both belong to the warbler family and are two of the most common summer visitors to Europe. They come from Africa. In winter a few Blackcaps stay in Europe.

Willow Warbler

Blackcap

Hoopoe

Starling

Many Starlings fly south in winter and are attracted to bright lights at night, such as lighthouses. Many of them are killed by flying into buildings where they see lights. Starlings are one of the most common birds in towns and cities.

Identifying birds by size

Sparrow-sized birds

The notes for each bird give size from beak to tail. Each panel has birds of a similar size. The dots beside each bird tell you where to look for it.

The birds inside this panel are all drawn to the same scale.

- Water
- Woods
- Towns and gardens
- Fields

Wren. 9 cm. Smallest bird you will see in gardens. Holds its tail cocked over its back.

Goldcrest. 9 cm. Smallest European bird. Feeds on insects and spiders.

Blue Tit. 11.5 cm. Only tit with blue head and wings. One of the most common garden birds.

Treecreeper. 12.5 cm. This mouse-like bird climbs trees.

Nuthatch. 14 cm. Has a sharp straight bill used for cracking open nuts.

Long-tailed Tit. 14 cm. Tail very long. Often seen in small flocks.

Great Tit. 14 cm. Has a black band down its belly.

Coal Tit. 11.5 cm. Has a white stripe on its neck.

Sand Martin. 12 cm. Has brown back and collar. Nests in holes in banks.

House Martin. 12.5 cm. Has a white rump and a shorter tail than the Swallow. Often nests in large flocks.

Swallow. 19 cm. Has long tail feathers and a dark throat. Feeds on insects.

Swift. 16.5 cm. Has very long curved wings.

Blackbird-sized birds

The birds inside this panel are all drawn to the same scale.

Adult   Female   Male

Juvenile

Starling. 21.5 cm. On the ground has an upright waddling walk. This common bird is often seen in large flocks.

Blackbird. 25 cm. The male is all black with an orange beak. The female and young are brown with a brown beak.

Song Thrush. 23 cm. Both sexes look the same, with a brown back and spotted breast. Often feeds on snails.

Mistle Thrush. 27 cm. A greyer bird than the Song Thrush and the spots on the breast are larger and closer together.

Remember - if you cannot see a picture of the bird you want to identify on these pages, turn to the pages earlier in this section which show birds that live in the sort of place where you saw your bird. Pages 6 and 32-33, which show bird shapes in flight, will help you too.

Adult   Juvenile

Robin. 14 cm. Can be very tame. Has an orange breast.

Female

Male

Bullfinch. 14.5-16 cm. Has a black cap and white rump.

Female

Male

Greenfinch. 14.5 cm. Has yellow wing bars and a greenish rump.

Goldfinch. 12 cm. Has a red face and a black and white head.

Male

Dunnock. 14.5 cm. Feeds on the ground and moves slowly with a kind of creeping walk.

Female

House Sparrow. 14.5 cm. The male has a grey and brown head and black throat.

Male

Tree Sparrow. 14 cm. Has a brown cap and a black spot on its white cheeks.

Female

Chaffinch. 15 cm. Has white wing bars and white outer tail feathers.

Pied Wagtail

White Wagtail

Kingfisher. 16.5 cm. Catches small fish, shellfish and tadpoles for food.

The **Pied Wagtail** (18 cm) lives in Britain, the **White** (18 cm) in Europe.

Male

Skylark. 18 cm. Has white outer tail feathers.

Female   Male

Female

Yellowhammer. 16.5 cm. The male has a yellow head.

Linnet. 13.5 cm. The male has a red forehead and chest.

Adult

Juvenile

Great Spotted Woodpecker. 23 cm. Has large white wing patches and a black line from beak to neck.

Juvenile   Adult

Green Woodpecker. 32 cm. Has a bright red head and yellow rump. Often feeds on ants on the ground.

Cuckoo. 33 cm. Has a long tail. It lays its eggs in the nests of other birds.

Male   Female

Kestrel. 34 cm. The most common falcon. Often hovers before dropping on its prey.

Remember - if you cannot see a picture of the bird you want to identify on these pages, turn to the pages earlier in this section which show birds that live in the sort of place where you saw your bird. Pages 6 and 32-33, which show bird shapes in flight, will help you too.

Crow-sized birds

The birds inside this panel are all drawn to scale.

Collared Dove. 32 cm. Has a black half collar at the back of the neck.

Woodpigeon. 41 cm. Has a white patch on each side of the neck.

Buzzard. 51-56 cm. Has broad wings and tail. Plumage is dark brown and cream.

Barn Owl. 34 cm. A large white-looking owl. It hunts in twilight or at night. The remains of meals can be found as pellets.

Lapwing. 30 cm. Has a thin crest and broad, black and white wings which show up when it is flying.

Herring Gull. 56-66 cm. Commonest gull on the coast. Has a large yellow beak with a red spot near the tip and grey wings.

Black-headed Gull. 35-38 cm. In winter, instead of a dark head, it has only a dark mark behind the eyes.

Mallard-sized birds

The birds inside this panel are all drawn to scale.

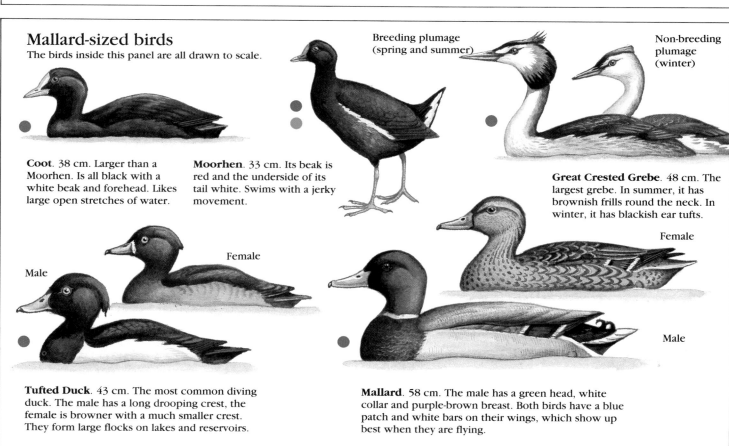

Breeding plumage (spring and summer)

Non-breeding plumage (winter)

Coot. 38 cm. Larger than a Moorhen. Is all black with a white beak and forehead. Likes large open stretches of water.

Moorhen. 33 cm. Its beak is red and the underside of its tail white. Swims with a jerky movement.

Great Crested Grebe. 48 cm. The largest grebe. In summer, it has brownish frills round the neck. In winter, it has blackish ear tufts.

Male

Female

Female

Male

Tufted Duck. 43 cm. The most common diving duck. The male has a long drooping crest, the female is browner with a much smaller crest. They form large flocks on lakes and reservoirs.

Mallard. 58 cm. The male has a green head, white collar and purple-brown breast. Both birds have a blue patch and white bars on their wings, which show up best when they are flying.

Jackdaw. 33 cm. Has a grey head and is smaller than the all-black crows.

Magpie. 46 cm. A large bird with a long tail and black and white plumage.

Carrion

Hooded

The northern form of the **Carrion Crow** (47 cm) has some grey feathers. It is called the **Hooded Crow** (47 cm).

Rook. 46 cm. Has a thinner beak than the crow, with a bare white face and "baggy trousers".

Curlew. 51-58 cm. Largest wader. Has a long downward curved beak, a brown body and long legs.

Pheasant. Male 66-89 cm. Female 53-63 cm. A large game-bird. The male is brightly coloured, the female browner with a shorter tail.

Male

Female

Large water birds

These birds are NOT drawn to the same scale.

Whooper Swan

Bewick's Swan

Juvenile Mute Swan

Female Mute Swan

Male Mute Swan

Grey Heron. 90 cm. A large grey bird, often seen standing at the water's edge. The nest is usually built in a tree.

Cormorant. 90 cm. This sea bird has a white chin and cheeks. Often seen sitting on rocks with its wings half open.

Mute Swan. 152 cm. Has an orange bill with a black knob at the base. Swims with its neck curved.

Bewick's and Whooper Swan. 122 cm and 152 cm. Bewick's has a shorter bill with a small yellow patch. Both hold their necks stiffly when swimming. They are winter visitors.

Birds in flight

Here are some illustrations to help you identify birds in flight. The sizes given are beak-to-tail measurements.

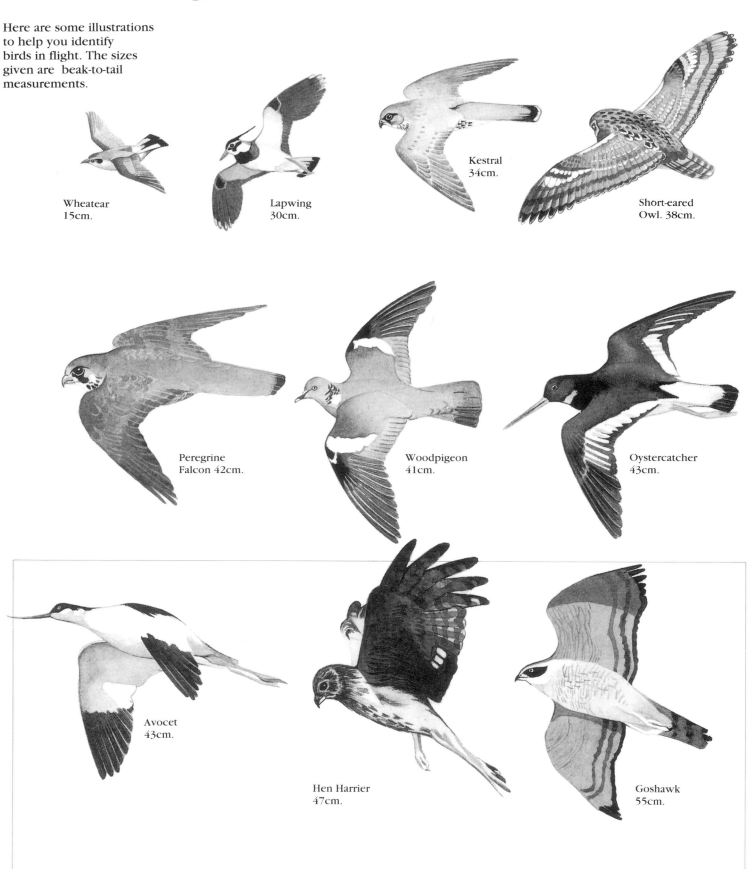

Wheatear
15cm.

Lapwing
30cm.

Kestral
34cm.

Short-eared
Owl. 38cm.

Peregrine
Falcon 42cm.

Woodpigeon
41cm.

Oystercatcher
43cm.

Avocet
43cm.

Hen Harrier
47cm.

Goshawk
55cm.

Buzzard
54cm.

Osprey
54cm.

Black Kite
54cm.

Herring Gull
60cm.

Mallard
58cm.

White-tailed
Eagle 69-91cm.

Greylag goose
76-89.

White Stork
102cm.

Pheasant
66-89.

Mute Swan
152cm.

Trees are everywhere. Only deserts and the tops of mountains are without them. This part of the book tells you about trees and how to study them. It shows you the different parts of a tree, how they work and how they can help you to identify the tree.

It tells the whole story of a tree, from the moment a seed sprouts to when a mature tree dies or is cut down for timber. There are also special tips on how to collect information and specimens.

If you want to identify a tree, look first at pages 60 to 63, called *Common trees you can spot*. If you fail to find a picture of your tree there, turn to the pages that deal with the part of the tree you are looking at, such as a leaf or a piece of the bark.

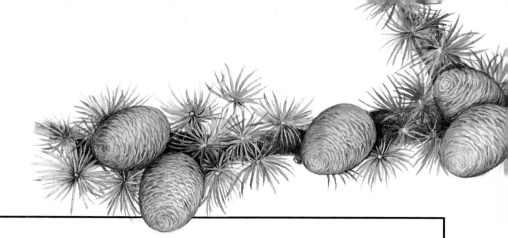

TREES & LEAVES

Contents

How a tree grows	36	Annual rings	52
How to identify trees	38	Wood	53
What to look for on a tree		Pests and fungi	54
Leaves	40	Injuries	55
Winter buds	42	Woodland life	56
Shape	44	Making a tree survey	58
Bark	45	Common trees you can spot	
Flowers	46	Conifers	60
Fruits and seeds	48	Broadleaved trees	61
Grow your own tree seedling	50	Trees in winter	64
Forestry	51		

How a tree grows

This is the life story of a Sycamore, but all trees grow in a similar way. Although there are many different kinds of trees, they all sprout from seeds, grow larger, have flowers, form fruits and shed seeds.

You can study many of these steps in a tree's life. You can watch a tiny seedling sprout and then keep a record of its growth. You can count the girdle scars on a young tree to find out its age.

Older trees have flowers and fruits, although they may be hard to see on some trees. Not all trees have flowers as large as the Horse Chestnut's or fruits as big as the Apple tree's. Most fruits ripen in autumn, but some appear in early summer and spring.

An important part of a tree that you do not usually see is the roots. If you find an overturned tree, look at the roots and try to measure them. Look also at logs and tree stumps for the layers of wood and bark. They can tell you the age of the tree and how quickly it has grown.

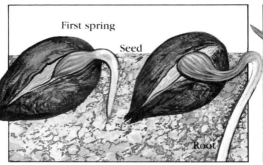

The tree starts growing in spring from a seed which has been lying in the soil all winter. At this time, with the help of the food stored inside it, the seed sends down a root into the soil to suck up water and minerals.

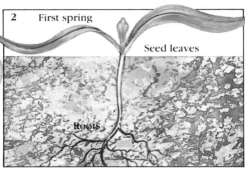

Next, the seed sends up a tiny shoot which pokes above the ground and into the light. Two fleshy seed leaves open up with a small bud between them. These leaves are not the same shape as the tree's real leaves will be.

Buds

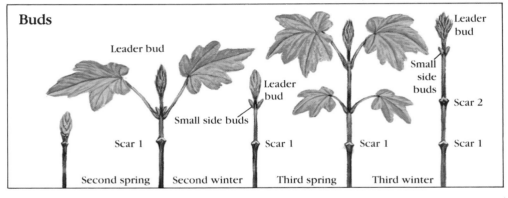

In the second spring, the bud opens and there are two new leaves. A new shoot grows too, with another bud at the tip. In autumn, the leaves drop off. Every year the same thing happens, and every time the leaves fall off, they leave a girdle scar on the stem. Buds on the sides of the stem also grow shoots, but they do not grow as fast as the leader shoot at the top of the tree. Each year the tree grows taller, and the roots grow deeper.

Pollen on the flowers

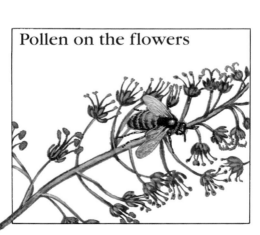

When the tree is about twelve years old, it grows flowers on its branches in the spring. Bees and other insects, searching for nectar, visit the flowers and some of the pollen from the flowers sticks on to their hairy bodies.

Fruits

When the bees visit other flowers from the same tree, some of the pollen on their bodies rubs off on to the female parts of the flowers. When the pollen and female parts are joined, the flowers are fertilized and become fruits.

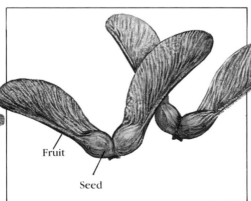

Later that year, the fruits fall off the tree. The Sycamore fruits here spin like tiny helicopters, carrying the seeds away from the parent tree. The wings rot on the ground, and the seeds are ready to grow the following spring.

3 Leaves

Seed leaves

First summer

The seed leaves have stored food in them to help the seedling grow. Soon the bud opens, and the first pair of real leaves appears. These will trap light from the sun to grow more food. The seed leaves then drop off. The roots grow longer.

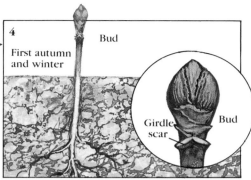

4 First autumn and winter

Bud

Girdle scar

Bud

In the autumn, all the leaves change colour and drop off, leaving a "girdle scar" around the stem where they were attached. A bud is left at the end of the shoot. The bud does not grow during the winter. It stays dorment.

Holly leaf

Many broadleaved trees are deciduous, which means that they lose their leaves in autumn. They do this because their leaves cannot work properly in cold weather, and there is not enough sunlight in winter for the leaves to make food for the tree.

Most conifers are evergreens. Their needles are tougher than most broadleaves, and they can keep making food even in the dark of winter.

A few broadleaved trees, such as Holly, are also evergreen. Like conifer needles, their leaves have a waxy coating which helps them survive the winter.

Inside a tree

Each year, a tree grows more branches. The trunk thickens by adding a new layer of wood to hold the branches up, and the roots grow deeper and wider. This picture shows you the inside of the trunk, and all its different parts.

1 Heartwood. This is old sapwood which is dead and has become very hard. It makes the tree strong and rigid.

2 Rays. In a cross-section of a log you can see pale lines. These are called rays and they carry food sideways.

3 Cambium. This layer is so thin that you can hardly see it. Its job is to make a new layer of sapwood (see page 20) each year. This makes the trunk thicker and stronger.

4 Sapwood. This layer also has tiny tubes in it which carry the sap (water and minerals) to all parts of the tree from the roots. Each year a new ring of this wood is made by the cambium.

5 Phloem. Just inside the bark are tubes which carry food down from the leaves to all parts of the tree, including the roots.

6 Bark is the outer layer which protects the tree from sun, rain and fungi which might attack it.

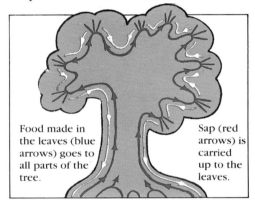

Food made in the leaves (blue arrows) goes to all parts of the tree.

Sap (red arrows) is carried up to the leaves.

To help it grow, the tree makes food for itself in the leaves, which contain a green chemical called chlorophyll. In sunlight, the chlorophyll can change oxygen from the air, water, and minerals brought up from the soil into food for the tree. If a tree gets no light to make food it will die.

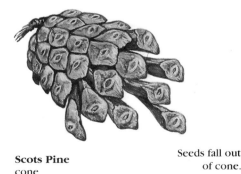

Scots Pine cone

Seeds fall out of cone.

Some trees, such as the Scots Pine, have fruits called cones, which stay on the tree, but open up to let the seeds fall out by themselves. When the cones are old and dried up, they usually fall off the tree too.

How to identify trees

One of the best ways of identifying a tree is to look at its leaves. Be careful though, because some trees have leaves that are very similar. For example, a London Plane leaf could be confused with a Norway Maple leaf. So when you have named your tree just by identifying a leaf, always check that you are correct by looking at other parts of the tree, such as the flowers or bark.

Trees can be divided into three groups: broadleaved, coniferous, and palm trees (see the pictures to the right here). Try to decide which group your tree belongs to. There is something to give you clues in every season of the year. In spring and summer, look at the leaves and flowers. In autumn, look at the fruits. Winter is the best time to study buds, twigs, bark and tree shapes.

You do not need to go into a woodland or forest to study trees. Look at the many different kinds that grow in gardens, parks and roads. Sometimes you can find rare trees in gardens.

Broadleaved trees

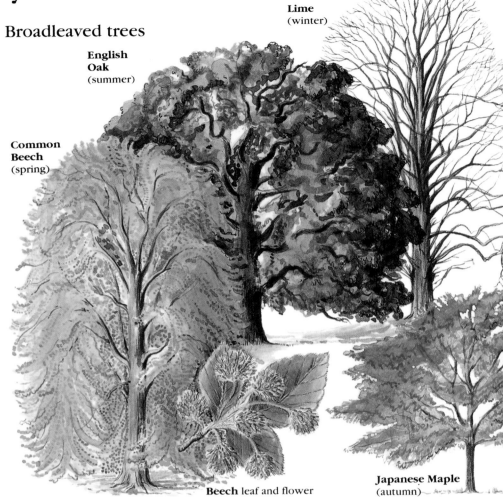

Lime (winter)

English Oak (summer)

Common Beech (spring)

Beech leaf and flower

Japanese Maple (autumn)

Most broadleaved trees have wide, flat leaves which they drop in winter. Some broadleaved trees, though, such as Holly, Laurel, Holm Oak and Box, are evergreen and keep their leaves in winter.

Broadleaved trees have seeds that are encased in fruits. The timber of broadleaved trees is called hardwood, because it is usually harder than the wood of most conifers, or softwood trees.

Tree or shrub?

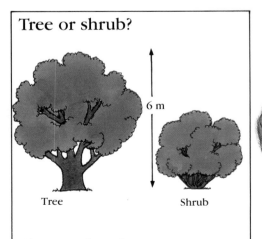

6 m

Tree

Shrub

Trees are plants that can grow to over 6 m high on a woody stem. Shrubs are smaller, and have several stems. See page 59 for how to measure trees.

What to look for

Leaves

Yew (conifer)

Common Beech (broardleaf)

Oak (broadleaf)

The leaves will give you the biggest clue to the identity of the tree, but look at other parts of the tree as well. There is a guide to leaves on page 40.

Shape and bark

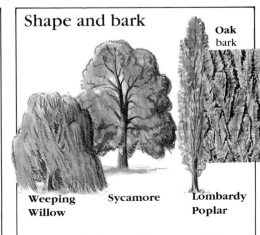

Oak bark

Weeping Willow

Sycamore

Lombardy Poplar

The overall shape of the tree and its crown is also a good clue (see page 44). Some trees can be identified just by looking at their bark.

Conifers

Norway Spruce

Palms

Leaf

Scots Pine

Cone and needles

European Larch (in winter)

European Larch (in summer)

Canary Palm

Most conifers have narrow, needle-like or scaly leaves, and are evergreen, that is they keep their leaves in winter. The Larch is one conifer that is not evergreen, as the tree loses its leaves in winter.

Conifer fruits are usually woody cones, but some conifers, such as the Yew, have berry-like fruits. The overall shape of conifers is more regular and symmetrical than the shape of most broadleaved trees.

Palms have trunks that have no branches. They look like giant stalks. The leaves grow from the top of the tree. Unlike other trees, palms grows taller without getting thicker.

Winter buds

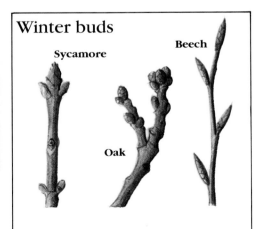

Sycamore

Beech

Oak

In winter, when there are often no leaves to look at, you can identify some trees from their buds, bark and shape. See page 43 for bud shapes.

Flowers

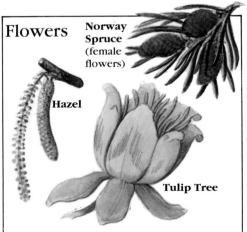

Norway Spruce (female flowers)

Hazel

Tulip Tree

In certain seasons a tree's flowers can help you to identify it. But some trees do not flower every year. For tree flowers, see pages 46-47.

Fruits and seeds

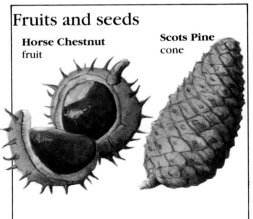

Horse Chestnut fruit

Scots Pine cone

All trees have fruits bearing seeds which may grow into new trees. This Horse Chestnut conker and the pine cone are both fruits. See pages 48-49.

Leaves

One of the things that most people notice about a tree is its leaves. A big Oak tree has more than 250,000 leaves and a conifer tree may have many millions of needles.

The leaves fan out to catch as much sunlight as possible. With the green chlorophyll inside them, they make food for the tree. They take in gases from the air through tiny holes, and give out water vapour and gases in the same way. Once the food is made, it is carried through veins to other parts of the leaf. The veins make the leaf strong like a skeleton.

The leaf stem carries water from the twig and also helps the leaf to move into the light. It is tough so that the leaf does not break off in strong winds.

The leaves of broadleaved trees and conifers look different, but they do the same work. Most conifer leaves can survive the winter, but the leaves of most broadleaves fall off in the autumn. A conifer needle stays on a tree for about three to five years.

Tracking down your mystery leaf

1. Decide if the leaf is from a conifer or a broadleaved tree.

2. Look at its shape and its edge.

3. Notice the way the leaves are arranged on the twig.

4. Look at the colour and leaf surface.

40

Conifer Leaves

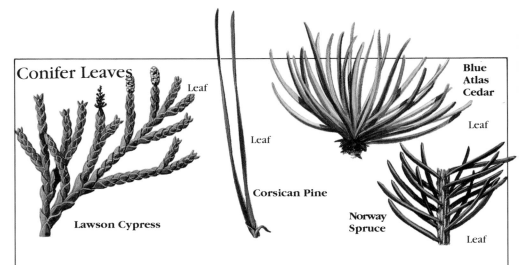

Here you can see three types of conifer leaf. Many conifers have narrow needle-like leaves which are either single, in small bunches or in clusters. They can be very sharp and spiky. But other conifers, such as the Cypresses, have tiny scale-like leaves, overlaping one another.

Broadleaves
Simple

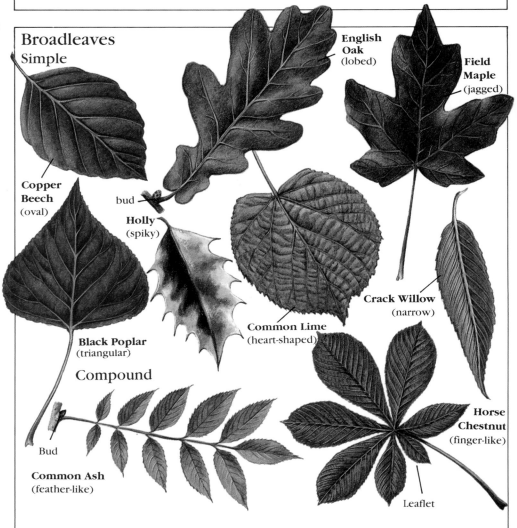

Compound

The leaves of broadleaved trees have many different shapes. Leaves in one piece are called simple. Those made up of many leaflets, such as Common Ash and Horse Chestnut shown here, are called compound. Simple leaves and compound leaves both have one bud at the base of their stems.

These leaves are not drawn to the same scale.

Copper beach

Maidenhair Tree

Rowan

Dawn Redwood

Opposite

Alternate

Horse Chestnut

Silver Birch

Red Oak

Common Pear

White Poplar

Underside

Magnified veins of underside

Twigs

Leaves are arranged on twigs in various ways. They can be opposite each other in pairs, or they can be single and alternate from one side of the twig to the other.

Colour

Leaves are green because of the chlorophyll inside them. In autumn, the chlorophyll in broadleaves decays. They change colour before they fall.

Leaf close-up

Leaves have a network of tiny veins. Their upper surface is tough and often glossy, to stop the sun from drying them out. The underside is often hairy.

Leaf scrapbook

Heavy object

Blotting paper

Leaf skeleton

Keep a scrapbook of the leaves you find. Place each leaf between two sheets of blotting paper. Then put a book and a heavy object on top.

Leave them for about a week. When the leaves are flat and dry, mount them in a scrapbook with sticky tape. Label the leaves and write down where and

when you found them. When a dead leaf has crumbled, the strong stem and veins remain as a skeleton. You will often find these in winter.

Leaf tiles

Press the leaf on to the "clay" with a rolling pin.

The finished tile can be painted or varnished.

Make your clay by mixing together:
2 cups flour (not self-raising)
1 cup salt
1 cup water
2 tablespoons cooking oil

Scatter some flour onto a surface top and shape your "clay" into a ball. Roll it out flat with a floured rolling pin, until it is about 2 cm thick. Press your leaf, vein side down, onto the clay so that it

leaves a mark. Remove the leaf and bake the clay in the oven at 150°C (250°F) for about two hours. When the tile has cooled, you can paint it or varnish it.

Winter buds

Most broadleaved trees have no leaves in winter, but you can still identify them by their winter buds. These contain the beginnings of a shoot, leaves and flowers, which will appear in the next year.

The thick, overlapping bud scales protect a shoot from the cold and from attack by insects. In places where winter is the dry season, the bud scales keep a new shoot from drying out. If the tiny undeveloped leaf has no bud scales, it may be covered with furry hairs to protect it.

In spring, when it gets warmer, a new shoot swells and breaks open the protective hard scales. At the end of the growing season, each shoot will have a new winter bud at the tip. There are many buds on a twig. The leading bud, which is usually at the tip, contains the shoot which will grow most. Shoots become twigs and eventually branches.

Other buds hold leaves and flowers. They are also reserves in case the leading bud is damaged.

Inside a bud there are tiny leaves and flowers, all folded up. If you cut a bud in half and look at it through a lens, you can see the different parts.

Outer scales of bud.

Leaf

Complete flower head.

This is a three-year-old Horse Chestnut twig. You can tell its age by counting the girdle scars. It has large brown buds in opposite pairs. The bud scales are sticky.

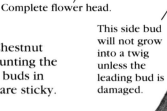

This side bud will not grow into a twig unless the leading bud is damaged.

The leading bud contains next year's shoot.

A leaf scar left by last year's leaf.

This side twig is two years old.

These buds will become leaves.

Last year's leading bud was here. Notice the girdle scar.

Leading bud

One year's growth.

Last year's buds were here.

An undeveloped twig.

A two-year-old **Norway Spruce** twig.

Forcing buds indoors

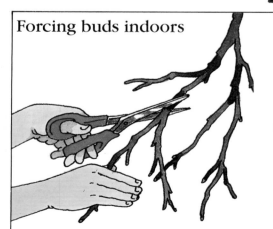

You can "force" buds to open in winter or early spring by bringing them indoors. The best ones to try are Horse Chestnut, Birch, Willow and Forsythia.

Cut the twigs with scissors. Don't break them! Always ask the owner before cutting and don't take too much. Place twigs in water in a vase or jam jar. Place

them in a sunny spot indoors, then wait for the buds to open. This may take some weeks. Draw the buds before and after they have opened.

Winter bud indentification chart

What to look for

If you try to identify trees by their winter buds, you will see that they vary a great deal. Here is a list of things to look for:

1 How are the buds positioned on the twig? Like leaves, buds can be in opposite pairs or single and alternate.

2 What colour are the buds and the twig?

3 What shape is the twig? Are the buds pointed or rounded?

4 Is the bud covered with hairs or scales? If there are scales, how many? Is the bud sticky?

Ash. Smooth, grey twig. Large, black opposite buds.

Sycamore. Large, green, opposite buds with dark-edged scales.

Beech. Slender twig. Alternate, spiky, brown buds sticking out.

Willow. Slender twig. Alternate buds close to twig.

False Acacia. Grey twig. Thorns next to tiny, alternate buds.

English Elm. Zigzag twig. Alternate, blackish-red buds.

Common Lime. Zigzag twig. Alternate, reddish buds with two scales.

Walnut. Thick, hollow twig. Big, black, velvety, alternate buds.

Turkey Oak. Clusters of alternate buds with whiskers.

Wild Cherry. Large, glossy, red buds grouped at tip of twig.

Magnolia. Huge, furry, green-grey buds.

These twigs are drawn life size.

Female flowers

Male catkin

Common Alder. Alternate, stalked, purple buds often with male catkins.

White Poplar. Twig and alternate buds covered with white down.

Sweet Chestnut. Knobbly twig. Large, reddish, alternate buds.

London Plane. Alternate, cone-shaped buds. Ring scar around bud.

Whitebeam. Downy, green, alternate buds.

Shape

Look at all these different tree shapes. Each type of tree has its own typical shape made up from the arrangement and shape of its branches. Winter is the best time of year to see the shapes of broadleaved trees because their branches are not hidden by leaves.

Practise making quick shape sketches when you are outside.

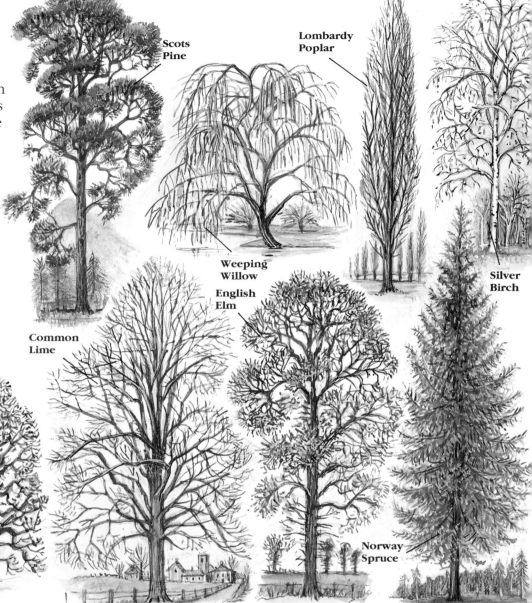

Scots Pine

Lombardy Poplar

Weeping Willow

English Elm

Silver Birch

Common Lime

Norway Spruce

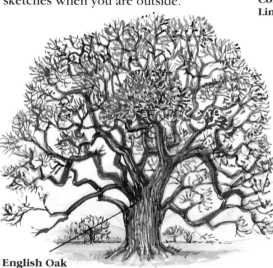

English Oak

How trees are shaped

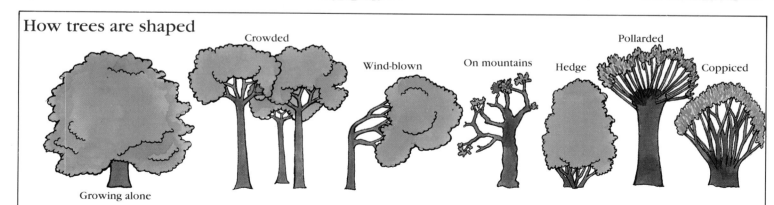

Growing alone

Crowded

Wind-blown

On mountains

Hedge

Pollarded

Coppiced

Trees grow a wide crown or top, so their leaves will get lots of sunlight. Where trees crowd together, they grow thin and tall to try and reach the light. Weather changes the shape of trees. Steady wind from one direction or salty sea winds can make trees grow bent and one-sided. On mountains, trees are dwarfed and gnarled by the cold and drying wind. Trees are also pruned or cut by man to grow in special ways. Pollarding means cutting off the branches of a tree. Coppicing is cutting the trunk down to the ground. This causes long, new shoots to grow.

Bark

The outside of the tree is covered in a hard, tough layer of bark. It protects the tree from drying out and from damage by insects or animals. It also keeps the inside of a tree at a steady temperature. Under the bark there are tubes (phloem) carrying food (sap) which can be damaged if the bark is stripped off. If this happens, the tree may die.

When the tree is young, the bark is thin and smooth, but with age it thickens and forms different patterns. You can identify trees by their bark.

Silver Birch bark peels off in wispy strips that look like ribbons.

English Oak bark has deep ridges and cracks.

How bark patterns form

The old bark splits and new bark forms underneath.

Bark is dead and cannot grow or stretch. As wood inside the bark grows outwards, the bark splits, peels or cracks in a way that is special to each type of tree.

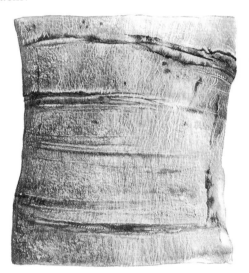

The bark of Scots Pine flakes off in large pieces.

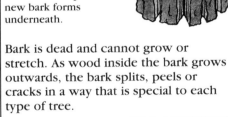

Beech has smooth thin bark, which flakes off in tiny pieces.

Bark rubbings

Sticky tape

You need strong thin paper, sticky tape and wax crayons or heel-ball. Tape the paper securely to the tree. Rub firmly with the crayon, but do not tear the paper. Watch the bark pattern appear.

Candle

Rubbing that has been painted.

You can also rub the paper with candle wax. Then at home, paint over the rubbing done in this way. The bark pattern will stay the colour of the candle.

Cork

The bark of the Cork Oak is so thick that it can be removed without damaging the tree. Cork is used in many ways to keep in moisture and to resist heat. Table mats are often made from cork.

Flowers

All trees produce flowers in order to make seeds that can grow into new trees. The flowers vary from tree to tree in size, shape and colour. Some are so small that you may not notice them.

Flowers have male parts called stamens and female parts called ovaries. The stamen produces pollen, while the ovary contains ovules. When pollen from the stamen reaches the ovules in the ovary, the flower is fertilized. Fertilized flowers grow into fruits which contain seeds.

Flowers which have both ovaries and stamens, such as the Cherry, are called "perfect". On other trees the ovaries and the stamens are in different flowers. Then, the female flowers grow in separate clusters to male the flowers. The clusters can be cone shaped or long and dangling. A few trees, such as Yew, Holly and Willow, have their male and female flowers on entirely separate trees.

Parts of a flower

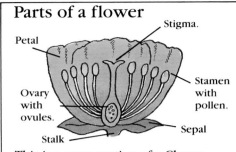

This is a cross-section of a Cherry blossom, which is a typical "perfect" flower as it has male and female parts.

European Larch

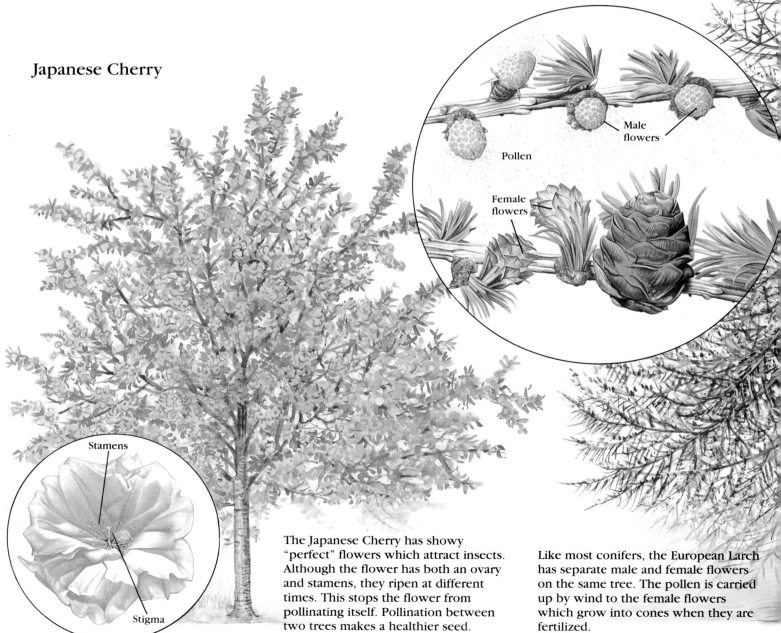

Japanese Cherry

The Japanese Cherry has showy "perfect" flowers which attract insects. Although the flower has both an ovary and stamens, they ripen at different times. This stops the flower from pollinating itself. Pollination between two trees makes a healthier seed.

Like most conifers, the European Larch has separate male and female flowers on the same tree. The pollen is carried up by wind to the female flowers which grow into cones when they are fertilized.

Pollination

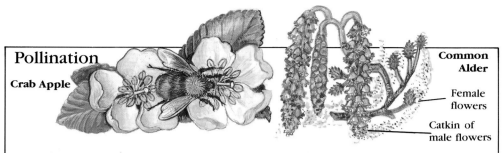

Crab Apple

Common Alder

Female flowers

Catkin of male flowers

Some flowers are pollinated by insects. Insects, feeding on flowers, accidentally pick up pollen on their bodies. The pollen rubs off on the next flower they visit. This is called cross-pollination. Most catkins and conifer flowers are wind-pollinated. They are small and dull because they do not need to attract insects. The wind blows pollen off the long stamens, and the sticky stigmas at the end of each ovary catch the pollen.

Fertilization

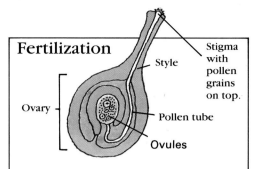

Stigma with pollen grains on top.

Style

Ovary

Pollen tube

Ovules

Once the pollen grains have reached the stigma, they make tubes down to the ovary. There they fertilize the ovules, which later become seeds.

Crack Willow

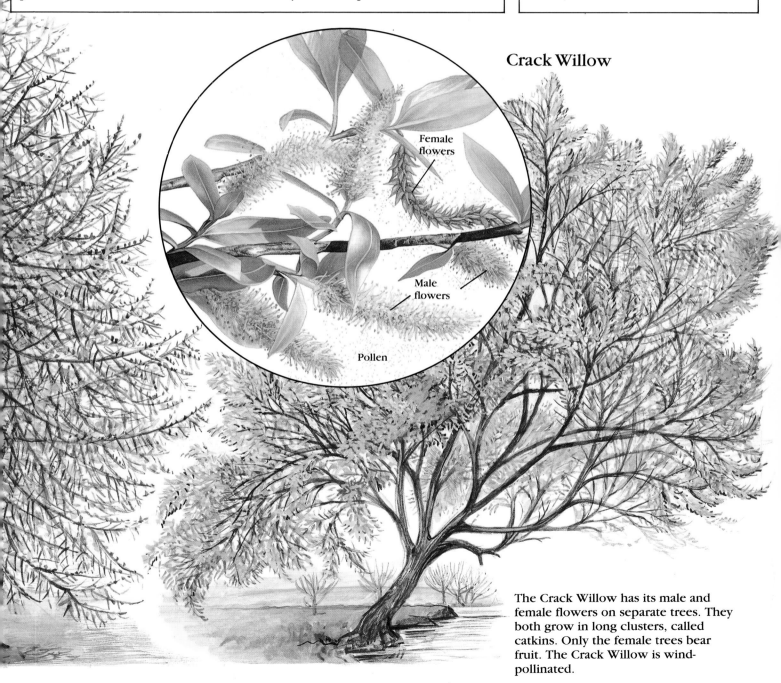

Female flowers

Male flowers

Pollen

The Crack Willow has its male and female flowers on separate trees. They both grow in long clusters, called catkins. Only the female trees bear fruit. The Crack Willow is wind-pollinated.

Fruits and seeds

Fruits containing seeds grow from fertilized flowers. An apple and the prickly conker case of the Horse Chestnut are both fruits. They look different, but they do the same job, protecting the seeds and helping them to spread to a place where they can grow.

Broadleaved trees have fruits which completely encase their seeds. These fruits can come in many different forms, such as nuts, berries and soft fruits. Conifer seeds are uncovered and not in a fruit that encases them. They are usually held in a scaly cone.

Many fruits and cones are damaged by insects and disease, eaten by birds and animals, or fall off the trees before they can ripen. The seeds inside undamaged healthy fruits ripen in the autumn. They need to get far away from the parent tree, as it will take all the food and light.

Seeds are spread by birds, animals, wind and water. Very few seeds ever get to a place where they can reach full growth. About one in a million acorns becomes an Oak tree.

How a cone ripens

The fertilized ovules become seeds.

Scale

Cross-section of a cone.

Female flowers in spring.

Each scale holds two seeds.

Young cone in summer.

Male flowers in spring.

Seeds

Last year's cone which is now empty.

Douglas Fir

Cones develop from the female flowers. After pollination, the scales harden and close. The stalk often bends, so the cone hangs down. The cone turns from green to brown. When the seeds are ripe and the weather is warm and dry, the scales open. The seeds flutter out on papery wings. Most cones stay on the tree for a year. Others take two years to ripen, and some remain after the seeds have gone.

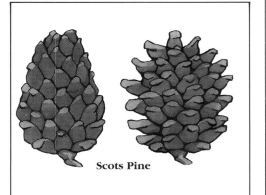

Scots Pine

Cones open in warm, dry weather to release the seeds. If it is wet, the scales close. Find a cone and make it open by placing it near a heater. Then put it in a damp place, and it will close.

Fruits of conifers

Most cones have woody scales and vary in size from 1 cm to 35 cm, and can weigh as much as 2 kg. See how many different kinds of cones you can collect.

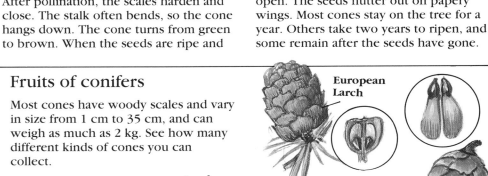

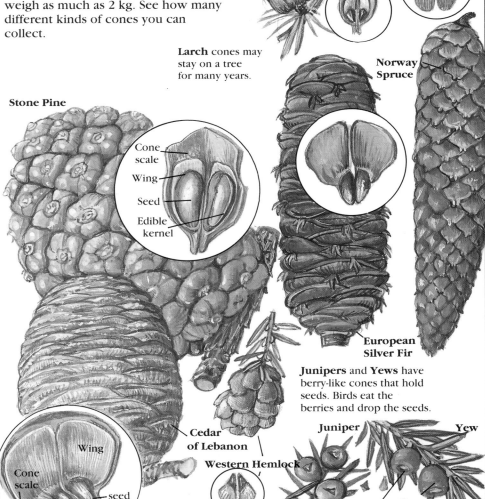

European Larch

Larch cones may stay on a tree for many years.

Stone Pine

Cone scale
Wing
Seed
Edible kernel

Norway Spruce

European Silver Fir

Junipers and **Yews** have berry-like cones that hold seeds. Birds eat the berries and drop the seeds.

Wing
Cone scale
seed

Cedar of Lebanon

Western Hemlock

Juniper

Yew

Seed   Cone

The conifer seeds are drawn life size.

How the fruit of a Peach tree ripens

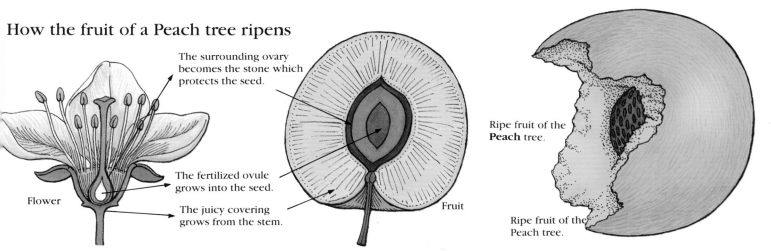

The surrounding ovary becomes the stone which protects the seed.

The fertilized ovule grows into the seed.

The juicy covering grows from the stem.

Flower

Fruit

Ripe fruit of the **Peach** tree.

Ripe fruit of the Peach tree.

The pictures show how the different parts of a flower grow into the different parts of a fruit. The flower is from a Peach tree.

Water from the stem and sunshine make the fleshy part of the fruit swell. As the fruit ripens, it turns golden pink and

softens. The bright colour and sweet smell attract animals or people, who eat thee juicy outer layer and throw away the stone.

Fruits of broadleaved trees

Broadleaved trees produce many different kinds of fruits. Some are nuts with hard outer shells, some are soft fruits, some are pods, some have wings or hairs.

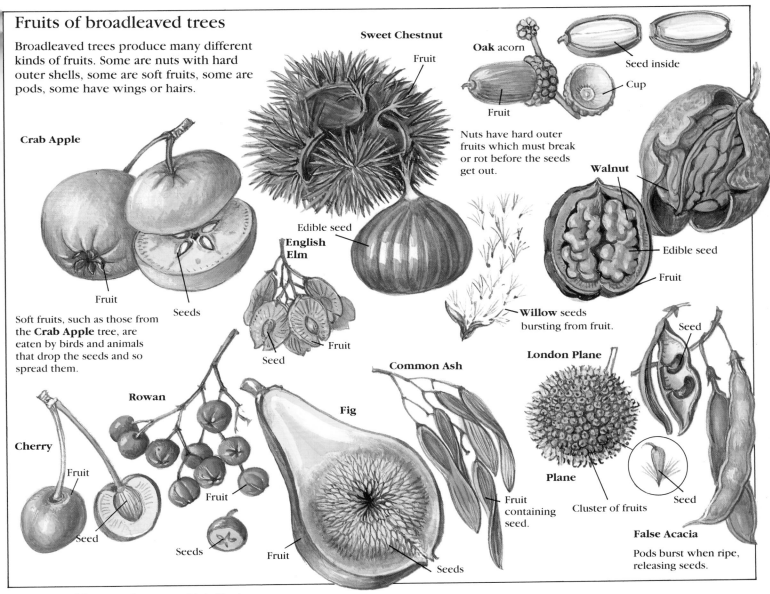

Sweet Chestnut

Fruit

Oak acorn

Seed inside

Cup

Fruit

Nuts have hard outer fruits which must break or rot before the seeds get out.

Walnut

Edible seed

Fruit

Edible seed

Crab Apple

Fruit

Seeds

Soft fruits, such as those from the **Crab Apple** tree, are eaten by birds and animals that drop the seeds and so spread them.

English Elm

Seed

Fruit

Willow seeds bursting from fruit.

London Plane

Seed

Common Ash

Plane

Seed

Cluster of fruits

Rowan

Fig

Fruit

Cherry

Fruit

Seed

Seeds

Fruit

Seeds

Fruit containing seed.

False Acacia

Pods burst when ripe, releasing seeds.

The cones and fruits are drawn two thirds life size.

Grow your own tree seedling

Try growing your own tree from a seed. Pick ripe seeds from trees or collect them from the ground if you know that they are fresh. The time a seed takes to sprout varies, but an acorn takes about two months. Some seeds, like those from conifers, may need to lie in the ground for over a year. Once the seedling has sprouted, keep a diary of its growth with drawings or photographs.

What you need

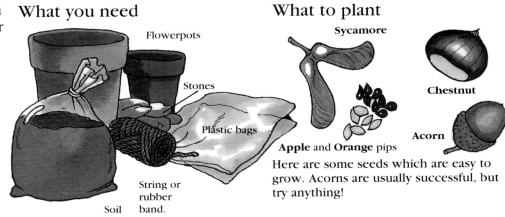

Flowerpots

Stones

Plastic bags

String or rubber band.

Soil

What to plant

Sycamore

Chestnut

Acorn

Apple and Orange pips

Here are some seeds which are easy to grow. Acorns are usually successful, but try anything!

1 Soak acorns or other hard nuts in warm water overnight. Peel off the hard outer shells. Do not cut shells from nuts.

2 Put a handful of stones in the bottom of your pot. This is to help the water to drain properly. Place a saucer under the pot.

3 Fill a pot with some soil, or compost, until it is about two thirds full. Water the soil until it is moist, but not soggy.

4 Place one acorn, or other nut, on top of the soil. They need lots of room to grow, so only put one acorn in each pot.

5 Cover the acorn, or other nut, with a layer of soil. This layer should be about as thick as the acorn itself.

Fasten with string or rubber band.

6 Place a plastic bag over the pot. This will keep the seed moist without watering Put the pot in a sunny place and wait.

The soil should be moist, but not wet.

7 As soon as the seedling appears, remove the plastic bag. Water the seedling once or twice a week.

8 In the summer, put your seedling outside, if you can. In autumn, plant it in the ground. (You can leave it in its pot.)

9 Dig a hole a bit larger than the pot. Gently lift out the seedling and soil from the pot. Plant it in the hole and water it.

Forestry

Trees have been growing on Earth for about 350 million years. Much land was once covered by natural forests, but they have been cut down for timber and cleared. New forests are often planted to replace the trees that have been cut down.

Because conifers grow faster than broadleaved trees and produce straight timber, they are preferred for wood production.

On this page you can read about the story of a Douglas Fir plantation, and what the foresters do to care for the trees.

Seedbeds

The seeds are sown in seedbeds. When the seedlings are 15-20 cm high, they are planted in rows in another bed where they have more room. They are weeded regularly.

Planting out

When the seedlings are about 50 cm high, they are planted out in the forest ground, which has been cleared and ploughed. There are about 2,500 trees per hectare.

Fire towers on hills help to spot fire - the forest's worst enemy. Fires can be started by a carelessly dropped match or an unguarded campfire.

Plantations can be sprayed with weedkillers and fertilizers from the air.

When the trees are felled, they are taken away to sawmills to be cut up.

Every few years the weaker trees are weeded out to give more light and room to the stronger ones. These thinnings are used for poles or are made into paper.

Trees are felled when they are fully grown (about 70 years for conifers and 150 years for Oaks). About one in every ten trees reaches its full growth.

Dead and lower branches are cut off trees. This lessens the risk of fire and stops knots from forming in the wood.

Annual rings

Inside the bark is the wood which is made up of many layers (see page 37). Each year the cambium makes a ring of wood on its inner side and grows outwards. This layer is called an annual ring. The early wood made in spring is pale and has wide tubes (phloem) to carry sap. Late wood, which is formed in summer, is darker and stronger. In wet years, the layers of wood are broad and the annual rings are far apart, but in dry years they are narrow. They are also narrow if the trees are not thinned.

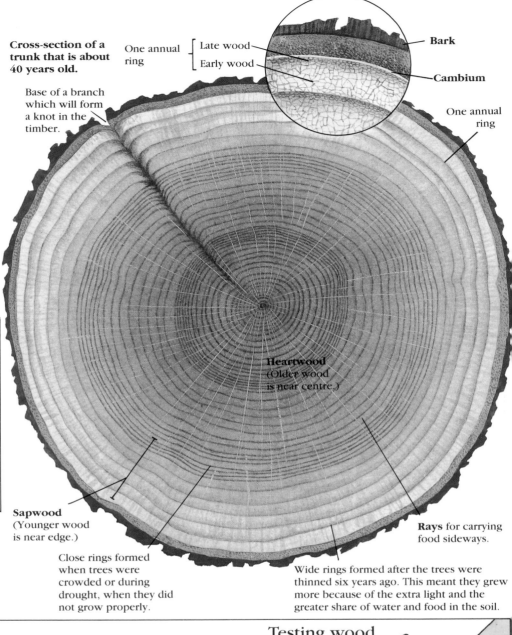

Cross-section of a trunk that is about 40 years old.

Base of a branch which will form a knot in the timber.

One annual ring

Late wood
Early wood

Bark

Cambium

One annual ring

Heartwood
(Older wood is near centre.)

Sapwood
(Younger wood is near edge.)

Close rings formed when trees were crowded or during drought, when they did not grow properly.

Rays for carrying food sideways.

Wide rings formed after the trees were thinned six years ago. This meant they grew more because of the extra light and the greater share of water and food in the soil.

Palms

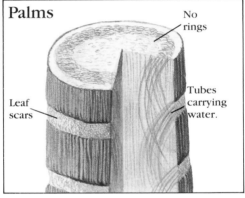

No rings

Leaf scars

Tubes carrying water.

Palm trees do not have annual rings because they have no cambium to grow new wood. Their trunks are like giant stalks which do not grow thicker.

How old is a tree?

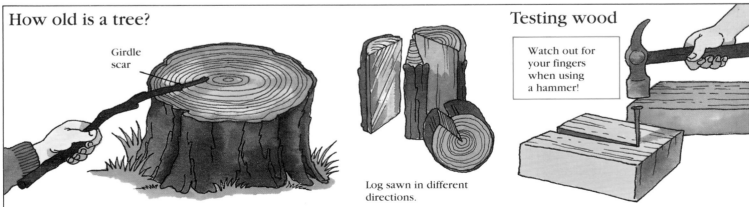

Girdle scar

You can find out the age of a tree by counting the annual rings in a cross-section of its trunk, as in this tree stump here. It is easiest to count the dark rings

Log sawn in different directions.

of late wood. Twigs also have annual layers. Cut off a twig on the slant and count its rings. Then count the girdle scars on the outside. Do they agree?

Testing wood

Watch out for your fingers when using a hammer!

Saw a small log in different ways and look at the patterns the wood makes. Test the strength of different woods by hammering nails into them.

Wood

The wood inside different types of trees varies in colour and pattern, just as the bark varies. Different kinds of wood are suited for certain uses. Wood from conifers, called softwood, is mainly used for building and making paper. Wood from broadleaved trees, called hardwood, is used to make furniture.

At the sawmill, the person operating the saw decides the best way to cut each log. A log can be made into many different sizes of planks, as well as into paper pulp.

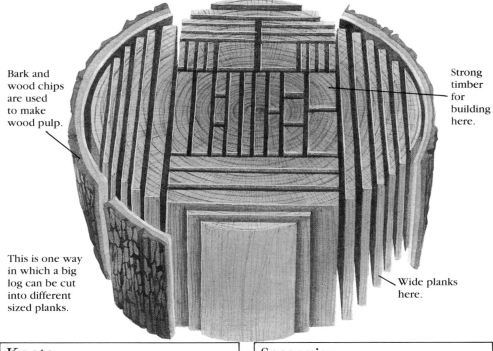

Bark and wood chips are used to make wood pulp.

Strong timber for building here.

This is one way in which a big log can be cut into different sized planks.

Wide planks here.

Grain

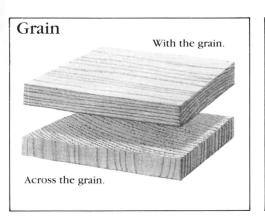

With the grain.

Across the grain.

When a plank is cut from a log, the annual rings make vertical lines which may be wavy or straight. This pattern is called the grain. Wood cut with the grain is stronger than wood cut across the grain..

Knots

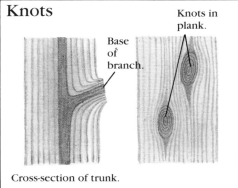

Knots in plank.

Base of branch.

Cross-section of trunk.

In a plank you may notice dark spots, called knots. This is where the base of a branch was buried in the trunk of the tree. This distorts and colours the grain, and so leaves a knot.

Seasoning

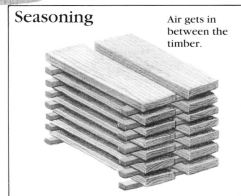

Air gets in between the timber.

Fresh wood contains water which is why green logs spit in the fire. As wood dries, it shrinks and often cracks or warps. Planks must be dried out, or seasoned, before they can be used.

Processed wood

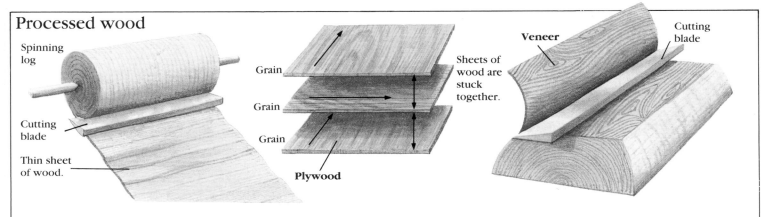

Spinning log

Cutting blade

Thin sheet of wood.

Grain

Grain

Grain

Plywood

Sheets of wood are stuck together.

Veneer

Cutting blade

Much of the wood that you see around you has been "processed". Plywood is thin layers of wood which are glued together with the grain lying in different directions. It is stronger than ordinary wood and does not warp. The thin sheet of wood is peeled off the log like a Swiss roll. Veneer is a thin sheet of wood with a beautiful grain which is used on the surface of plain furniture. Chipboard (not shown) is made of small chips and shavings mixed with glue.

Pests and fungi

Trees are attacked by insects and diseases caused by fungi. Insects use trees for food and shelter, and as places to breed. They can cause serious damage to trees, but they rarely kill them.

Fungi are a group of plants which do not flower. Mushrooms are fungi. Because fungi cannot make their own food, they may feed off plants and animals, and sometimes kill them. Fungi spread by releasing microscopic spores, like seeds, into the tree. These spores can spread and rot the tree.

Leaves and shoots

Spangle galls

Cherry galls

Pine Looper

Green Tortrix

Gall Wasp

Kidney galls

The **Tent Caterpillar** lives in a "tent", which it spins among the branches.

Pine Sawfly

Many moth and butterfly caterpillars and other larvae eat leaves. Often each species only feeds on a certain type of tree.

Oak apple galls

Some insects lay their eggs in leaves or shoots. The tree forms swellings, called galls, around the eggs. The larvae feed inside the galls.

Leaf Roller

Leaf Miner

"Pineapple" gall

Aphid

Leaf Miners eat tunnels through leaves. **Leaf Rollers** fold leaves over themselves for protection.

An **Aphid** made this "pineapple" gall by piercing a shoot to suck out the sap.

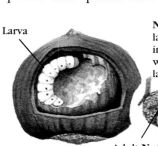

Larva

Nut Weevils lay their eggs inside nuts, where the larvae grow.

Adult **Nut Weevil**

Bark and wood

Conifer Heart Rot is caused by this bracket fungus. It attacks conifers and rots the inside of trees until they die.

Elm Bark Beetles make tunnels under Elm bark. They spread the fungus which causes Dutch Elm Disease.

Honey Fungus attacks the roots of many trees. In autumn, their toadstools appear at the base of infected trees.

White Pine Blister Rust is a fungus which causes swellings on pine trunks and branches.

Look for **Scale** insects on bark. If you pull one off, you may see the grub which sucks sap from the tree.

The **Pine Weevil** strips the bark off newly planted conifers.

Roots

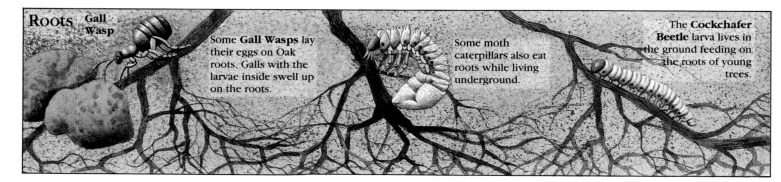

Gall Wasp

Some **Gall Wasps** lay their eggs on Oak roots. Galls with the larvae inside swell up on the roots.

Some moth caterpillars also eat roots while living underground.

The **Cockchafer Beetle** larva lives in the ground feeding on the roots of young trees.

Keeping an Oak apple gall

Netting top tied on with string.

Release **Wasp** when it emerges.

Oak Apple

In summer, collect Oak apples and other galls which do not have holes in them. Keep them in a jar with netting on top. The wasps living inside the galls should emerge in a month.

Making spore prints

Mushrooms or toadstools

Cap

Spore print

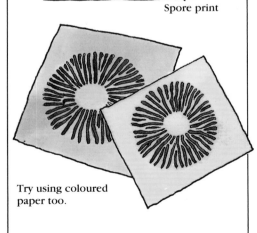

Try using coloured paper too.

Make spore prints from mushrooms. Cut off the stalk and place the cap on some paper. Leave it overnight. It will release its spores on the paper, leaving a print. Always wash your hands after handling a fungus.

Injuries

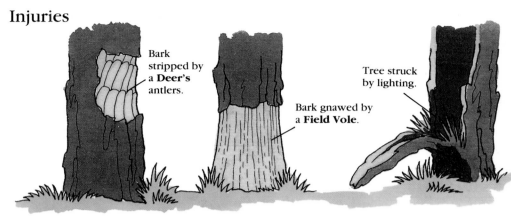

Bark stripped by a **Deer's** antlers.

Bark gnawed by a **Field Vole**.

Tree struck by lighting.

Sometimes trees are damaged by animals. Deer strip the bark off trees when they scrape the "velvet" off their antlers. Squirrels, voles and rabbits eat young bark, which can kill young saplings. If lightning strikes a tree, the trunk often cracks. This happens because the sap gets so hot that it becomes steam. It expands and then explodes, shattering the tree.

How a tree heals itself

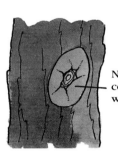

Recent pruning cut.

Bare wood

Three years later.

New bark covering wound.

Six years later.

If a branch is pruned off a tree properly, the wound usually heals. A new rim of bark grows from the cambium around the cut. This finished seal will keep out fungi and diseases. It takes years for a wound to heal. But if a wound completely surrounds the trunk, the tree will die because its food supply is cut off. This can happen when animals strip off the bark.

How trees die

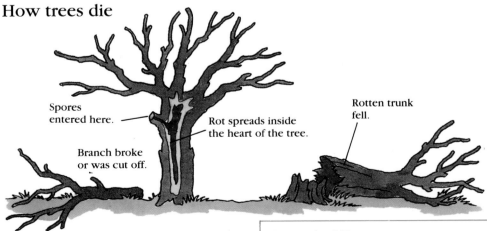

Spores entered here.

Branch broke or was cut off.

Rot spreads inside the heart of the tree.

Rotten trunk fell.

Fungus kills many trees. Spores in the air enter an opening and spread through the tree. The heartwood rots until the tree dies and falls down.

Remember! Never carve your initials or anything else on a tree. It looks ugly and can leave an opening for fungi to enter.

Woodland life

The forest is home to many plants and animals. Trees protect wildlife from bad weather, wind and too much sun. Fallen leaves and twigs make a rich soil called humus. This helps plants to grow. The wildlife in broadleaved and coniferous forests is not the same, although it may overlap.

Trees change carbon dioxide into oxygen. Chopping down trees leaves too much carbon dioxide in the atmosphere which is bad for our planet, making it warmer. This is called the "greenhouse" effect.

A coniferous forest

A coniferous forest is dark and dense. Few plants grow on the ground because of the thick layer of needles and the lack of light. Here are some animals and plants you might see in a coniferous forest.

Pine Marten

Squirrel's drey

Long-eared Owl's nest

Long-eared Owl

Great Spotted Woodpecker

Red Deer

Crossbill

Bracken

Black Grouse

Fox

Norway spruce cones

Wood Ant-hill

Broad Buckler Fern

Timberman

Goldcrest

Fly Agaric

Treecreeper

Red Squirrel

Lichen

Black Slug

A broadleaved forest

A broadleaved forest is more light and open and so attracts many more plants and animals. There are many flowers in spring before the trees' leaves have blocked out the light. As you can see, an Oak wood supports many different kinds of wildlife.

Tree roots help to hold the soil firm. If forests are cut down and the land cleared, the soil can become very loose and dry. This is called erosion.

Mistletoe

Nuthatch

Green Woodpecker

Rook in nest

Tawny Owl

Long-eared Bat in tree

Poor Man's Beefsteak

Blue Tit

Oak

Wood Anemone

Roe Deer

Badger

Rabbit

Bluebells

Pheasant

Ivy

Common Shrew

Hedgehog

Primrose

Moss

Common Toad

Earthworm

Greater Stag Beetle

Speckled Wood Butterfly

Making a tree survey

You will gather many interesting facts about trees and the wildlife they shelter by doing a tree survey. Start with a small area and choose one that has many trees of different types. A piece of countryside, a park, garden or street will all do.

With a friend, make a rough map of your area and add any landmarks, such as roads or buildings. Try to work out a scale for your map - 2 cm for every 50 paces is a good one. Plot each tree on your map and be careful not to miss any.

What to take

Notebook
Tree field guide
Tape measure
Pencils
String

Identifying a tree

Try to identify the trees using this book or another guide. Remember that there are many clues to help you identify them. One type of clue, such as a leaf, is not enough.

Making a map

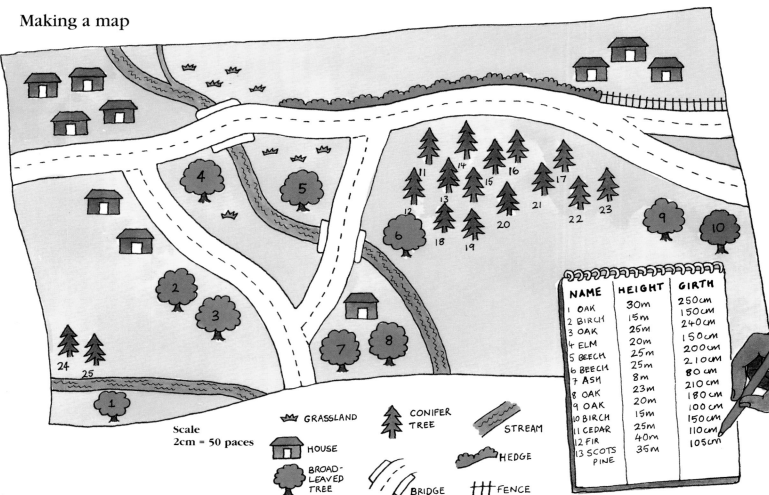

Scale
2cm = 50 paces

| | GRASSLAND |
| CONIFER TREE |
| HOUSE |
| BROAD-LEAVED TREE |
| STREAM |
| HEDGE |
| BRIDGE |
| FENCE |

NAME	HEIGHT	GIRTH
1 OAK	30m	250cm
2 BIRCH	15m	150cm
3 OAK	25m	240cm
4 ELM	20m	150cm
5 BEECH	25m	200cm
6 BEECH	25m	210cm
7 ASH	8m	80cm
8 OAK	23m	210cm
9 OAK	20m	180cm
10 BIRCH	15m	100cm
11 CEDAR	25m	150cm
12 FIR	40m	110cm
13 SCOTS PINE	35m	105cm

After you have identified and measured the trees (as shown on these pages), make a neater and more detailed copy of your map. Show the scale of your map. Then make a key of the symbols you used, like the one above.

Write down the findings of your survey. Give the name, height and girth of each tree. Repeat the survey later to see if there are any new trees, or if anything else has changed. If you enjoyed making the survey, you can write to the Tree Council * to find out how to do a more complicated one.

Measuring a tree

The friend here is 1.5 m tall.

The tree here is four times the height of your friend. 4 x 1.5 m = 6 m. This is the height of the tree.

Mark stick here where your thumb lined up with your friend's feet.

Ask a friend to stand by a tree. From a short distance, hold up a stick at arm's length. Line up the stick's tip with the top of your friend's head. Then move your thumb up the stick until it lines up with your friend's feet. Mark the stick where your thumb is.

From the same spot, hold out the stick again. How many times does the piece of stick above the mark go into the height of the tree. (Look carefully at the pictures here to see how this is done.) Now multiply the answer by your friend's height (1.5 m here).

Measure the girth of a tree at chest height. Ask your friend to hold one end of some string while you hold the other. Walk right around the tree until you meet your friend. Now measure the length of string.

Studying a tree

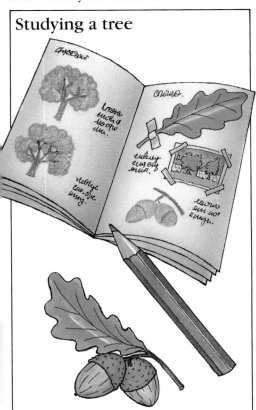

Make a careful study of one tree all through the year. Choose a tree which you can get to easily and often. Make a notebook in which you keep a record of when it comes into leaf, when it flowers and fruits, and when it drops its leaves. Include sketches or photos of the tree at these different times and keep specimens from it.

Squirrel's drey

Insects on the bark.

Nest

Do not touch birds' nests or go too near to them.

White sheet to catch insects.

Study the animals that live in or near your tree. Look for birds' nests and squirrels' dreys in the tree top. Look on the trunk for insects and on the ground for other traces of animals, such as owl pellets, and nuts or cones which have been eaten by animals. To examine the insects in the tree, beat a branch gently with a stick. With a white sheet, catch the insects that fall out.

Leaf litter

Light bulb

Jar covered with black paper.

Funnel

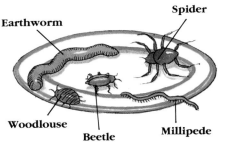

Earthworm

Spider

Woodlouse

Beetle

Millipede

Leaf litter is made up of dead and rotting leaves and contains many small animals. To study these animals, take a large funnel (or make one out of tin foil), and place it in a jar. Cover the jar with black paper. Fill the funnel with damp leaf litter. Place a lamp about 10 cm above the leaves and switch it on. Wait a few hours. The heat and light from the lamp will drive the animals into the dark jar. Then you can take them out and study them.

Common trees you can spot

Conifers

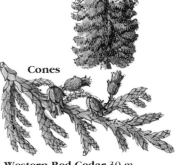

Lawson Cypress 25 m. Narrow shape. Drooping top shoot. Small, round cones. Common as a hedge.

Western Red Cedar 30 m. Branches curve upwards. Tiny, flower-like cones. Hedges.

Yew 15 m. Dark green. Trunk gnarled. Bark reddish. Leaves and red-berried fruits poisonous.

Western Hemlock 35 m. Branches and top shoot droop. Small cones. Needles various lengths.

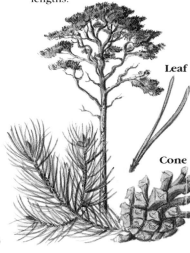

Norway Spruce 30 m. Christmas tree. Long, hanging cones. Parks, gardens, plantations.

Douglas Fir 40 m. Hanging, shaggy cones. Deep-ridged bark. Important timber tree.

European Silver Fir 40 m. Large, upright cones at top of tree. Parklands.

Scots Pine 35 m. Uneven crown. Bare trunk. Flaking bark. Common wild and planted.

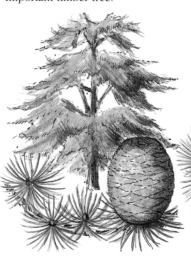

Corsican Pine 36 m. Shape rounder and fuller than Scots Pine. Long, dark green needles. Dark brown bark.

Blue Atlas Cedar 25 m. Broad shape. Barrel-shaped, upright cones. Blue-green needles. Parks.

European Larch 38 m. Upright cones egg-shaped. Soft, light-green needles fall off in winter.

Japanese Larch 35 m. Upright, rosette-like cones. Orange twigs. Blue-green needles fall in winter.

60

Broadleaved trees

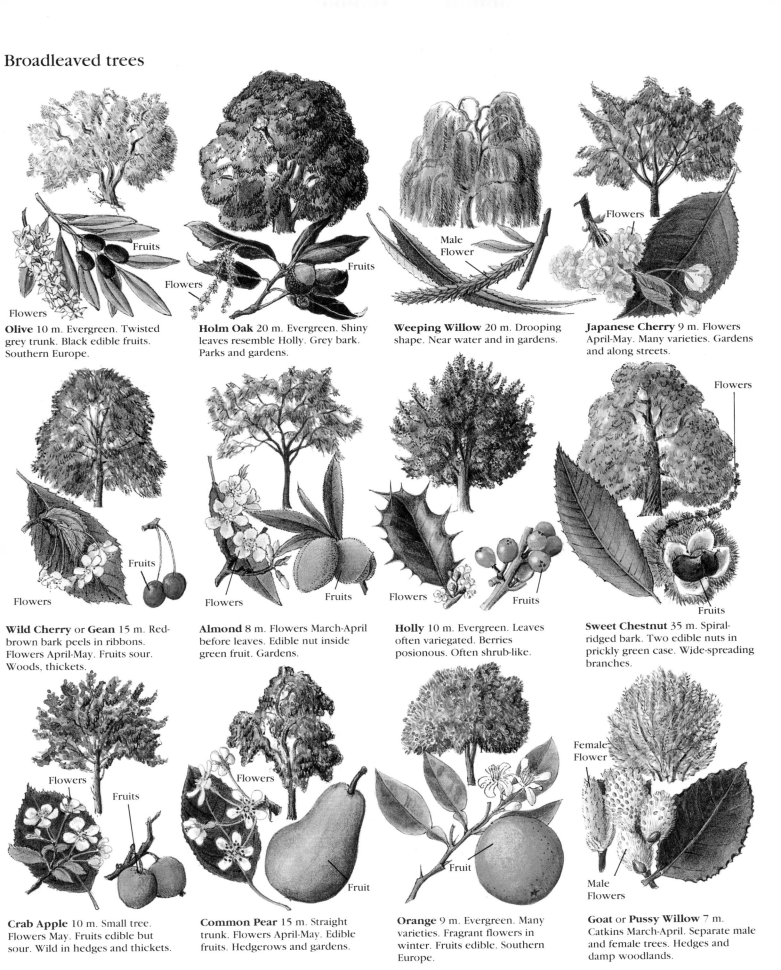

Olive 10 m. Evergreen. Twisted grey trunk. Black edible fruits. Southern Europe.

Holm Oak 20 m. Evergreen. Shiny leaves resemble Holly. Grey bark. Parks and gardens.

Weeping Willow 20 m. Drooping shape. Near water and in gardens.

Japanese Cherry 9 m. Flowers April-May. Many varieties. Gardens and along streets.

Wild Cherry or **Gean** 15 m. Red-brown bark peels in ribbons. Flowers April-May. Fruits sour. Woods, thickets.

Almond 8 m. Flowers March-April before leaves. Edible nut inside green fruit. Gardens.

Holly 10 m. Evergreen. Leaves often variegated. Berries posionous. Often shrub-like.

Sweet Chestnut 35 m. Spiral-ridged bark. Two edible nuts in prickly green case. Wide-spreading branches.

Crab Apple 10 m. Small tree. Flowers May. Fruits edible but sour. Wild in hedges and thickets.

Common Pear 15 m. Straight trunk. Flowers April-May. Edible fruits. Hedgerows and gardens.

Orange 9 m. Evergreen. Many varieties. Fragrant flowers in winter. Fruits edible. Southern Europe.

Goat or **Pussy Willow** 7 m. Catkins March-April. Separate male and female trees. Hedges and damp woodlands.

The trees are arranged by leaf shape. The height given is of a large full-grown tree.

More broadleaved trees

Common Beech 25 m. Smooth, grey bark. Nuts eaten by animals. Leaves can also be purple coloured.

Hornbeam 10 m. Smooth, grey, fluted trunk. Green winged fruits hanging in clusters. Hedges.

Wych Elm 20 m. Round, even crown. Woods and hedgerows. More common than English Elm in the north.

English Elm 30 m. Tall narrow crown, often irregular shape. Hedgerows and woods. Attacked by Dutch Elm Disease.

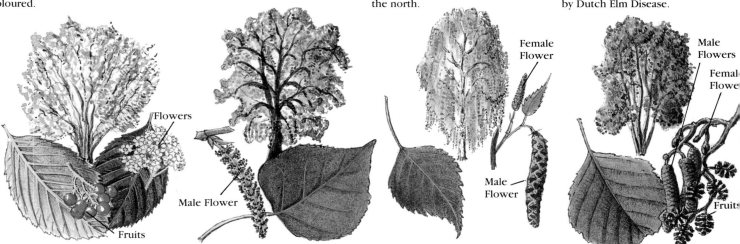

Whitebeam 8 m. Leaves white-felted underneath. Flowers May-June. Sour red berries. Grows wild.

Black Poplar 25 m. Dark trunk often with bumps. Common in city parks.

Silver Birch 15 m. White bark peels in ribbons. "Lamb's tail" catkins in April. Wild on heaths and mountains. Planted in gardens.

Common Alder 12 m. Cone-like fruits which stay on in winter. Catkins in early spring. Near water and damp woodlands.

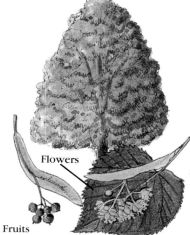

Common Lime 25 m. Heart-shaped leaves. Fragrant flowers attract bees in June. Parks and gardens.

Turkey Oak 25 m. Whiskers on buds and at base of leaves. Acorn cups mossy. Bark ridged.

English or **Pedunculate Oak** 23 m. Wide-spreading branches. Long-stalked acorns. Common alone and in woods.

White Poplar 20 m. Leaves covered with white down underneath. Bark whitish-grey with diamond marks.

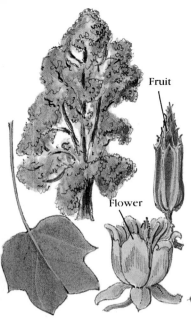

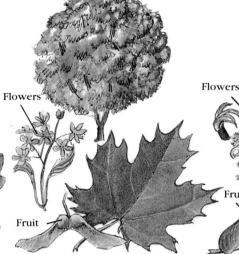

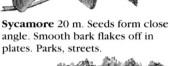

Tulip Tree 20 m. Tulip-like flowers, June-July. Upright brown fruits. Parks, gardens.

Field Maple 10 m. Rounded crown. Narrow-ridged bark. Winged seeds almost form straight line. Hedges and woods.

Norway Maple 15 m. Seeds form wide angle. Autumn leaves colourful. Parks, streets.

Sycamore 20 m. Seeds form close angle. Smooth bark flakes off in plates. Parks, streets.

London Plane 30 m. Bark flakes off leaving white patches. Spiky fruits stay on in winter. City streets.

Fig 6 m. Flower inside a pear-shaped receptacle which becomes the fruit. Gardens.

Horse Chestnut 25 m. Compound leaves. Upright flowers, May. Prickly fruits with conkers inside.

Laburnum or **Golden Rain** 7 m. Compound leaves. Flowers May-June. Seeds poisonous. Gardens.

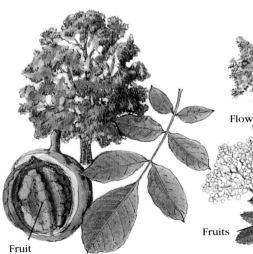

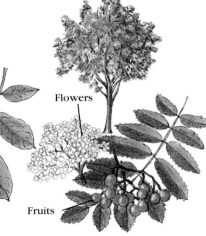

False Acacia or **Locust Tree** 20 m. Compound leaves. Ridged twigs spiny. Hanging flowers, in June. Gardens, parks.

Walnut 15 m. Compound leaves. Deep-ridged bark. Hollow twigs. Edible nuts inside thick green fruits.

Rowan or **Mountain Ash** 7 m. Compound leaves. Flowers May. Sour orange berries, September. Wild on mountains.

Common Ash 25 m. Compound leaves open late. Key-shaped fruits stay on in winter. Common woods, parks.

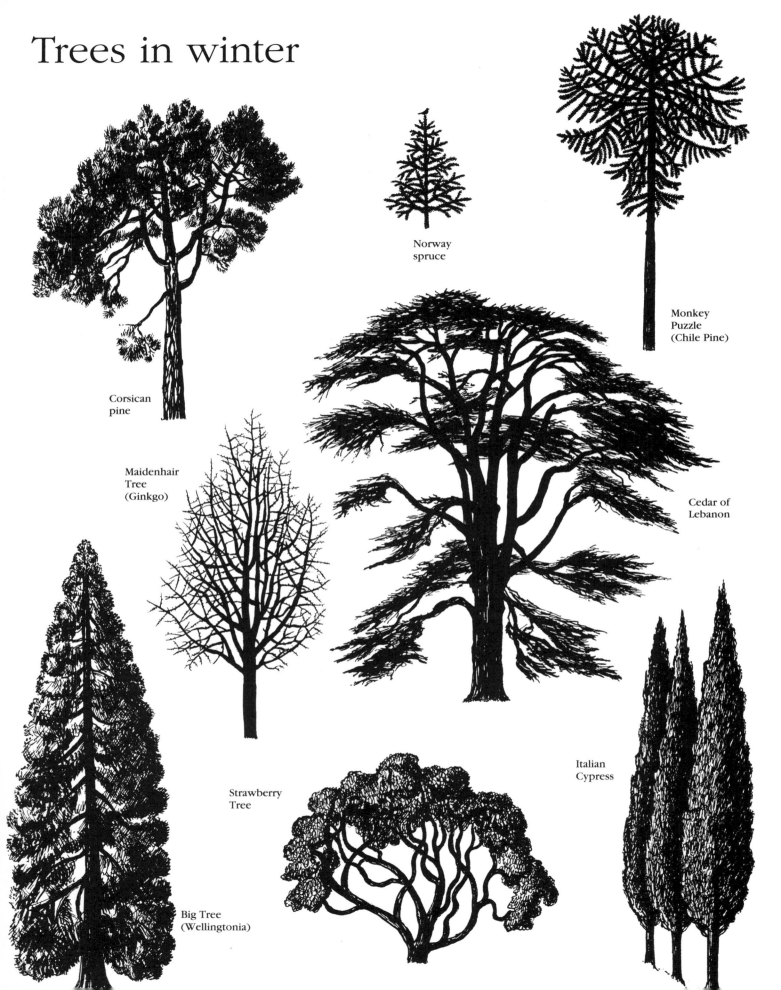

Trees in winter

Norway spruce

Monkey Puzzle (Chile Pine)

Corsican pine

Maidenhair Tree (Ginkgo)

Cedar of Lebanon

Strawberry Tree

Italian Cypress

Big Tree (Wellingtonia)

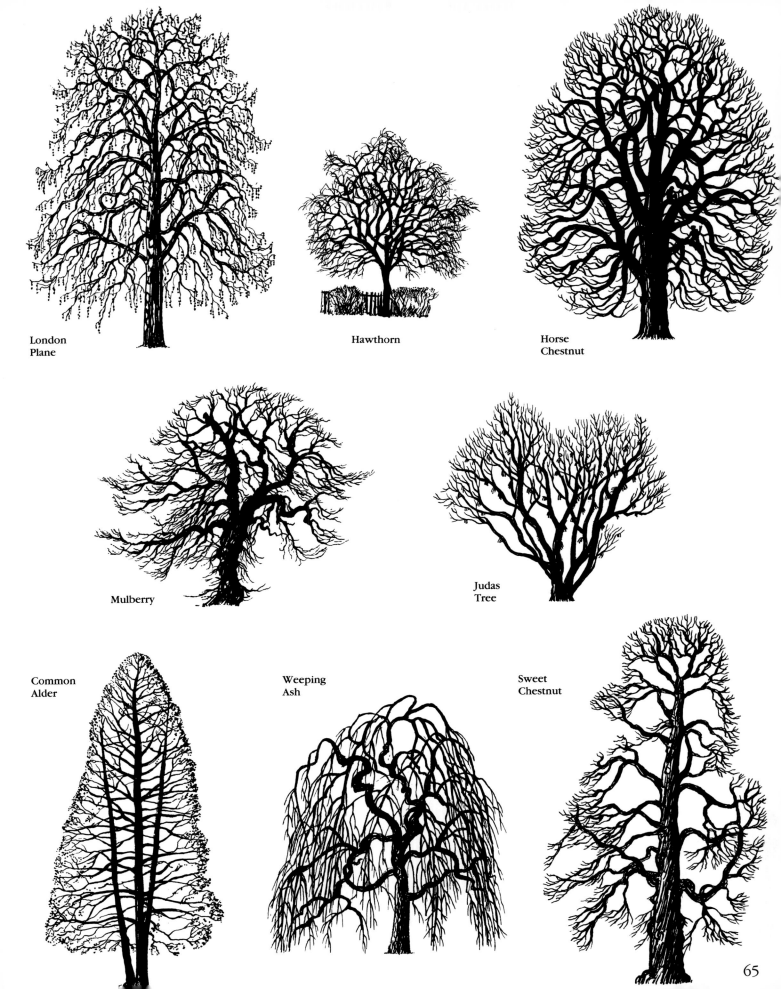

London
Plane

Hawthorn

Horse
Chestnut

Mulberry

Judas
Tree

Common
Alder

Weeping
Ash

Sweet
Chestnut

65

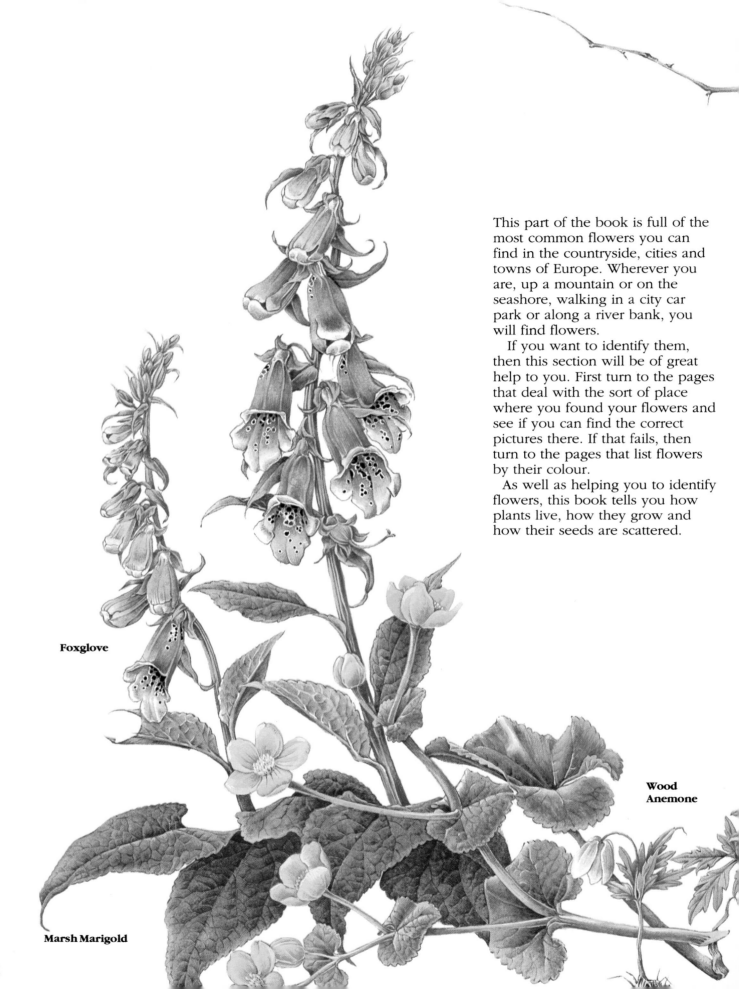

This part of the book is full of the most common flowers you can find in the countryside, cities and towns of Europe. Wherever you are, up a mountain or on the seashore, walking in a city car park or along a river bank, you will find flowers.

If you want to identify them, then this section will be of great help to you. First turn to the pages that deal with the sort of place where you found your flowers and see if you can find the correct pictures there. If that fails, then turn to the pages that list flowers by their colour.

As well as helping you to identify flowers, this book tells you how plants live, how they grow and how their seeds are scattered.

Foxglove

Wood Anemone

Marsh Marigold

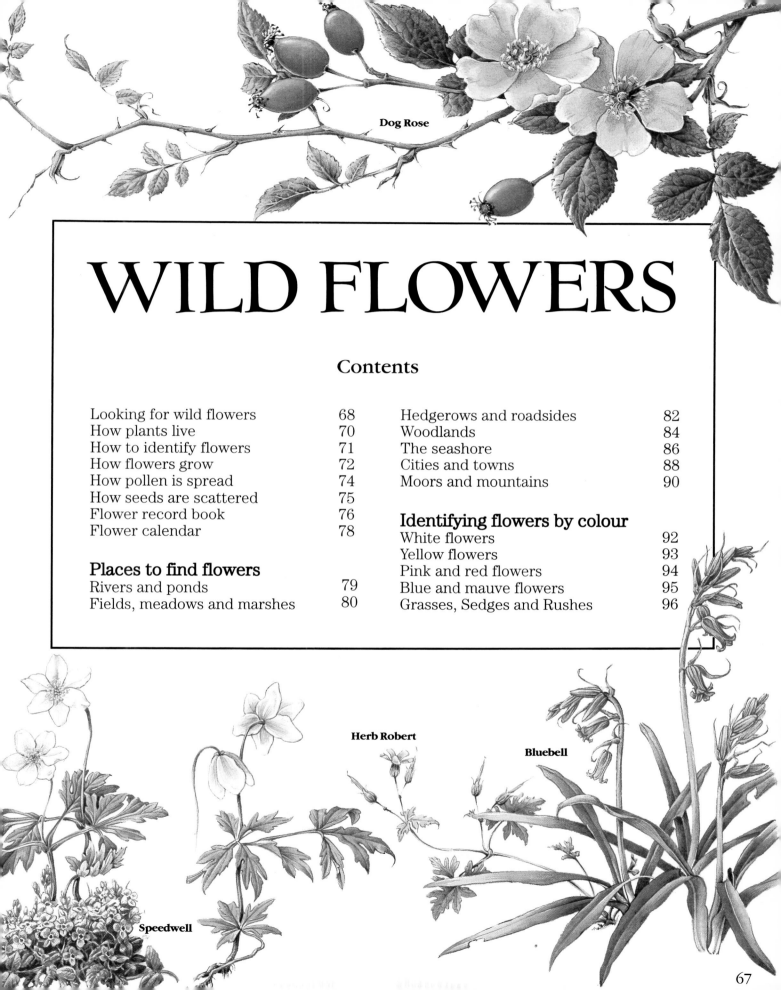

Dog Rose

WILD FLOWERS

Contents

Looking for wild flowers	68	Hedgerows and roadsides	82
How plants live	70	Woodlands	84
How to identify flowers	71	The seashore	86
How flowers grow	72	Cities and towns	88
How pollen is spread	74	Moors and mountains	90
How seeds are scattered	75		
Flower record book	76	**Identifying flowers by colour**	
Flower calendar	78	White flowers	92
		Yellow flowers	93
Places to find flowers		Pink and red flowers	94
Rivers and ponds	79	Blue and mauve flowers	95
Fields, meadows and marshes	80	Grasses, Sedges and Rushes	96

Herb Robert

Bluebell

Speedwell

Looking for wild flowers

When you go looking for wild flowers, take a notebook with you and two pencils for making notes and quick sketches. A tape measure, magnifying glass and outdoor thermometer are useful too. Record all you can about a flower, such as its height, colour and where it is growing. Use the magnifying glass to study the small parts.

Never dig up flowers and only pick them if you are sure they are common and there are lots of the same kind growing together. Take sheets of blotting paper to press them.

This is what the inside of a buttercup looks like. Other flowers may look different. Try to draw what you see inside the flower you have found.

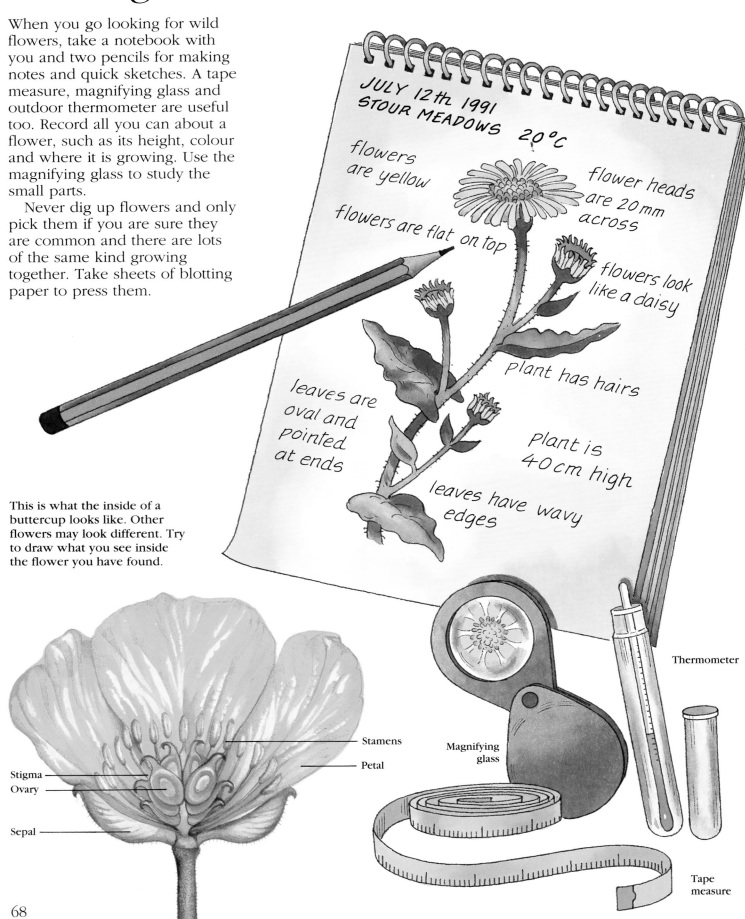

JULY 12th 1991
STOUR MEADOWS 20°C

flowers are yellow

flower heads are 20 mm across

flowers are flat on top

flowers look like a daisy

Plant has hairs

leaves are oval and pointed at ends

Plant is 40 cm high

leaves have wavy edges

Stamens

Petal

Stigma

Ovary

Sepal

Magnifying glass

Thermometer

Tape measure

Rare flowers

The three flowers shown on the right are very rare indeed. If you think you may have found a rare flower, do not pick it. If you do, the flower will become even more rare and it may disappear completely from the spot where you found it.

Instead, make a careful drawing of the flower and record in your notebook exactly where you found it. Show these to an adult who knows about rare flowers. If it is rare, you can report it to a conservation or nature club.

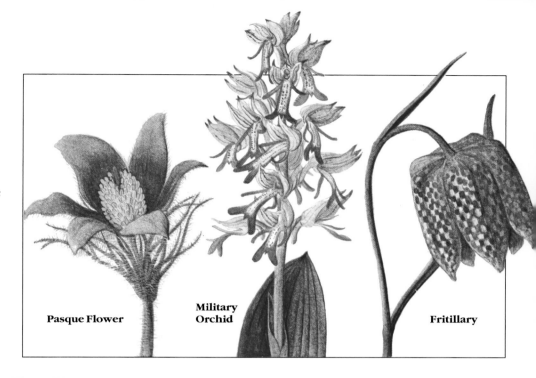

Pasque Flower

Military Orchid

Fritillary

How to make a flower map

The easiest way to make a map is to draw it as you walk along a route you know well. Draw lines for a road or path and make them turn in the same way you do.

Put in symbols for bridges, buildings and other special places. Wherever you find wild flowers, mark the place with a star. Use different colour stars for different types of flowers. Draw the symbols on the bottom of your map and write down next to them what they mean, so that everyone can understand them.

If you like, you can use a scale to show distance. Then anyone looking at it can understand how far apart everything is.

You can choose any scale you want. This map has a scale of 2 cm for every 50 paces.

SYMBOLS FOR YOUR MAP

 FLOWERS

WOODS

 STREAM

 GRASSLAND

 HILLS

 MARSHES, WATER

 BRIDGE

HOUSES

Our Church

John's house

My School

My house

50 paces

How plants live

The Rosebay Willowherb and the Field Buttercup have flowers with petals and sepals. They also have leaves, stems and roots. Most other plants have the same parts, but they can be different shapes and sizes.

Each part of a plant does one special thing that helps the plant to live. Leaves make food for a plant. During the day, they take in a gas from the air called carbon dioxide. This gas, the green colouring in the leaves, water and sunlight are used by the leaves to make food.

Leaves breathe out gases and water and take in gases from the air through tiny holes, so small you cannot see them with a magnifying glass.

Rosebay Willowherb

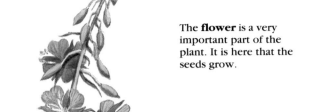

The **flower** is a very important part of the plant. It is here that the seeds grow.

The **sepals** protect the flower when it is in bud. When the flower is open, they lie underneath the petals. All the sepals together are called the calyx.

The **petals** may be brightly coloured or scented to attract insects. Some flowers need insects to carry pollen to other flowers for pollination (see pages 72 and 74), so the brighter the colours, the more insects the flower will attract.

Field Buttercup

The **leaves** make food and "breathe" for the plant. They also get rid of any water that the plant does not need. Because leaves need light to make food, the whole plant grows towards light. Some plants close their leaves at night.

The **stem** carries water from the roots to the leaves, and carries food made in the leaves to the rest of the plant. It also holds the leaves up to the light.

The **roots** hold the plant firmly in the ground and draw up water from the soil that the plant needs.

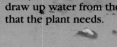

How to identify flowers

Colour and place

When trying to identify a flower the first thing you notice is colour. The shape of its petals, sepals and leaves and the place where you found it are useful also.

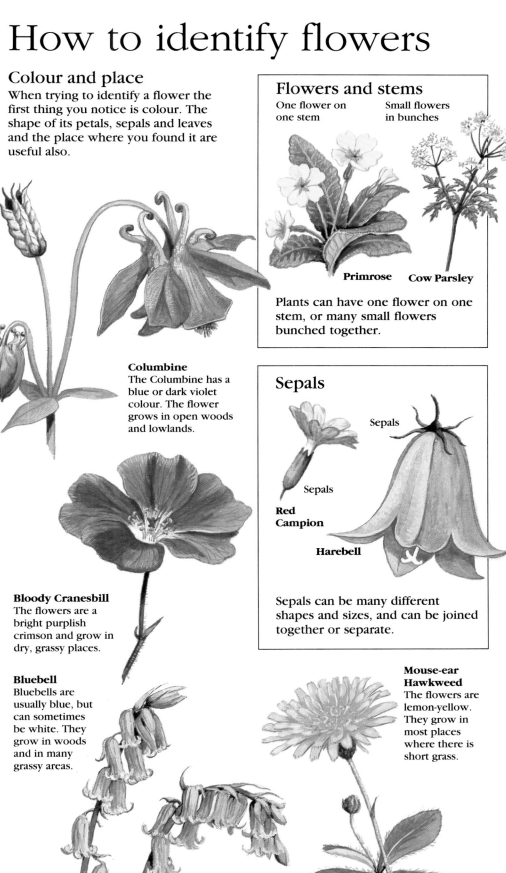

Columbine
The Columbine has a blue or dark violet colour. The flower grows in open woods and lowlands.

Bloody Cranesbill
The flowers are a bright purplish crimson and grow in dry, grassy places.

Bluebell
Bluebells are usually blue, but can sometimes be white. They grow in woods and in many grassy areas.

Mouse-ear Hawkweed
The flowers are lemon-yellow. They grow in most places where there is short grass.

Flowers and stems

One flower on one stem   Small flowers in bunches

Primrose   **Cow Parsley**

Plants can have one flower on one stem, or many small flowers bunched together.

Petals

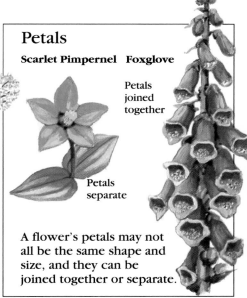

Scarlet Pimpernel   Foxglove

Petals joined together

Petals separate

A flower's petals may not all be the same shape and size, and they can be joined together or separate.

Sepals

Sepals

Sepals

Red Campion

Harebell

Sepals can be many different shapes and sizes, and can be joined together or separate.

Leaves

Wood Anemone

Leaf divides into three parts, joined at the base.

Leaves can be single, as in the Bugle (below). They can also be in separate parts. The Wood Anemone (above) has leaves which divide into three parts joined at the base. Sometimes the parts are on little stalks. These are called leaflets.

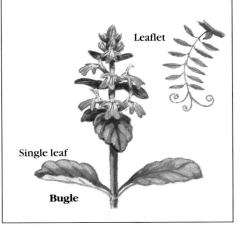

Leaflet

Single leaf

Bugle

How flowers grow

Almost every plant has a male part, called the stamen, and a female part, called the pistil. The Common Poppy has a group of stamens in the centre of the flower which grow around the pistil (see picture 3).

These pages tell you how the stamens and the pistil in a poppy work together to make seeds and how insects, such as bees, play a very important part by carrying pollen from flower to flower. These seeds will leave the plant and become new plants. Not all plants make seeds in this way, but many do.

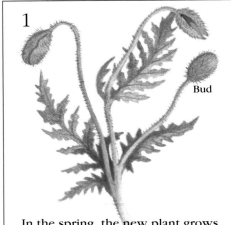

1 In the spring, the new plant grows from a seed buried in the ground. Later, many buds will develop on the plant.

Bud

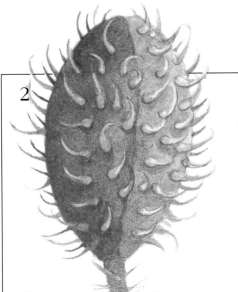

2 The sepals protect the flower when it is inside the bud. As the flower grows, the sepals begin to open.

6 When a bee visits another poppy some of this pollen may fall off onto the other flower's stigma. This is called pollination.

When the pollen grains land on top of the stigma, very thin tubes begin to grow down towards the ovary.

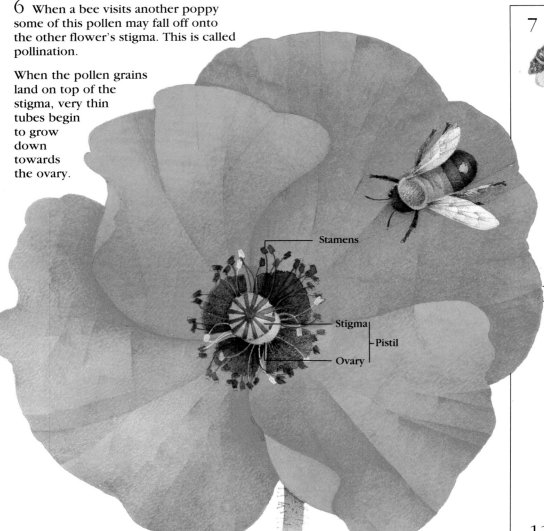

Stamens

Stigma

Pistil

Ovary

The **pistil** has two parts, the **stigma** and the **ovary**. The stigma is the top part. The ovary is the bottom part and holds "eggs", called ovules.

7 Pollen tube

Ovules

Ovary

The tubes eventually reach the ovules in the ovary. The contents of each pollen grain empty into an ovule. This is called fertilization.

11 Holes

The fruit ripens. Its outside walls dry up and holes appear at the top.

3

In the summer, the petals open. You can see the stamens (the male parts) and the pistil (the female parts).

4

Pollen

Anther

The small sacs at the end of the stamens, called anthers, open. The powder they hold, called pollen, escapes.

5

When a bee visits a poppy to feed, pollen from the stamens sticks to its hairy body or onto its legs.

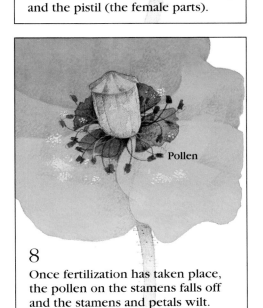

Pollen

8

Once fertilization has taken place, the pollen on the stamens falls off and the stamens and petals wilt.

9

Pistil

Petals

Stamens

The poppy does not need the stamens or the petals any more and they fall off. But the pistil is still needed. It remains strong.

10

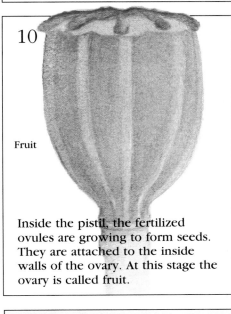

Fruit

Inside the pistil, the fertilized ovules are growing to form seeds. They are attached to the inside walls of the ovary. At this stage the ovary is called fruit.

12

Wind

Holes at top of fruit.

Seeds

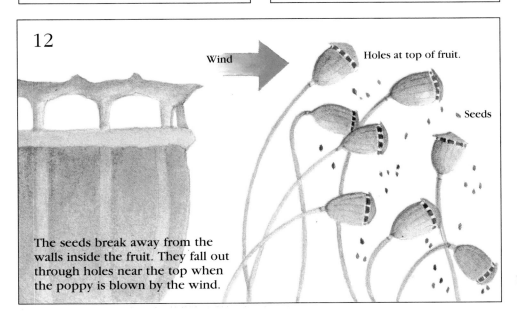

The seeds break away from the walls inside the fruit. They fall out through holes near the top when the poppy is blown by the wind.

13 The seeds which fall out of the fruit onto the soil in the autumn may grow into new plants the next spring.

How pollen is spread

In most plants, pollen must travel to another plant of the same sort to make seeds in an ovary. The pollen from a Common Poppy plant can only make seeds in another Common Poppy plant, not the one it came from (see pages 72-73). This is called cross-pollination.

In a few plants, such as the Red Helleborine on this page, pollen can make seeds grow in an ovary from the same flower. This is called self-pollination. Pollen can never make seeds grow in another sort of plant. Pollen from a rose cannot pollinate a daisy.

Insects feed on the nectar inside flowers and they can carry pollen from plant to plant when it sticks to their bodies. The colour of petals or scent can attract insects into the flowers. Some flowers have spots or lines on their petals called nectar guides. The insects follow these guides to find nectar.

The wind carries pollen too and in the summer the air is full of it. It can give people hayfever and make them sneeze.

By insects

Daisy

Some flowers make the shape of a platform with their petals for insects to land on easily.

Foxglove

Bees crawl inside some flowers to gather nectar.

By wind

Dog's Mercury

Some plants make it easy for the wind to blow away the pollen. They have a lot of pollen, and the stamens and pistils are not covered.

By itself

Red Helleborine

Some flowers, like the Red Helleborine, can pollinate themselves.

What plants need

Plants need to grow, spread their pollen, and make sure their seeds are scattered far away. To do all these things, they often depend on the weather, the soil and other living creatures - even people.

Some plants need insects to carry pollen.

Plants need the right amount of water and mineral salts in the soil to help them grow.

Plants need certain temperatures, whether they grow in cool or hot places. Most European flowers bloom when it is warm.

Plants need light to make food for themselves and to grow.

How seeds are scattered

Once the seeds have grown in the ovaries, it is important that they are scattered. Then they can begin to grow into another plant. Plants need light to grow, so it is best if they fall away from the parent plant, which might overshadow them and block out the light.

Seeds can be scattered by the wind, by animals and by water. Some plants scatter their seeds by themselves.

By animals

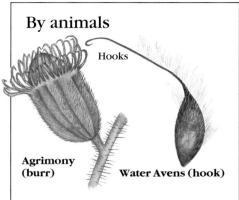

Agrimony (burr)

Hooks

Water Avens (hook)

Some seeds have burrs or hooks that stick to animal fur. The seeds eventually drop off the animal and in this way may be carried far from the parent plant.

By wind

Rosebay Willowherb

Seeds with hair "parachutes".

Dandelion ("clock")

Some seeds can float on the wind. Dandelion seeds are inside very small fruits, which have hairs that behave like parachutes.

By water

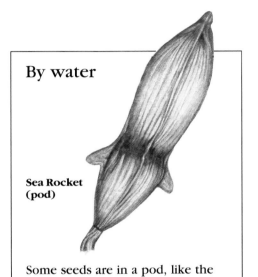

Sea Rocket (pod)

Some seeds are in a pod, like the Sea Rocket pod, that floats in the water until it opens, releasing the seeds.

By explosion

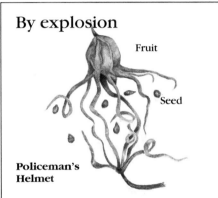

Fruit

Seed

Policeman's Helmet

Some plants have their seeds in a fruit that pops open. The seeds then shoot out, and travel away from the parent plant. The fruits of the Policeman's Helmet do this.

Animals carry seeds and nuts and drop them away from the parent plant.

Some plants need water to carry seeds away from the parent plant.

Birds may fly far from where they eat fruits. The seeds pass through their bodies and fall on the ground.

People often spread seeds without knowing. They get seeds in the soles of their shoes.

Flower record book

You could keep everything you discover about wild flowers in a record book. The best sort of book is a loose-leaf binder, which lets you add pages whenever you wish. This is the perfect place to copy out notes from flower hunting expeditions and keep drawings, maps you have made and photographs.

Everything to do with wild flowers belongs in your book. Record your experiments too. Draw and write about every step of an experiment as it happens.

A flower record book will be a permanent reminder of all the interesting bits of information you discover about the flowers you find.

Common Mallow
Found in a grassy field
on July 25th

Stick pressed flowers in your book.

Collecting pictures

Stick magazine pictures or postcards of wild flowers into your book. This way you can add to your record book even in the winter.

Pressing and mounting

Press only a common flower. Place it between two sheets of blotting paper and rest some heavy books on top for about a week.

When it is completely dry, put a dab of glue on the stem. Then fix it carefully to the inside of a clear plastic bag, so you can see both sides.

Stick the bag to a page in your record book with sticky tape. If you know the name of the flower, write it on the page. Write the date and place you found it as well.

Common Fleabane

Found in a damp meadow on August 8th at 11 a.m.
40 cm high
21°C

A simple experiment

Turn a plant away from the light. In a few days time, you will see that the plant is leaning towards the light. Plants grow towards light because they need it to make food. Plants die without light.

Make a collection of flower seeds and pods. Fix them in your book with sticky tape. Remember to label them with their flower's name.

When flowers such as poppies or daises are in bloom, make a list of the insects that visit them. Record this in your notebook.

Drawing and painting

Make coloured drawings or paintings of the quick sketches you did in your notebook when you were outside. Be sure to write down the time of day when you saw the flowers, as plants may look different in the afternoon from in the morning.

Write in your record book any information you can find about customs and festivals where flowers are used.

Leaf rubbing

Put a leaf onto a flat surface with its underside facing you.

Cover it with a piece of thin white paper. Rub backwards and forwards gently over the paper with a crayon or pencil until the shape shows through.

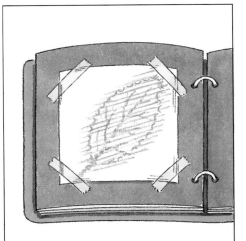

Stick your leaf rubbings into your record book.

Flower calendar

You will find that different plants flower at different times of the year. Make a calendar to help you remember when their flowers appear.

You will also discover that plants change appearance as the seasons change. Draw plants at different stages of their life, first when they are in bud, when the flowers come out and later when the fruits develop.

The pictures of the Arum on the right show how a plant can change its appearance, both inside and out at different stages in its life.

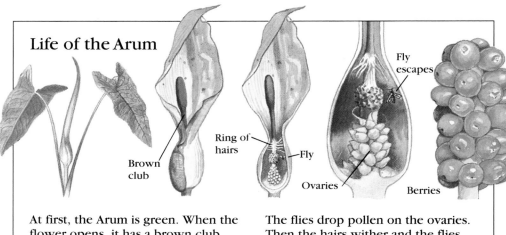

Life of the Arum

Fly escapes

Ring of hairs

Brown club

Fly

Ovaries

Berries

At first, the Arum is green. When the flower opens, it has a brown club. This attracts flies with its smell, and they get trapped inside the lower part of the flower by a ring of hairs.

The flies drop pollen on the ovaries. Then the hairs wither and the flies escape. In autumn, the ovaries become very poisonous red berries which must never be picked.

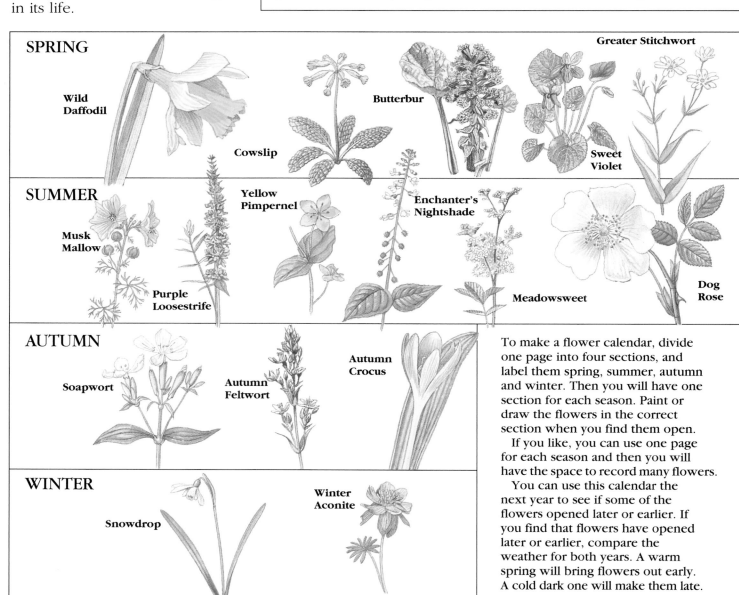

SPRING

Wild Daffodil

Cowslip

Butterbur

Greater Stitchwort

Sweet Violet

SUMMER

Musk Mallow

Purple Loosestrife

Yellow Pimpernel

Enchanter's Nightshade

Meadowsweet

Dog Rose

AUTUMN

Soapwort

Autumn Feltwort

Autumn Crocus

WINTER

Snowdrop

Winter Aconite

To make a flower calendar, divide one page into four sections, and label them spring, summer, autumn and winter. Then you will have one section for each season. Paint or draw the flowers in the correct section when you find them open.

If you like, you can use one page for each season and then you will have the space to record many flowers.

You can use this calendar the next year to see if some of the flowers opened later or earlier. If you find that flowers have opened later or earlier, compare the weather for both years. A warm spring will bring flowers out early. A cold dark one will make them late.

Rivers and ponds

Look for plants in different places around fresh water. If they actually grow in the water, they may be rooted to the bottom or their roots may float freely. Their leaves may be under the water or floating on top of it. If plants are growing on land, they may be at the water's edge, on the banks, or in swamps. Most water plants have their flowers above the water. They are usually pollinated by insects or wind, not by water.

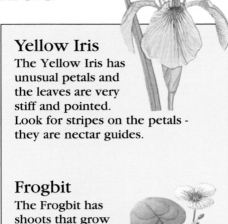

Yellow Iris

The Yellow Iris has unusual petals and the leaves are very stiff and pointed. Look for stripes on the petals - they are nectar guides.

Frogbit

The Frogbit has shoots that grow sideways. New plants grow upwards from these shoots.

Duckweed

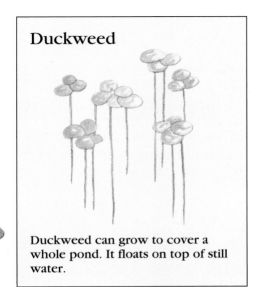

Duckweed can grow to cover a whole pond. It floats on top of still water.

Reedmace

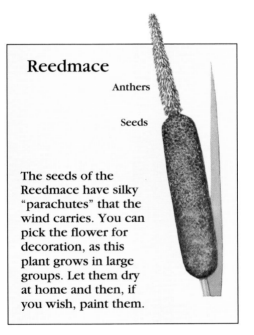

Anthers

Seeds

The seeds of the Reedmace have silky "parachutes" that the wind carries. You can pick the flower for decoration, as this plant grows in large groups. Let them dry at home and then, if you wish, paint them.

Water Lily

The petals of the Water Lily give shade to pond creatures in hot weather. They can rest on the broad, thick leaves.

Policeman's Helmet

This flower has its seeds in a fruit. When the seeds are fully grown, the fruit explodes if anything touches it. You can collect these seeds in the late summer and plant them in spring.

The leaves of fresh-water plants

The leaves of plants growing in fresh water can be all shapes and sizes - oval, round, short or long. This is because some grow under the water's surface and some on top of it, and the water

itself can be still or fast-moving.

The Water Crowfoot has broad leaves above the water and thread-like leaves below the water. The Water Soldier floats completely below the water's surface.

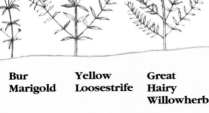

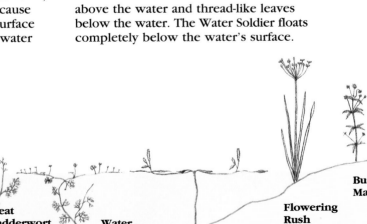

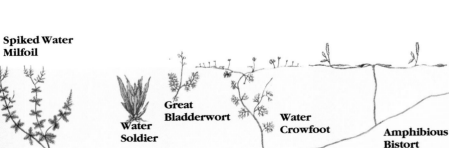

Spiked Water Milfoil

Water Soldier

Great Bladderwort

Water Crowfoot

Amphibious Bistort

Flowering Rush

Bur Marigold

Yellow Loosestrife

Great Hairy Willowherb

Fields, meadows and marshes

Some fields are used for animals to graze in and others for growing crops such as wheat and barley. You will see different flowers in different kinds of fields.

Grass grows in meadows and this is often cut to make hay. Marshes are grassy areas that are waterlogged all or almost all of the time. The flowers you find in a meadow will often be different from those you find in a marsh.

Wet soil is rich in many things that plants need to grow. This means you will find a lot of flowers in wet areas.

Marsh Marigold

This flower grows in wet meadows and looks like a large, thick-petalled buttercup.

Meadow Clary

This flower is quite common. It can be confused with Wild Clary, which has more jagged leaves and is more rare.

Marsh Thistle
The flowers are in clusters. There are prickly leaves on the dark green stems.

Yellow Rattle
When the wind blows the ripe seeds rattle inside their fruits.

Common Comfrey
The flowers are bell-shaped and hang down. You can make tea from the leaves.

Red Clover
The flower heads are made up of dozens of sweet-smelling flowers.

Wild Pansy
The flowers are violet or yellow, or a mixture of both colours.

Marsh Orchid

This plant has very unusual pink flowers. You should never pick it, or dig up the roots, as it is quite rare.

It is important to notice where flowers are growing when you find them. Marsh Orchids, for example, will often be found in the shade of a tree. Write in your notebook as many facts as possible, such as how wet or dry the soil was, if a stream was nearby, or if the land was being used for a crop or grazing animals. Often the position of a flower can be a great help when trying to identify it.

Creeping Buttercup
This plant has creeping stems which root easily.

Meadowsweet
The flowers are in clusters and smell sweet to attract insects.

Water Avens
The sepals and petals are both red, and the flowers hang in a nodding position. The fruits are easy to spot.

Fruit

Creeping Jenny
The flowers are bell-shaped and the creeping stems are matted on the ground.

Common Valerian
These red-pink flowers are common near water. They smell very unpleasant. The stem is quite stout.

Water Forget-me-Not
This plant grows near water. It is covered in soft hairs and the flower has a yellow centre.

Hedgerows and roadsides

A hedgerow is a line of specially planted bushes, usually along the edges of fields. Often other bushes start to grow in between the planted ones to give a mixture of plants. Hedgerows are important because many flowers, such as Cow Parsley, grow alongside them. As fields are cultivated and meadows mown for hay, hedgerows are often the only place left where flowers can live and grow. This means that when hedgerows are destroyed, the flowers near them usually die.

Hedgerows give shade and shelter to flowers. Often seeds are blown into a hedge and get trapped. Later they fall to the ground and start to grow.

Flowers growing on grassy verges at the roadside must be tough and strong to survive car exhaust fumes and the litter dumped on them.

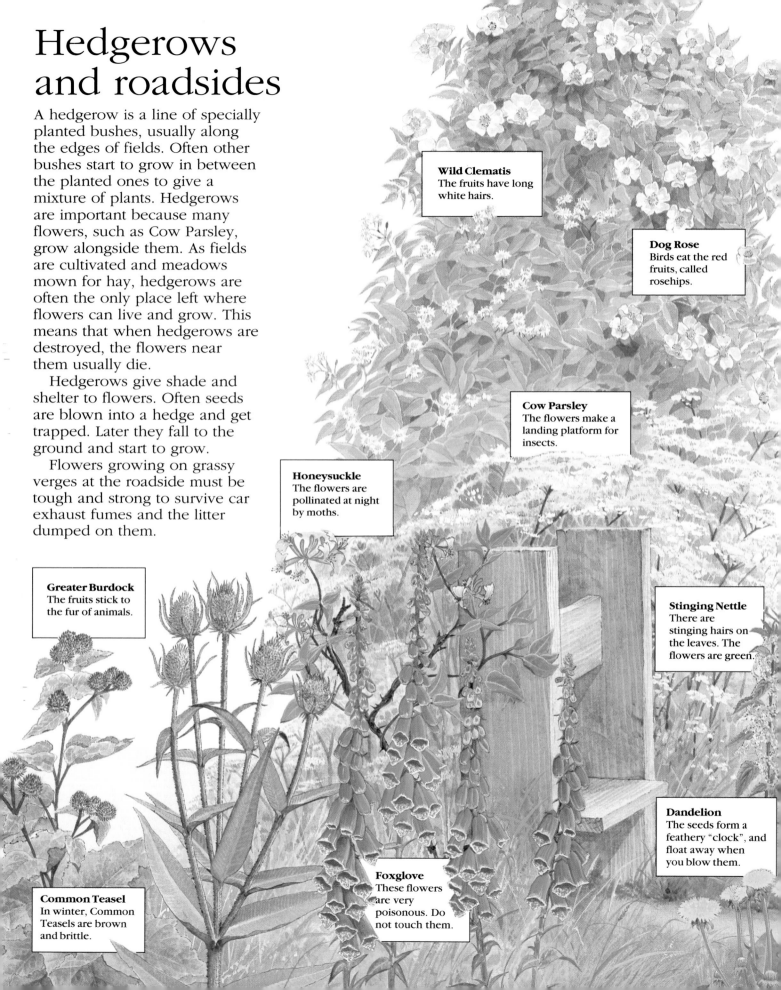

Wild Clematis
The fruits have long white hairs.

Dog Rose
Birds eat the red fruits, called rosehips.

Cow Parsley
The flowers make a landing platform for insects.

Honeysuckle
The flowers are pollinated at night by moths.

Greater Burdock
The fruits stick to the fur of animals.

Stinging Nettle
There are stinging hairs on the leaves. The flowers are green.

Dandelion
The seeds form a feathery "clock", and float away when you blow them.

Common Teasel
In winter, Common Teasels are brown and brittle.

Foxglove
These flowers are very poisonous. Do not touch them.

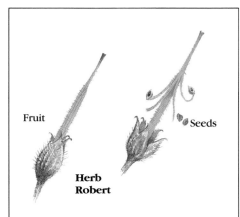

Fruit

Seeds

Herb Robert

Look for the fruit of the Herb Robert. When the seeds are fully grown, the fruit explodes, and the seeds shoot out.

Stinging Nettle

Tortoiseshell Butterfly

The small Tortoiseshell Butterfly lays its eggs on the leaves of the Stinging Nettle. If you find any eggs, do not touch them.

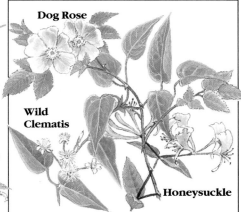

Dog Rose

Wild Clematis

Honeysuckle

Wild Clematis and Honeysuckle wrap themselves around the Dog Rose. This rose has hook-like thorns to help it climb.

Make a scent jar

Make a scent jar from any flower petals that have a nice smell, such as Honeysuckle or Wild Strawberry. Put the petals between two sheets of blotting paper (picture 1) and press them under a pile of books for about a week, or until they are dry. Put the dried petals in a jar with some pieces of dried orange or lemon peel, and a bay leaf. Prepare the lid of your scent jar by punching holes with a pencil in a circle of tin foil (picture 2). Fix the foil lid carefully over and fasten it with

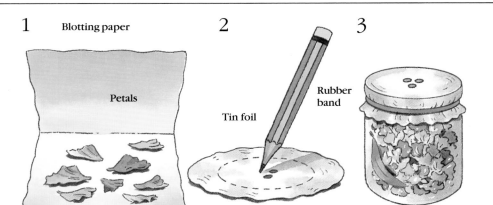

1

Blotting paper

Petals

2

Tin foil

3

Rubber band

a rubber band (picture 3).
   You can also put the petals in little bags that you have sewn out of fabric.

Leave one side of the bag open until you have put the dried petals inside. Then sew it up completely.

Creeping Cinquefoil
The creeping stems are called runners.

Greater Stitchwort
The delicate stem is square, not round.

Herb Robert
The flowers droop at night or in bad weather.

Wild Strawberry
The flowers have a nice scent.

Bird's-foot Trefoil

Coltsfoot
The seeds form a feathery "clock" like the Dandelion's.

Woodlands

In the summer and autumn, when all the trees are in full leaf, you will probably find only a few flowers on the ground beneath them. This is because the leaves are blocking the sunlight from reaching the flowers. The time when you usually find a lot of flowers in woodlands is in spring before the leaves have come out on the trees. Another reason for not seeing many flowers in woods is that the roots of trees take almost all the food from the soil. The kinds of flowers you will find change with the type of trees growing and the season.

At the edge of woods there will be more flowers because there is more sunlight. See for yourself how many grow near the edge and how many where it is very shady.

Primrose
A pale yellow flower, it blooms early in the year, before the leaves come out on the trees.

Dog's Mercury
It often carpets the ground and is very poisonous.

Oak tree in winter

Oak leaf

Acorn

Oak woods
The top picture shows an oak wood. When oak trees grow big, very little light filters down through their leaves. Even grasses find it hard to grow. A good place to hunt for flowers in an oak wood is near a path at the edge of the wood.

Beech woods
The bottom picture shows a beech wood. Beech trees grow best where the soil does not hold much water. The flowers in beech woods also prefer soil that is not too wet. See if the flowers you find in a beech wood are different from those in an oak wood.

Note
In these pictures we have left out some of the trees so you can see the flowers. In real woodlands the trees would be closer together. The scenes here are like those on the edge of woodland. Many flowers here appear before the leaves are fully out on the trees.

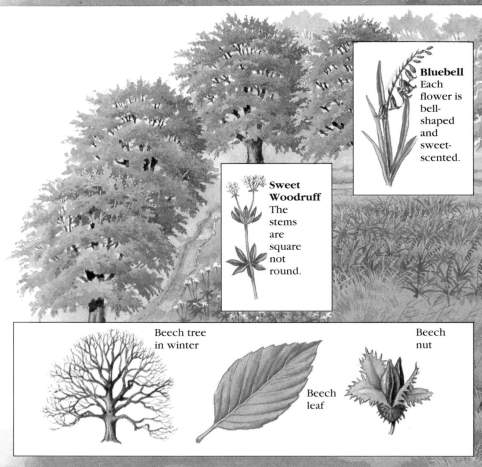

Bluebell
Each flower is bell-shaped and sweet-scented.

Sweet Woodruff
The stems are square not round.

Beech tree in winter

Beech leaf

Beech nut

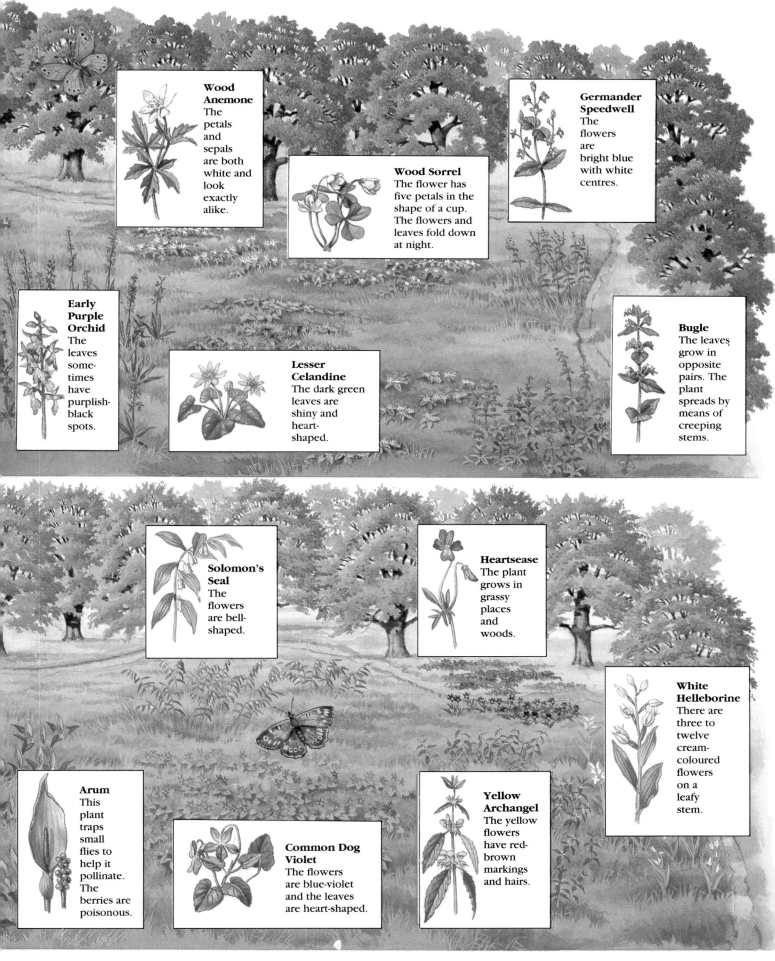

Wood Anemone The petals and sepals are both white and look exactly alike.

Wood Sorrel The flower has five petals in the shape of a cup. The flowers and leaves fold down at night.

Germander Speedwell The flowers are bright blue with white centres.

Early Purple Orchid The leaves sometimes have purplish-black spots.

Lesser Celandine The dark green leaves are shiny and heart-shaped.

Bugle The leaves grow in opposite pairs. The plant spreads by means of creeping stems.

Solomon's Seal The flowers are bell-shaped.

Heartsease The plant grows in grassy places and woods.

White Helleborine There are three to twelve cream-coloured flowers on a leafy stem.

Arum This plant traps small flies to help it pollinate. The berries are poisonous.

Common Dog Violet The flowers are blue-violet and the leaves are heart-shaped.

Yellow Archangel The yellow flowers have red-brown markings and hairs.

85

The seashore

Plants near the seashore must survive in very difficult conditions. The hot sun can dry them out very quickly. Strong winds can dry them out too or blow them over.

They must find ways of not losing the water inside them. To stop water escaping, some plants have a thick outer layer to trap the water, while others have a waxy coat over their leaves, or roll up their leaves when it is very hot and sunny.

Other plants may have small leaves, hairs on their leaves which shield them from the sun, or grow spines instead of leaves.

Plants must be sturdy enough not to blow over in the strong sea winds. This means they either have strong deep roots clinging onto mud, stones and rocks, or grow close to the ground so that there is less chance of them blowing over.

Salt marshes

Salt marshes are made of sand and mud. Be careful when you walk there. It is very easy to sink in. Go with a friend and wear rubber boots. The land in such places has slowly taken over from the sea. That is why the soil is salty.

There are different sections in salt marshes, called zones. Different plants grow in different zones. Many plants that grow in salt marshes do not grow further inland.

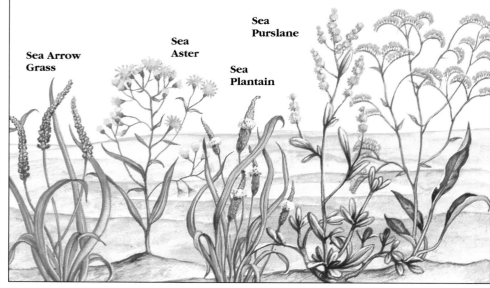

Sea Lavender

Sea Purslane

Sea Aster

Sea Plantain

Sea Arrow Grass

Sand dunes

Like salt marshes, sand dunes have different zones. The types of plants in each zone change according to how near the zone is to the sea and how much the dunes have been held together by plants such as Marram Grass. Couch Grass will be in a zone nearer to the sea than Ragwort.

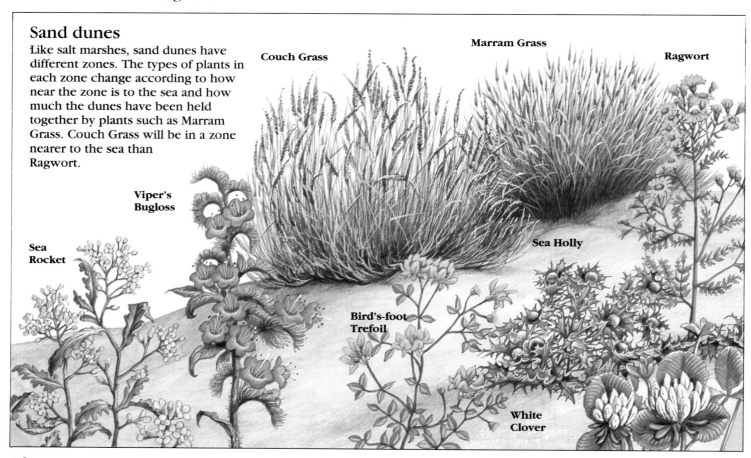

Marram Grass

Couch Grass

Ragwort

Viper's Bugloss

Sea Rocket

Sea Holly

Bird's-foot Trefoil

White Clover

Shingle Beaches

Not many plants can grow here. These beaches are made of pebbles that once were part of cliffs or rocks. The pebbles have been worn down by the pounding of the sea. There is some sand mixed in with the pebbles, and in many places the shingle is constantly on the move. Only plants with deep roots, such as the Yellow Horned Poppy and the Sea Pea, can anchor themselves firmly enough to survive in the shingle.

Shrubby Seablite

Yellow Horned Poppy

Sea pea

Sea Bindweed

Cliffs

Plants struggle to grow here. The winds can be very fierce and blow a lot of the time. Small plants whose roots are not deep can be torn up. The rainwater drains away very quickly, leaving little for the plants. There is almost no soil. Plants must send their roots deep into cracks in the rock. Sometimes they grow along the steep sides of a cliff and can be sprayed with salty water from the sea.

Cliffs may have more soil at the top and there you may be able to find some land plants. Be careful when you look at flowers there. Do not climb any cliffs, and keep well back from the edge.

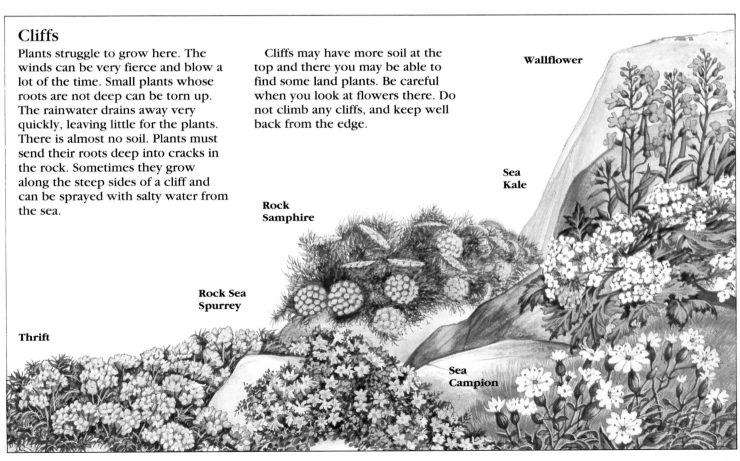

Wallflower

Sea Kale

Rock Samphire

Rock Sea Spurrey

Thrift

Sea Campion

Cities and towns

Flowers grow in waste lands, streets, car parks, gardens, on walls, or any other place in towns and cities where they can find enough soil.

Many flowers can spread quickly over open ground. Some of these flowers are called weeds. Weeds are often stronger than the plants people grow in their gardens, and they can take over. This is a big problem for gardeners.

The flowers in this section are not drawn to scale.

Seed experiment

Heat some soil in an old pan in the oven for about an hour. This will kill any seeds in the soil. Put the pan outside. After a while do wild flowers start to grow? If so, how do you think they get there?

Wallflower
This is a garden flower, but it often "escapes" and can survive from year to year in the wild.

Pellitory of the Wall
This plant looks rather like a Stinging Nettle, but it has no stinging hairs. The stem is reddish-brown.

Prickly Sow Thistle
The leaves are spiny and clasp the stem. The flowers are pale yellow, about 2.5 cm across.

Ivy-leaved Toadflax
The plant is delicate and trailing, with tiny purple flowers, which have curved spurs. The stems are weak.

Dandelion
There is one flower head, made up of many tiny flowers, on each hollow stalk, which contains a milky juice.

Shepherd's Purse
A common weed in cities and towns. The seeds are held in a heart-shaped fruit. Flowers are white.

Ribwort Plantain
The flowers grow on small dark brown spikes. The anthers are pale yellow or purple.

White Clover
The leaves have three (and very rarely four) leaflets. The white flowers have a sweet smell to attract insects.

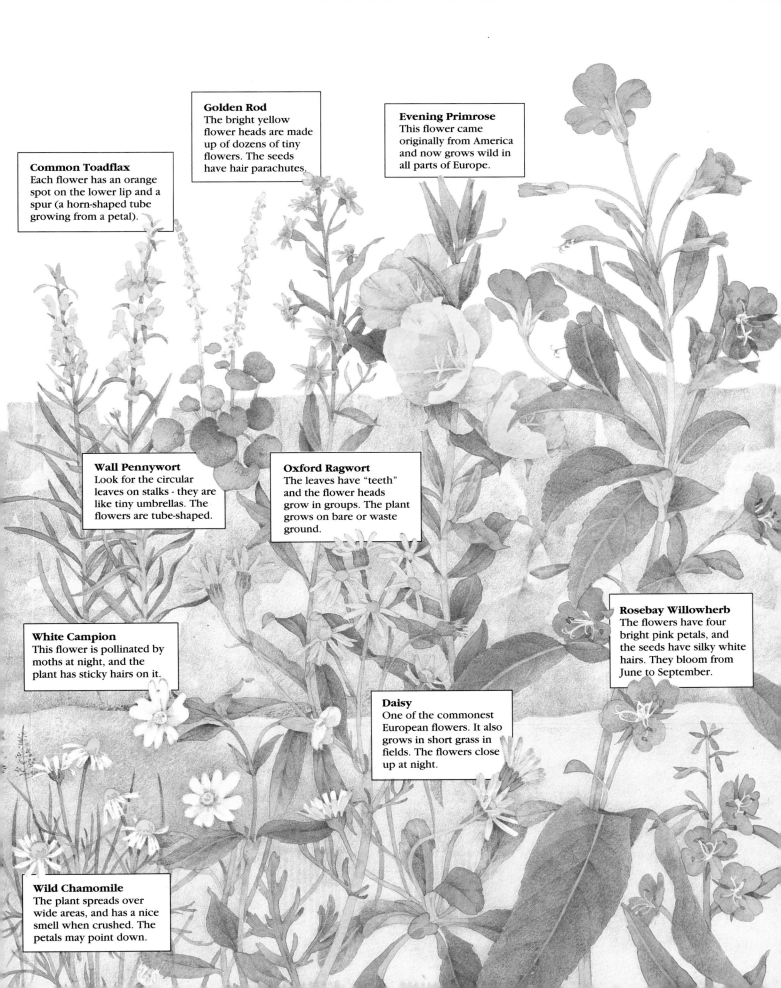

Common Toadflax
Each flower has an orange spot on the lower lip and a spur (a horn-shaped tube growing from a petal).

Golden Rod
The bright yellow flower heads are made up of dozens of tiny flowers. The seeds have hair parachutes.

Evening Primrose
This flower came originally from America and now grows wild in all parts of Europe.

Wall Pennywort
Look for the circular leaves on stalks - they are like tiny umbrellas. The flowers are tube-shaped.

Oxford Ragwort
The leaves have "teeth" and the flower heads grow in groups. The plant grows on bare or waste ground.

White Campion
This flower is pollinated by moths at night, and the plant has sticky hairs on it.

Rosebay Willowherb
The flowers have four bright pink petals, and the seeds have silky white hairs. They bloom from June to September.

Daisy
One of the commonest European flowers. It also grows in short grass in fields. The flowers close up at night.

Wild Chamomile
The plant spreads over wide areas, and has a nice smell when crushed. The petals may point down.

Moors and mountains

Moors

Moors are open lands that are swept by wind. Heathland is very similar. Some of these areas are very dry and some are waterlogged from time to time. Water collects in poor soil, such as in high land or near the coast. You will find fewer flowers on moors and heaths than in meadows and fields. The ones that do grow sometimes take over large sections of land.

Different flowers grow on different types of moors and heaths. The most common moorland plant is Common Heather. Sometimes it is burnt to encourage new shoots to grow. The Common Gorse is very widespread on heaths.

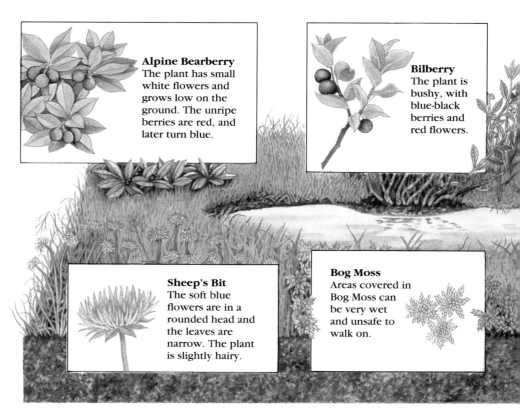

Alpine Bearberry
The plant has small white flowers and grows low on the ground. The unripe berries are red, and later turn blue.

Bilberry
The plant is bushy, with blue-black berries and red flowers.

Sheep's Bit
The soft blue flowers are in a rounded head and the leaves are narrow. The plant is slightly hairy.

Bog Moss
Areas covered in Bog Moss can be very wet and unsafe to walk on.

Mountains

The seeds of mountain flowers find it difficult to grow in the poor soils and the cold, windy weather of mountains. The higher up a mountain you go, the fewer flowers you will find. Trees cannot grow high up on a mountain because of the strong winds and lack of soil.

Some plants can grow high up on a mountain-side. They grow low so that the strong winds will not blow them away. Many mountain flowers spread by sending out creeping stems, which root.

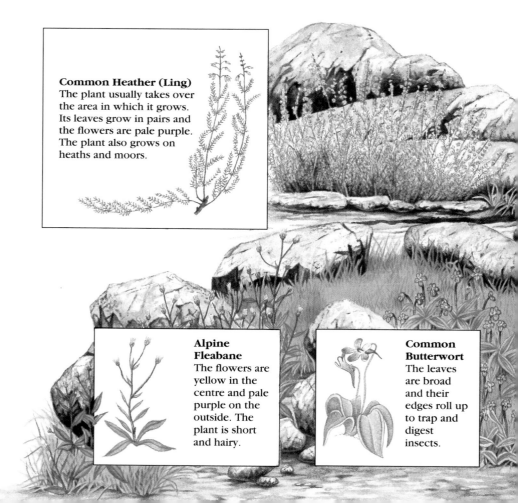

Common Heather (Ling)
The plant usually takes over the area in which it grows. Its leaves grow in pairs and the flowers are pale purple. The plant also grows on heaths and moors.

Alpine Fleabane
The flowers are yellow in the centre and pale purple on the outside. The plant is short and hairy.

Common Butterwort
The leaves are broad and their edges roll up to trap and digest insects.

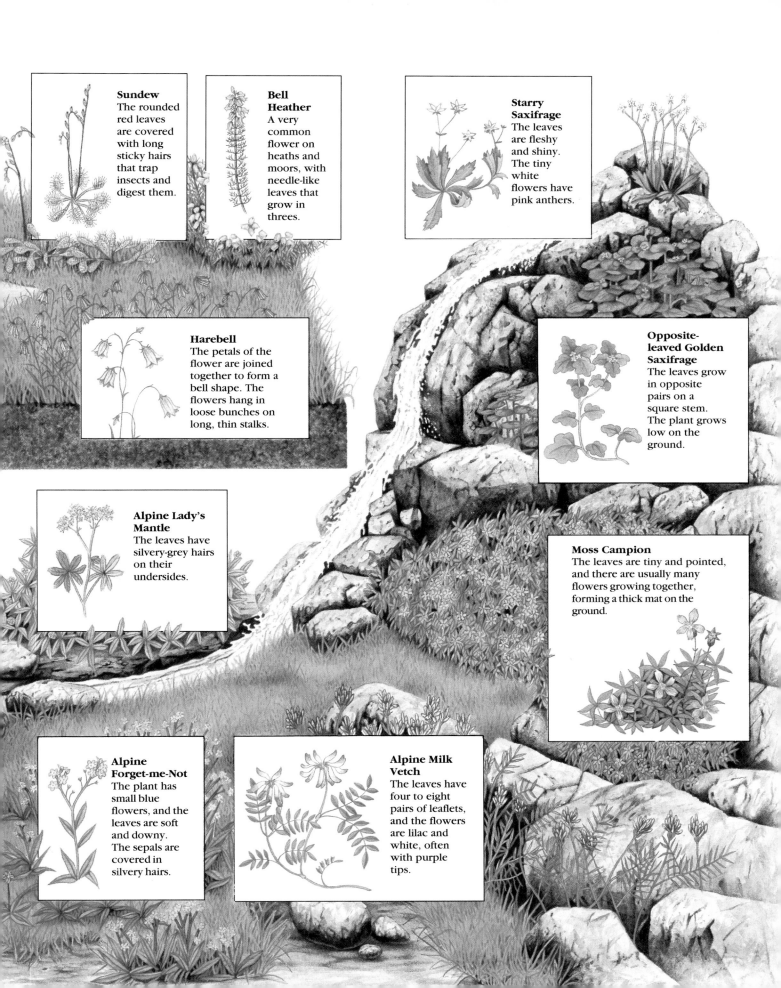

Sundew
The rounded red leaves are covered with long sticky hairs that trap insects and digest them.

Bell Heather
A very common flower on heaths and moors, with needle-like leaves that grow in threes.

Starry Saxifrage
The leaves are fleshy and shiny. The tiny white flowers have pink anthers.

Harebell
The petals of the flower are joined together to form a bell shape. The flowers hang in loose bunches on long, thin stalks.

Opposite-leaved Golden Saxifrage
The leaves grow in opposite pairs on a square stem. The plant grows low on the ground.

Alpine Lady's Mantle
The leaves have silvery-grey hairs on their undersides.

Moss Campion
The leaves are tiny and pointed, and there are usually many flowers growing together, forming a thick mat on the ground.

Alpine Forget-me-Not
The plant has small blue flowers, and the leaves are soft and downy. The sepals are covered in silvery hairs.

Alpine Milk Vetch
The leaves have four to eight pairs of leaflets, and the flowers are lilac and white, often with purple tips.

Identifying flowers by colour

White flowers

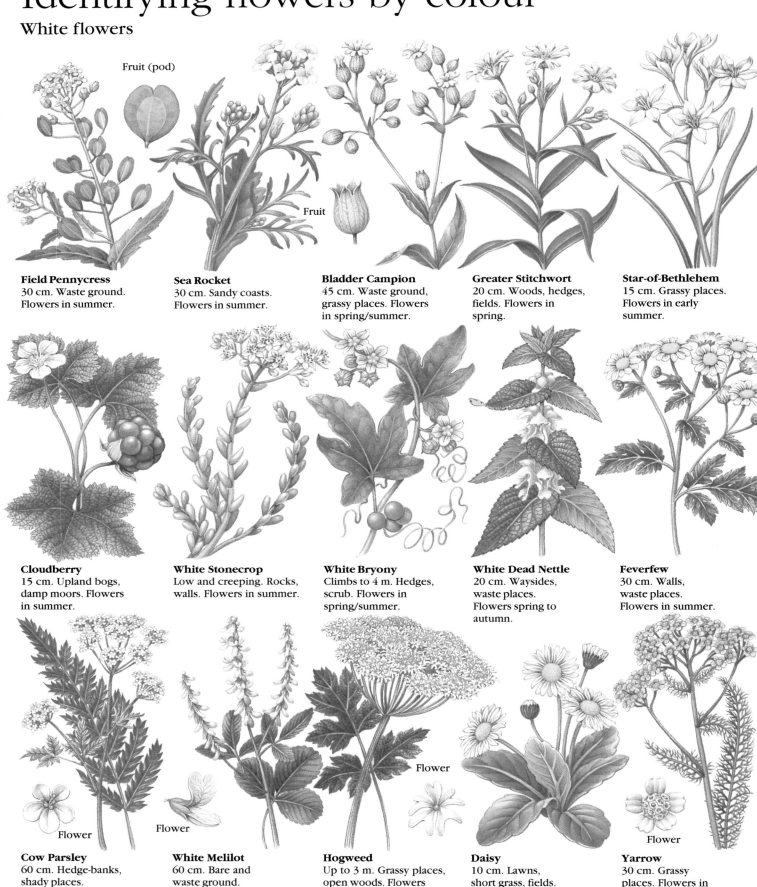

Fruit (pod)

Fruit

Field Pennycress
30 cm. Waste ground.
Flowers in summer.

Sea Rocket
30 cm. Sandy coasts.
Flowers in summer.

Bladder Campion
45 cm. Waste ground,
grassy places. Flowers
in spring/summer.

Greater Stitchwort
20 cm. Woods, hedges,
fields. Flowers in
spring.

Star-of-Bethlehem
15 cm. Grassy places.
Flowers in early
summer.

Cloudberry
15 cm. Upland bogs,
damp moors. Flowers
in summer.

White Stonecrop
Low and creeping. Rocks,
walls. Flowers in summer.

White Bryony
Climbs to 4 m. Hedges,
scrub. Flowers in
spring/summer.

White Dead Nettle
20 cm. Waysides,
waste places.
Flowers spring to
autumn.

Feverfew
30 cm. Walls,
waste places.
Flowers in summer.

Flower

Flower

Flower

Flower

Flower

Cow Parsley
60 cm. Hedge-banks,
shady places.
Flowers in spring.

White Melilot
60 cm. Bare and
waste ground.
Flowers in summer.

Hogweed
Up to 3 m. Grassy places,
open woods. Flowers
spring to autumn.

Daisy
10 cm. Lawns,
short grass, fields.
Flowers all year.

Yarrow
30 cm. Grassy
places. Flowers in
summer/autumn.

92   On these pages you will find the average height of the plant from ground level to the top, the season when the plant comes
into flower, and the place where it is most likely to be found.

Yellow flowers

Bulbous Buttercup
15 cm. Grassland.
Flowers in spring.

Marsh Marigold
15 cm. Wet places.
Flowers in spring/
summer.

Yellow Horned Poppy
60 cm. Sea shingle,
waste places inland.
Flowers in summer.

Monkey Flower
20 cm. Wet
places. Flowers
in summer.

Yellow Rattle
30 cm. Grassy places,
and fields. Flowers
in spring/summer.

Flower

Wild Cabbage
60 cm. Sea cliffs.
Flowers in summer.

Silverweed
Low, creeping. Damp
grassy places. Flowers
in spring/summer.

Lady's Bedstraw
10 cm. Dry, grassy
places. Flowers
in summer.

Yellow Chamomile
30 cm. Dry, bare
and waste places.
Flowers in summer.

Groundsel
10 cm. Gardens
and waste ground.
Flowers all year.

Flower

Common Gorse
Up to 2.5 m. Heaths,
grassland.
Flowers all year.

Common Rockrose
Close to the ground.
Grassy and rocky places.
Flowers in summer.

Kidney Vetch
15 cm. Dry grassland,
by sea, mountains.
Flowers spring/summer.

**Perforate St John's
Wort**
45 cm. Grassy places.
Flowers in summer.

Yellow Water Lily
4 cm above water. Still
water, slow streams.
Flowers in summer.

**Remember - if you cannot see a picture of the flower you want to identify here, then look on the pages earlier in this section which
link flowers with the places where they grow.**

Pink and red flowers

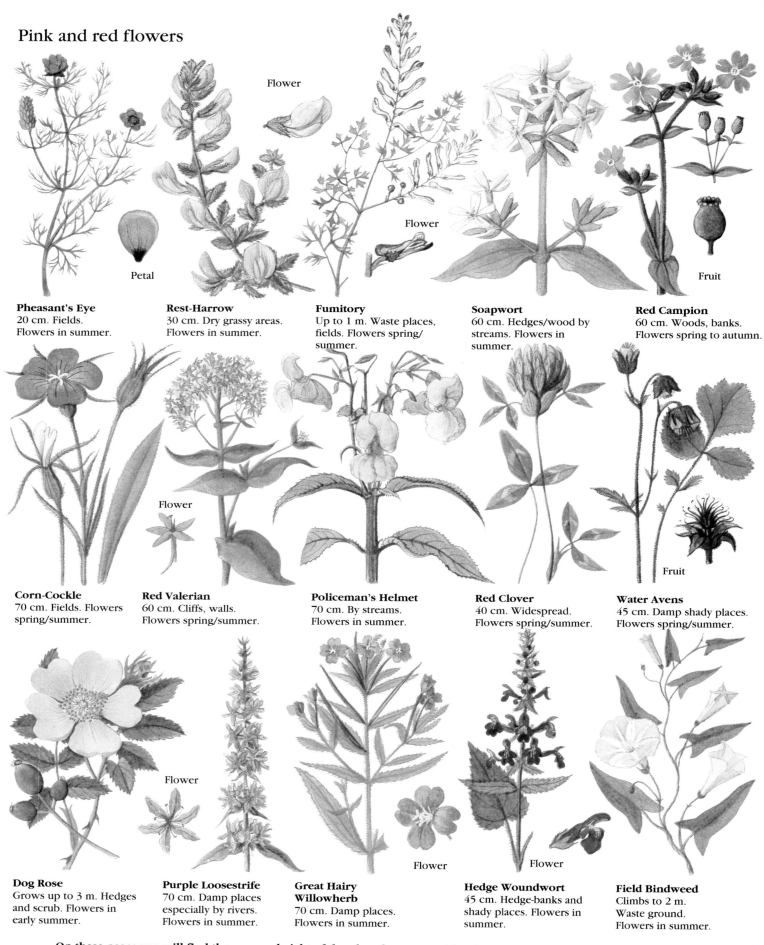

Flower

Petal

Flower

Flower

Fruit

Pheasant's Eye
20 cm. Fields.
Flowers in summer.

Rest-Harrow
30 cm. Dry grassy areas.
Flowers in summer.

Fumitory
Up to 1 m. Waste places,
fields. Flowers spring/
summer.

Soapwort
60 cm. Hedges/wood by
streams. Flowers in
summer.

Red Campion
60 cm. Woods, banks.
Flowers spring to autumn.

Flower

Fruit

Corn-Cockle
70 cm. Fields. Flowers
spring/summer.

Red Valerian
60 cm. Cliffs, walls.
Flowers spring/summer.

Policeman's Helmet
70 cm. By streams.
Flowers in summer.

Red Clover
40 cm. Widespread.
Flowers spring/summer.

Water Avens
45 cm. Damp shady places.
Flowers spring/summer.

Flower

Flower

Flower

Dog Rose
Grows up to 3 m. Hedges
and scrub. Flowers in
early summer.

Purple Loosestrife
70 cm. Damp places
especially by rivers.
Flowers in summer.

**Great Hairy
Willowherb**
70 cm. Damp places.
Flowers in summer.

Hedge Woundwort
45 cm. Hedge-banks and
shady places. Flowers in
summer.

Field Bindweed
Climbs to 2 m.
Waste ground.
Flowers in summer.

**On these pages you will find the average height of the plant from ground level to the top, the season when the plant comes into
flower, and the place where it is most likely to be found.**

Blue and mauve flowers

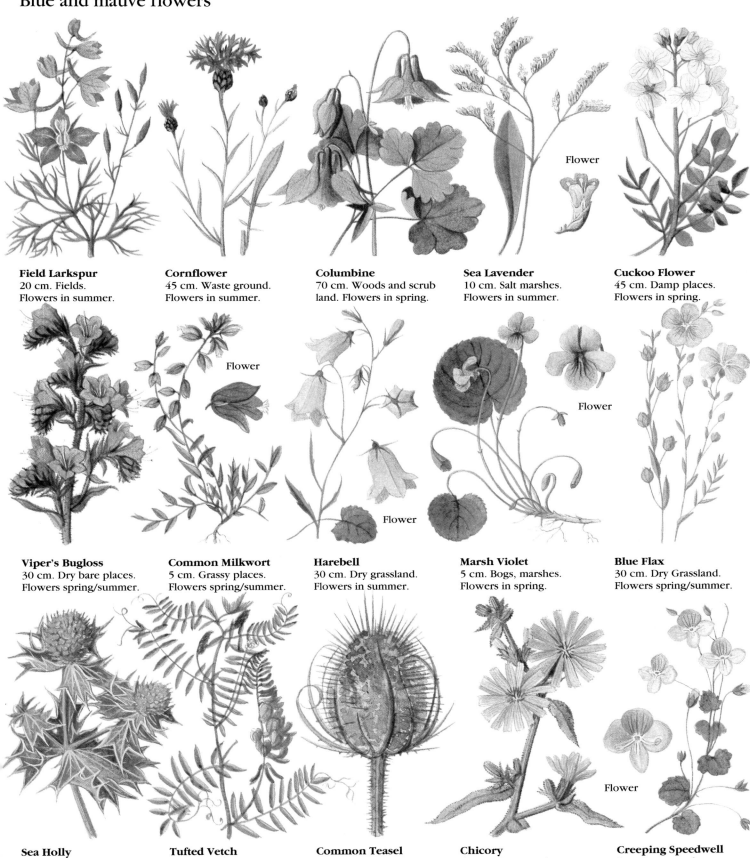

Field Larkspur
20 cm. Fields.
Flowers in summer.

Cornflower
45 cm. Waste ground.
Flowers in summer.

Columbine
70 cm. Woods and scrub
land. Flowers in spring.

Sea Lavender
10 cm. Salt marshes.
Flowers in summer.

Flower

Cuckoo Flower
45 cm. Damp places.
Flowers in spring.

Flower

Viper's Bugloss
30 cm. Dry bare places.
Flowers spring/summer.

Common Milkwort
5 cm. Grassy places.
Flowers spring/summer.

Harebell
30 cm. Dry grassland.
Flowers in summer.

Flower

Marsh Violet
5 cm. Bogs, marshes.
Flowers in spring.

Flower

Blue Flax
30 cm. Dry Grassland.
Flowers spring/summer.

Sea Holly
30 cm. By the sea on
sand and shingle.
Flowers in summer.

Tufted Vetch
Climbs to 1.5 m.
Hedges and bushy places.
Flowers in summer.

Common Teasel
70 cm. Grassy and
bushy places.
Flowers in summer.

Chicory
60 cm. Grassy and
waste places.
Flowers in summer.

Flower

Creeping Speedwell
Low. Lawns and
grassy places.
Flowers in spring.

**Remember - if you cannot see a picture of the flower you want to identify here, then look on the pages earlier in this section which
link flowers with the places where they grow.**

Grasses, Sedges and Rushes

Grasses

Most grasses have round hollow stems, long narrow leaves and spikes or sprays of tiny flowers.

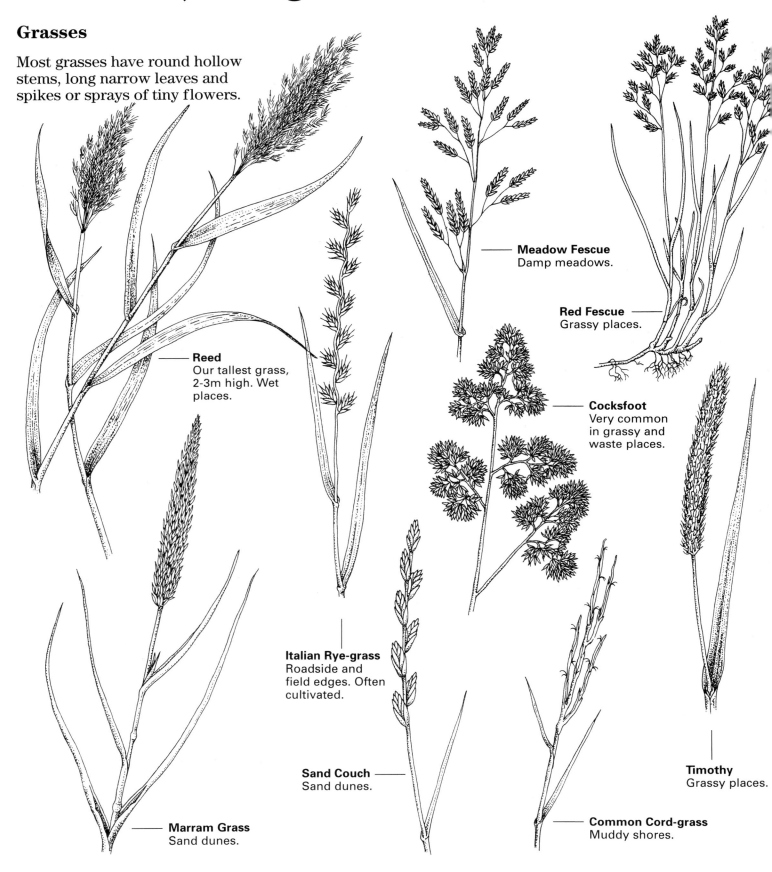

Meadow Fescue
Damp meadows.

Red Fescue
Grassy places.

Reed
Our tallest grass, 2-3m high. Wet places.

Cocksfoot
Very common in grassy and waste places.

Italian Rye-grass
Roadside and field edges. Often cultivated.

Sand Couch
Sand dunes.

Timothy
Grassy places.

Marram Grass
Sand dunes.

Common Cord-grass
Muddy shores.

Sedges

Sedges look rather like grasses, but their stems are often three-sided, and never hollow like grass stems.

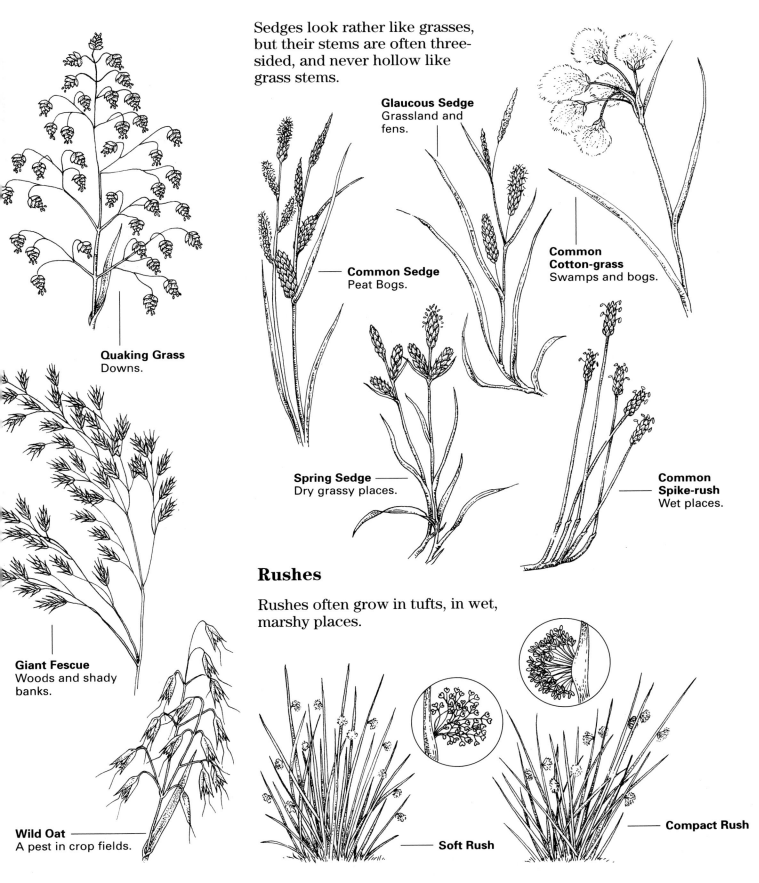

Quaking Grass
Downs.

Giant Fescue
Woods and shady banks.

Wild Oat
A pest in crop fields.

Glaucous Sedge
Grassland and fens.

Common Sedge
Peat Bogs.

Common Cotton-grass
Swamps and bogs.

Spring Sedge
Dry grassy places.

Common Spike-rush
Wet places.

Rushes

Rushes often grow in tufts, in wet, marshy places.

Soft Rush

Compact Rush

This part of the book is about the many kinds of animals and plants that live and grow in gardens. Any garden, however small, is a fascinating place to explore. You have only to turn over a stone, disturb a small area of soil, or move a pile of dead leaves to find a world filled with tiny creatures, such as woodlice, ants and centipedes.

This part of the book tells you how and where to look for wildlife in gardens. It shows you how many of the animals and plants live, and how to collect and study them. Most important of all, you can learn how to protect wildlife, by providing food and shelter which will encourage animals and plants to live in your garden.

GARDEN WILDLIFE

Wildlife in your garden 100
Life in the soil 102
How to attract wildlife 104
Plants in the garden 106
More about plants 108
Butterflies and moths 110
Garden insects 112
Snails and other small animals 114

Spiders 116
Birds 118
Ponds and trees 120
The garden at night 122
Visitors to the garden 124
More wildlife in the garden 126
Water flowers 128

Wildlife in your garden

If you think that gardens are only full of flowers, with a vegetable patch and the odd bird or spider, you are wrong. Even in a backyard with a few flower pots and a hedge or wall, all kinds of animals and wild flowers can be found, if you look closely.

The kinds of wildlife in your garden will depend partly on where you live (see page 124), how old the garden is, and the food and shelter it offers.

Most of the animals have a special job to do in the garden. By watching them and learning how they all live together, you will be able to enjoy your garden all the more.

Each part of the garden, from the flower beds to the compost heap, is a separate world with its own wildlife. This is called a habitat.

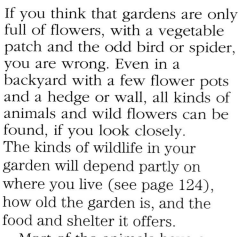

You will not find any animals in a new garden like this one because there is no food or shelter for them. You can help attract wildlife straightaway by making a bird table (see page 105) and a pond (see page 120). More animals will come as plants begin to grow.

Insects, such as hoverflies, rest on walls, especially in sunny spots. The Wall Mason Wasp builds its nest in holes in walls.

Wall Mason Wasp

Hoverfly

Great Spotted Woodpecker

Smooth Newt

A pond will attract frogs and newts, and insects such as dragonflies.

Cardinal Beetle

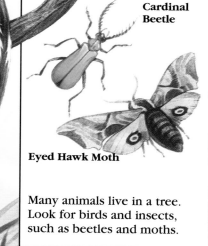

Eyed Hawk Moth

Common Frog

Many animals live in a tree. Look for birds and insects, such as beetles and moths.

Shrubs hide insects such as the Speckled Bush-cricket. Hedgehogs may hibernate in leaves under hedges.

Speckled Bush-cricket

Hedgehog

Rotting compost heaps hide many small animals. Look for worms, beetles, millipedes, centipedes, and harvestmen.

Centipede

Brandling Earthworm

In winter, look in corners of garden sheds for spiders and hibernating ladybirds. You may find a Wood Mouse in a shed.

Two-spot Ladybird

Spider

Wood Mouse

Bees and butterflies visit flowers to feed on nectar.

Bumble Bee

Orange-tip Butterfly

Look under logs and stones, and in other damp, dark places for animals like this woodlouse.

Woodlouse

Flower borders provide shelter for snails, caterpillars and slugs.

Dot Moth caterpillar

Brown-lipped Snail

Blackbird

101

Life in the soil

The soil in your garden is full of small animals, although many can be too tiny to see. Different kinds of animals and plants need different types of soil. Snails, for example, need lime in the soil for making their shells. Moles will visit your garden only if the soil is soft enough for them to dig in.

You will be able to find some of the garden animals shown on these pages, by digging in the soil. Some animals, such as earthworms, help to keep the soil healthy, but other animals can damage plants by feeding on the roots and shoots.

Making a wormery

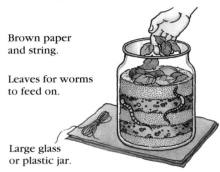

Brown paper and string.

Leaves for worms to feed on.

Large glass or plastic jar.

Put alternate layers of fine sand and soil in a large jar. Then put in a few worms and some leaves for them to feed on. Wrap paper round the jar to keep the light out. Remove the paper two days later and you will see how the worms have mixed up the layers.

Looking at soil

Round Worms

Soil Mite

Measure out a square metre of soil and then scoop up its top layer. In it will be millions of minute animals. Try to find some of them by putting a little of the soil in a dish with some water. Pick up the creatures on a paint brush and use a magnifying glass to examine them.

Underground slugs

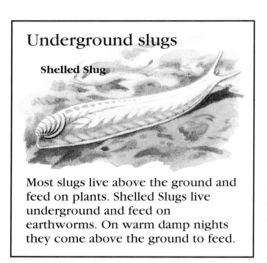

Shelled Slug

Most slugs live above the ground and feed on plants. Shelled Slugs live underground and feed on earthworms. On warm damp nights they come above the ground to feed.

Food webs

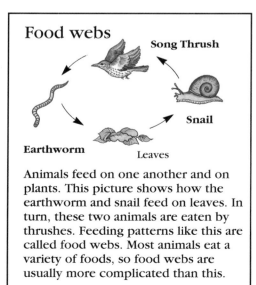

Song Thrush

Snail

Earthworm

Leaves

Animals feed on one another and on plants. This picture shows how the earthworm and snail feed on leaves. In turn, these two animals are eaten by thrushes. Feeding patterns like this are called food webs. Most animals eat a variety of foods, so food webs are usually more complicated than this.

Worms

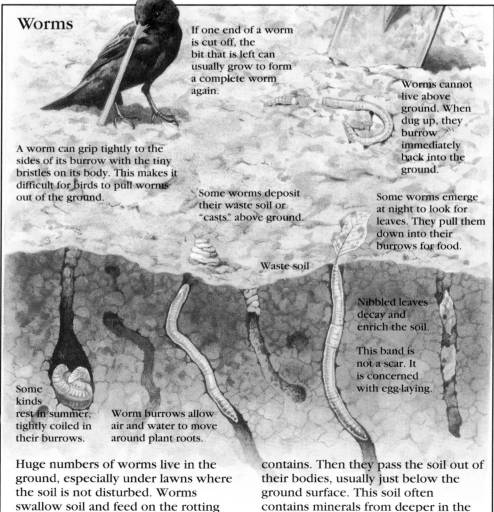

If one end of a worm is cut off, the bit that is left can usually grow to form a complete worm again.

Worms cannot live above ground. When dug up, they burrow immediately back into the ground.

A worm can grip tightly to the sides of its burrow with the tiny bristles on its body. This makes it difficult for birds to pull worms out of the ground.

Some worms deposit their waste soil or "casts" above ground.

Some worms emerge at night to look for leaves. They pull them down into their burrows for food.

Waste soil

Nibbled leaves decay and enrich the soil.

This band is not a scar. It is concerned with egg-laying.

Some kinds rest in summer, tightly coiled in their burrows.

Worm burrows allow air and water to move around plant roots.

Huge numbers of worms live in the ground, especially under lawns where the soil is not disturbed. Worms swallow soil and feed on the rotting parts of dead plants and animals it contains. Then they pass the soil out of their bodies, usually just below the ground surface. This soil often contains minerals from deeper in the ground which are valuable to plants.

Animals that come out of the ground

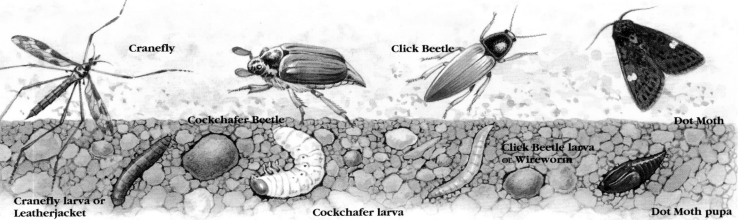

Cranefly

Cockchafer Beetle

Click Beetle

Dot Moth

Click Beetle larva or Wireworm

Cranefly larva or Leatherjacket

Cockchafer larva

Dot Moth pupa

Several insects found in gardens start life in the soil. For example, some beetles and flies lay their eggs in soil. When the young insects, called larvae, hatch they feed on plant roots. It may be several years before the adult insects emerge above ground. Some moth caterpillars form pupae (see page 110) in the soil. If you dig up a pupa, try keeping it in a cool place until the adult moth emerges. Put the pupa on sand in a box with a few twigs and check it every day.

Moles

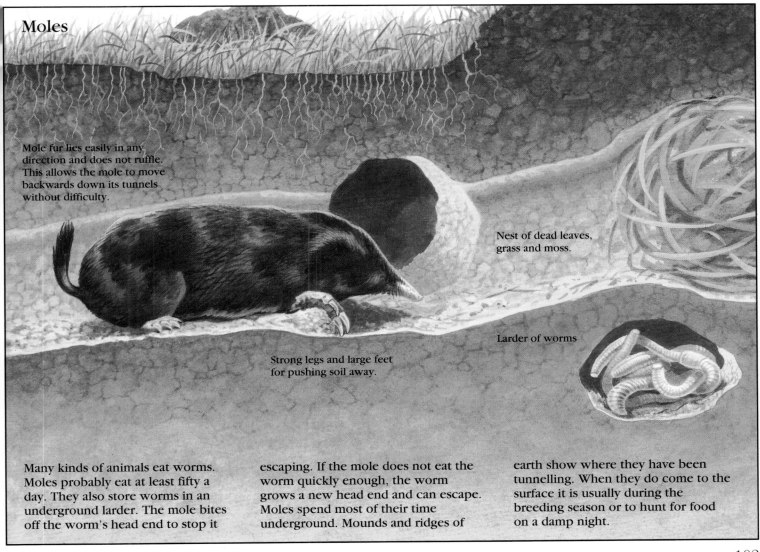

Mole fur lies easily in any direction and does not ruffle. This allows the mole to move backwards down its tunnels without difficulty.

Nest of dead leaves, grass and moss.

Larder of worms

Strong legs and large feet for pushing soil away.

Many kinds of animals eat worms. Moles probably eat at least fifty a day. They also store worms in an underground larder. The mole bites off the worm's head end to stop it escaping. If the mole does not eat the worm quickly enough, the worm grows a new head end and can escape. Moles spend most of their time underground. Mounds and ridges of earth show where they have been tunnelling. When they do come to the surface it is usually during the breeding season or to hunt for food on a damp night.

How to attract wildlife

A neat, tidy garden with no overgrown patches gives little shelter to wildlife. A small corner of long grass and nettles, where dead plants are left to rot instead of being cleared away, attracts many insects. These insects then attract visits from larger animals that feed on them.

You could create your own habitats where animals can hide, build their nests or hibernate. You could also grow some of the plants, shown here and on page 111, which provide food for insects and birds.

Some flowers, such as **Michaelmas Daisies**, attract butterflies to feed on their nectar.

Magpie

Wedge a flower pot or an old jug in a hedge or bank to provide a nesting site for birds. Put some dried grass in it.

Some climbing plants give food and shelter to animals. In spring birds may build their nests in them, and in winter feed on any berries. The Holly Blue Butterfly survives the winter as a pupa (see page 110) in Ivy leaves.

Song Thrush

Ivy

Wren

Holly Blue Butterfly

Cotoneaster

Peacock Butterfly

If you leave a fallen log or branch on the ground, fungi and mosses will grow on it, while beetles and other small animals will live in the decaying wood.

Leave fallen fruit for butterflies and wasps to feed on.

Dead leaves under a hedge or shrub might encourage a Hedgehog to hibernate there.

Some bees and wasps live alone in small holes, such as those in a ventilation brick. You could put one in your garden.

Nesting materials

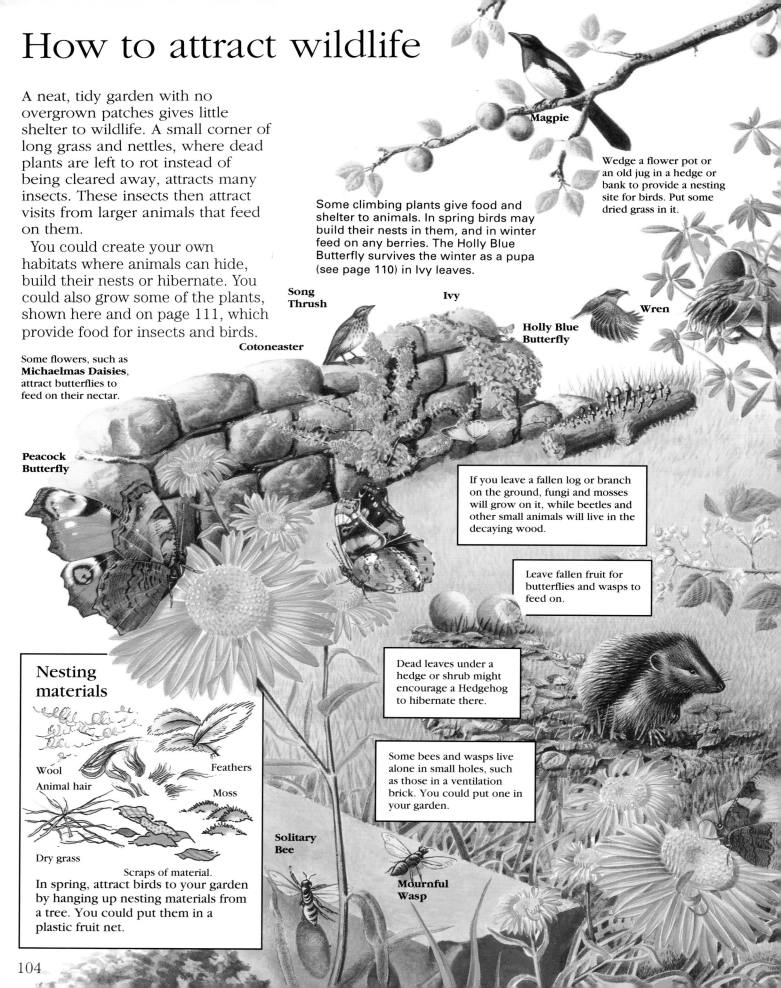

Wool

Feathers

Animal hair

Moss

Dry grass

Scraps of material.

In spring, attract birds to your garden by hanging up nesting materials from a tree. You could put them in a plastic fruit net.

Solitary Bee

Mournful Wasp

The wildlife on these pages is not drawn to scale.

A piece of corrugated iron or a plank of wood on rough grass could shelter a toad, Slow Worms, beetles or a Field Mouse's nest.

Common Toad

Devil's Coach Horse Beetle

Feeding birds

A bird table in your garden will attract many different types of birds, especially in winter. To make this simple bird table, use a piece of plywood for the base and thin strips of wood for the edges. To make a roof for the table, use another piece of plywood and a thick strip of wood to support it. Fix the table to a post or hang it from a tree. Remember to wash it regularly.

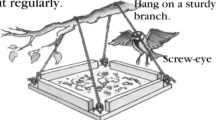
Hang on a sturdy branch.

Screw-eye

Food

Bread

Bacon

Dried fruit

Cheese

Cooked potato

Banana

Shelled peanuts in a net bag (not salted).

These are some foods that birds like to eat. Collect seeds for them to eat in the winter. Try thistles, groundsel and other wild plants, together with berries like hips and haws, and nuts like acorns.

Water

Dustbin lid

Bricks

Dangers to wildlife

Pest-killers do not only kill the creatures they are meant to kill. They are also likely to poison other animals that feed in the same area. Animals are also harmed when they eat the poisoned creatures.

Slug pellets

Chemical spray

Bird table

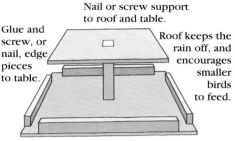

Nail or screw support to roof and table.

Glue and screw, or nail, edge pieces to table.

Roof keeps the rain off, and encourages smaller birds to feed.

Leave gaps for rain to drain off.

To hang your table from a tree, fix a screw-eye at each corner and make two loops with thick string. When you put food out on the table, put some on the ground as well, for ground-feeding birds. Keep a record of the types of food different birds eat.

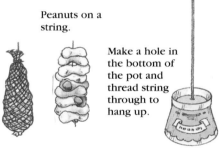

Peanuts on a string.

Make a hole in the bottom of the pot and thread string through to hang up.

You can make a bird pudding by mixing kitchen scraps and uncooked porridge oats with melted fat. (Ask an adult to melt the fat.) Carefully pour the mixture into an empty yoghurt pot. Hang the pot upside down.

Birds need water for drinking and bathing all through the year. Use an old tin tray, a dustbin lid or a pie dish. Change the water daily and keep it free of ice in winter.

Cats scare and attack birds. They also attack small mammals such as mice, voles and shrews.

Plants in the garden

For hundreds of years, gardens were full of fruit, vegetables and herbs. These were thought to be more important than flowers. Today, most gardens have more flowers than any other plant. Flowers are grown for their beauty, and not for food.

All garden flowers have been bred from wild plants. Some flowers are grown in gardens in one part of the world, but still grow wild in another part.

Wild flowers often grow in gardens. Look for them in lawns and vegetable plots.

Where garden flowers come from

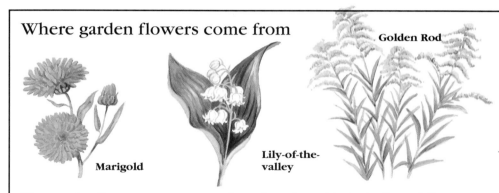

Marigold

Lily-of-the-valley

Golden Rod

Many garden flowers were once used to make medicines and cosmetics. Marigolds were used to colour cheese, and rubbed on sore eyes as a soothing lotion. Lily-of-the-valley was used to make a skin tonic. Several flowers that we grow in our gardens grow wild in other countries and are thought of as weeds. Golden Rod is a common weed in North America.

The lawn

A lawn that is mown regularly provides the same kind of habitat for wild flowers as a field where animals graze. Some flowers, such as the Daisy and Plantain, survive the mowing and grazing because they grow close to the ground in rosettes. Other flowers, such as Clover and Bird's-foot Trefoil, send out long creeping shoots. If the grass is not cut down, it will grow up quickly and produce flowers in summer.

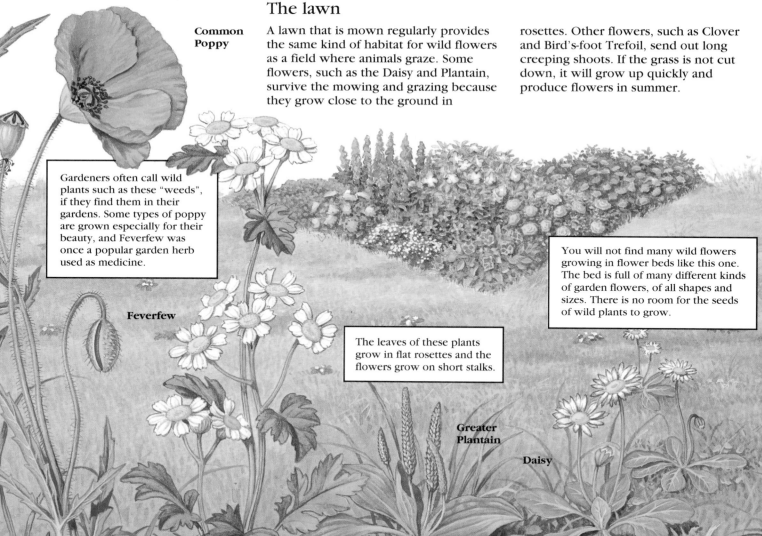

Common Poppy

Gardeners often call wild plants such as these "weeds", if they find them in their gardens. Some types of poppy are grown especially for their beauty, and Feverfew was once a popular garden herb used as medicine.

Feverfew

The leaves of these plants grow in flat rosettes and the flowers grow on short stalks.

You will not find many wild flowers growing in flower beds like this one. The bed is full of many different kinds of garden flowers, of all shapes and sizes. There is no room for the seeds of wild plants to grow.

Greater Plantain

Daisy

Three special breeds

Chrysanthemum

Dahlia

Rose

Many flowers have been specially bred for the garden and look quite different from the original plants. Flowers like these three are grown for their colour and size. They attract little wildlife.

Feeding the soil

Compost heap

Rotted **Stinging Nettles** are very good for feeding soil.

Soil needs feeding regularly, as growing plants use up its goodness. Decaying plants enrich soil, so when you cut plants down, leave them, or put them on a compost heap to rot.

Growing wild flowers

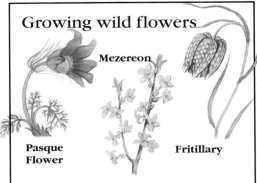

Mezereon

Pasque Flower

Fritillary

As more land is used for building, and hedges and grassland are lost, wild flowers are losing their natural habitats. Help protect plants in danger of dying out by growing some in your garden.

The vegetable patch

Vegetables are usually grown in neat rows like this. This makes it easy for the gardener to hoe out any wild plants. But every time the ground is hoed to remove weeds, large areas of bare soil are exposed. On this soil, more seeds from wild plants can settle and take root again.

If some wild plants are allowed to grow, they can help to attract insect pests away from the vegetables. Wild plants can also provide shelter for other insects that feed on the pests. So it is a good idea not to remove all the weeds from a vegetable patch.

The plants and flowers here are not drawn to scale.

Rye Grass

Couch Grass

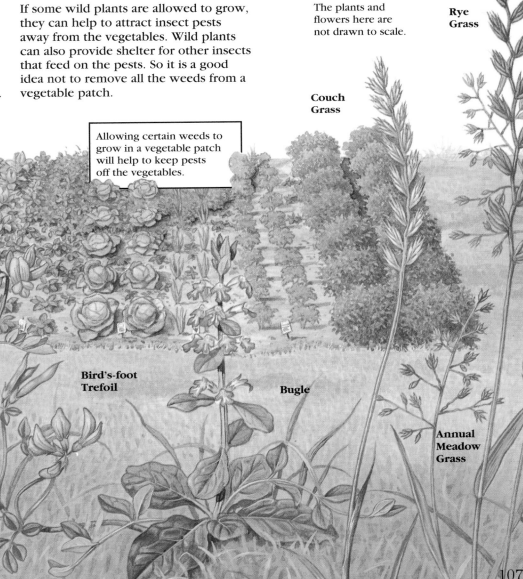

Allowing certain weeds to grow in a vegetable patch will help to keep pests off the vegetables.

White Clover

Bird's-foot Trefoil

Bugle

Annual Meadow Grass

More about plants

The common garden weeds shown on these pages are all wild plants. They are very tough and have developed excellent ways of spreading and surviving. Some produce thousands of seeds, while others grow very long, strong roots.

Many weeds choke out garden flowers and are difficult to get rid of. Gardeners must make sure they remove weeds such as clover from their flower beds.

Make a record of all the wild plants you can find in your garden. Press them and keep them in a scrap book.

Seeds in the mud

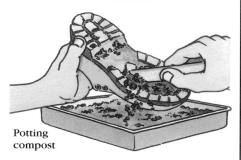

Potting compost

People help to spread seeds, especially on their shoes and on car tyres. Try scraping the mud from shoes or a tyre on to damp potting compost and see if any weeds grow.

Weeds and seeds

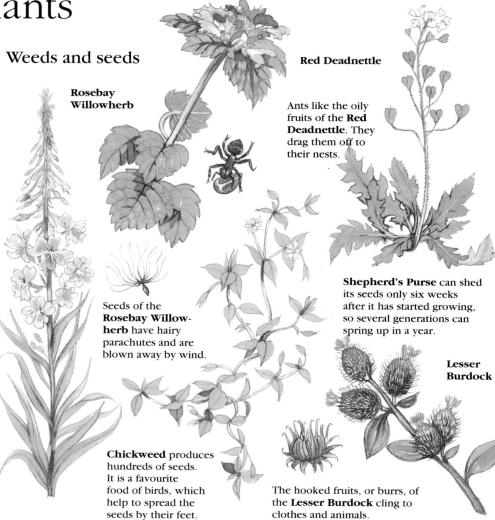

Rosebay Willowherb

Red Deadnettle

Ants like the oily fruits of the **Red Deadnettle**. They drag them off to their nests.

Seeds of the **Rosebay Willow-herb** have hairy parachutes and are blown away by wind.

Shepherd's Purse can shed its seeds only six weeks after it has started growing, so several generations can spring up in a year.

Lesser Burdock

Chickweed produces hundreds of seeds. It is a favourite food of birds, which help to spread the seeds by their feet.

The hooked fruits, or burrs, of the **Lesser Burdock** cling to clothes and animals.

The success of many weeds depends both on the large number of seeds they produce and also on how efficiently the seeds are scattered away from the parent plant. Most seeds are scattered, or dispersed, either by wind or by animals and humans. Some, such as those of Rosebay Willowherb, have more than one way. In wet weather, when the hairy seeds cannot blow away in the normal way, they become sticky and get carried away on birds' bodies.

Climbing plants

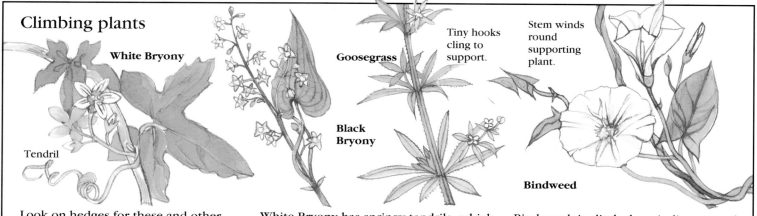

White Bryony

Tendril

Goosegrass

Black Bryony

Tiny hooks cling to support.

Stem winds round supporting plant.

Bindweed

Look on hedges for these and other climbing plants. Some grow so fast that they smother the hedge. Notice how each one climbs.

White Bryony has springy tendrils, which stretch when the plant is blown by the wind. Black Bryony has no tendrils and is not related to White Bryony. Like Bindweed, it climbs by winding around its support plant. Goosegrass has clinging hooks, too tiny to see, but they can still scratch you.

Changing shape

Dandelion

Some wild plants survive in the garden or the park by changing, or adapting, the way they grow to fit in with their habitat. Many plants that grow in lawns tend to do this. In short grass, where there is plenty of light, the Dandelion grows very close to the ground. Its leaves grow as a flat rosette, so the plant is not easily damaged by lawn mowers or trampling feet. In long grass, the Dandelion grows taller to reach the light, and has bigger, more upright leaves and a longer flower stem.

Long roots

Curled Dock

The main root of the Curled Dock may be two metres long and is hard to dig up. If it is broken off below ground level, new plants grow up from the bits of root left.

Coltsfoot

Coltsfoot has root-like underground stems which spread quickly and make it difficult to dig up. Its flowers look like Dandelions, but can be recognized by their stout stems covered with pink scales.

Plants without flowers

Mosses and ferns

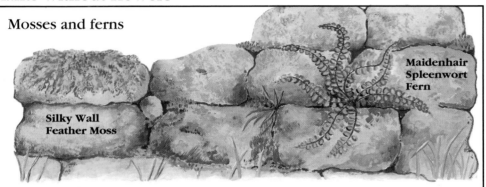

Maidenhair Spleenwort Fern

Silky Wall Feather Moss

Old walls in the garden are good places to look for mosses and ferns. Moss plants either grow in small dense cushions, or they form larger creeping patches like this Silky Wall Feather Moss. Mosses and ferns do not have flowers. They produce microscopic spores instead of seeds. Moss spores develop inside tiny capsules on long stalks. Fern spores can be seen as brown patches on the underside of the fronds.

Fungi

Grass in centre of ring grows thickly as nutrients from dead fungus threads make soil richer.

Grass around toadstools dies off as fungus threads strangle its roots.

Fairy-ring Toadstool

Purple Stereum grows on fruit trees.

Fungi also produce spores. They drop onto the ground from the underside of toadstool caps. The spores germinate, sending out masses of underground "threads" from which new toadstools can grow. The Fairy-ring Toadstool often grows in lawns. The ring gets larger every year as the threads reach out into fresh soil for food. Old threads inside the ring die. Rotted threads enrich the soil.

Some fungi grow on dead wood or living trees instead of in the ground. A few fungi are very poisonous, so never eat any you find and always wash your hands after touching them.

Butterflies and moths

Many butterflies and moths visit garden flowers in spring and summer to feed on the sugary fluid, called nectar, which flowers produce. During winter, some hibernate but others die, having laid their eggs earlier in the year. Few butterflies lay their eggs on garden plants but many moths do, so most of the caterpillars you find in gardens will belong to moths.

Moths mainly fly around at night, but you may spot them in the daytime when they are resting, hidden on tree trunks, among leaves and on walls.

Butterfly or moth?

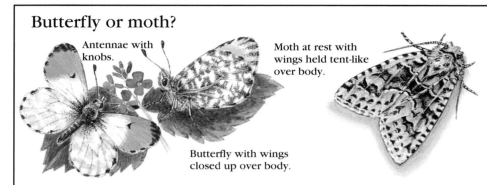

Antennae with knobs.

Moth at rest with wings held tent-like over body.

Butterfly with wings closed up over body.

You can tell the difference between butterflies and moths by looking at their feelers, called antennae. The antennae of butterflies always have knobs at the end. Moths' antennae are usually feathery or hair-like.

Another difference is that butterflies rest with their wings pressed tightly together over their bodies. Most moths rest with their wings held tent-like over their bodies, or else with each wing spread out on either side.

How they grow

Large White Butterfly

Male

Female

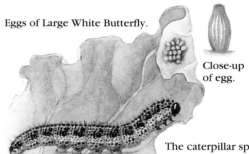

Eggs of Large White Butterfly.

Close-up of egg.

The caterpillar spends most of the time feeding. It sheds its skin (moults) several times as it grows.

Silky threads hold the Large White Butterfly pupa onto a fence. The pupae of other butterflies, and some moths, may be found on plant stems. Most moths pupate in the ground.

A male and female butterfly often circle around each other in the air before landing to mate. Female moths generally rest on plants until a male arrives to mate with them.

The female lays her eggs, singly or in clusters, on a plant. The caterpillars will feed on this plant when they hatch. Each kind of butterfly or moth has its own particular type of food plant.

When the caterpillar is fully grown, it stops feeding and changes into a pupa. The adult butterfly or moth develops inside the pupa and hatches out in spring or summer.

Feeding

Small Tortoiseshell Butterfly feeding on **Ice Plant.**

Proboscis

Lackey Moth caterpillars feeding on the leaves of a fruit tree inside their tent.

Close-up of mouth. Proboscis is coiled when butterfly is not feeding.

Some caterpillars spin a tent out of silky thread on their food plant. They feed on the leaves inside the tent and make the tent larger as they need more food.

Butterflies and moths feed on nectar which they suck from flowers with their long tube-like tongue, called a proboscis. Some moths do not feed at all, as they

only live for a very short time. These moths simply use the energy from the food they ate when they were caterpillars.

Keeping safe

The **Comma Butterfly** looks like a dead leaf when its wings are closed.

The **Poplar Hawk Moth** caterpillar is well disguised by colours and markings which match the leaves it feeds on.

This butterfly has been damaged by a bird's beak. The bird attacked the bright spot on the wing, not the body. So the insect escaped. A butterfly may be able to live with a damaged wing, but will die if its body is attacked.

The **Woolly Bear**, a Tiger Moth caterpillar, is protected by irritating hairs which put birds off eating it.

Meadow Brown Butterfly

Caterpillars, butterflies and moths protect themselves in different ways from birds which feed on them.

Some have colours and patterns that make them hard to see. Others have bright markings to frighten their

enemies away. Many butterflies have spots like eyes on their wings, to distract birds away from their bodies.

A butterfly garden

Some flowers, such as those shown here, are especially attractive to butterflies because they have bright colours and strong scent. Make a note of which plants attract butterflies in your garden.

Moths feed mainly at night and are attracted to pale coloured, night-scented flowers (see page 122).

Small Copper on **Michaelmas Daisy.**

Small Tortoiseshell on Buddleia

Small White

Green-veined White on **Wallflower.**

Red Admiral

Brimstone on **Aubretia.**

Peacock

Ice Plant

Garden insects

There are thousands of different insects, many of which live in gardens. All insects have six legs, and most have wings and can fly. Those that cannot fly are usually small and stay hidden. When disturbed they either keep still or scuttle out of sight.

A few insects damage garden plants, but many are useful to the gardener. Some feed on pests or dead plants. Bees are important to garden plants because they carry pollen from one flower to another. Pollen helps to produce seeds.

Insects and their young

Earwigs

If you touch an **Earwig's** head its body arches and its pincers snap in defence.

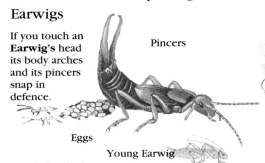

Pincers

Eggs

Young Earwig

Newly-hatched Earwigs.

The young Earwig grows directly into an adult and does not form a pupa. Unlike most insects, the female Earwig stays with her eggs after she has laid them, to protect them. She also licks them to stop mould growing and feeds her young when they first hatch.

Greenfly

Wingless female giving birth to live young.

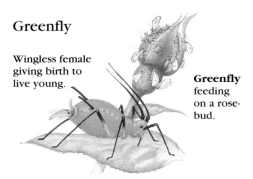

Greenfly feeding on a rose-bud.

Greenfly multiply very rapidly. In spring and summer, they give birth to live young and in autumn, they lay eggs. Not all Greenfly have wings, but those that do, fly to other plants to produce more young.

Living together

Ants

Nest hole

Ants carry food back to their nest.

Ants rub antennae when they meet.

Bread and jam.

Most insects live alone, but ants and some bees and wasps live together in colonies. Each colony has a queen, which lays eggs, and workers that look after the nest, eggs and young. At certain times in the year there are winged male and female ants too. You may spot a line of ants following a path between a nest hole and some food. The ants leave a scent trail which others follow. Rub your finger across the trail and see how the ants react.

Worker ants bring male and female winged ants out of the nest for the mating flight.

In summer, the winged males and winged females leave the nest on a mating flight. After mating, the males die. The new queens then break off their wings and make new nests.

Black Ant "milking" a **Greenfly**.

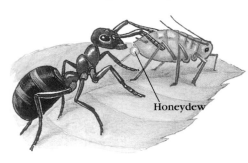

Honeydew

Ants feed on almost anything but they especially like sweet things. Some eat honeydew made by Greenfly. To make a Greenfly produce drops of honeydew, an ant strokes it with its antennae.

Bees

Bumble Bee gathering pollen.

Pollen

Bumble Bees live together in nests on, or under, the ground. They collect pollen from flowers and carry it to the nest in special pollen bags on their back legs.

Wasps

Common Wasp carrying a caterpillar back to its nest.

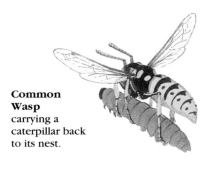

Common Wasps usually nest under the ground. The nest is made of paper which the queen and workers make by chewing bits of wood. Wasps feed their young on insects.

Insects that look alike

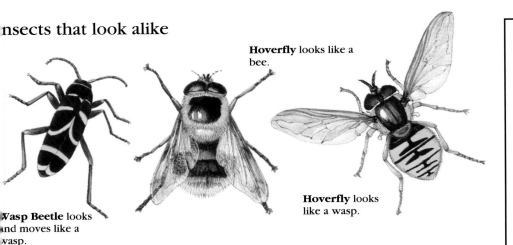

Hoverfly looks like a bee.

Wasp Beetle looks and moves like a wasp.

Hoverfly looks like a wasp.

Some insects, especially hoverflies, look like bees or wasps but have no sting. Birds learn to avoid stinging insects and anything that looks like a bee or a wasp. This means that they avoid the hoverflies as well. Hoverflies, like all true flies, have just one pair of wings. Bees and wasps have two pairs, but their back wings are small and very hard to see with the naked eye.

Clues to look for

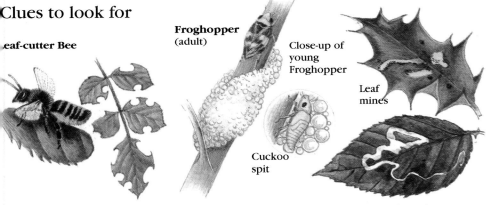

Leaf-cutter Bee

Froghopper (adult)

Close-up of young Froghopper

Cuckoo spit

Leaf mines

Some common garden insects are hard to find, but you can look for clues that will tell you where they are. Leaf-cutter Bees cut pieces out of rose leaves to make nests for their eggs. Young Froghoppers hide in white froth, called cuckoo spit, which they make as they feed on plant juices. The larvae of some insects feed inside leaves, causing blotches to appear on the surface of the leaves.

Insects and flowers

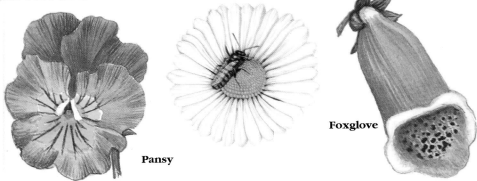

Pansy

Foxglove

Nectar guides

Some flowers, like these, have bold markings that guide insects to their nectar. Others appear to be plain, but have markings that only insects can see.

Trapping insects

Small stone under the rim, so that insects can get inside.

Place an empty grapefruit half in the garden overnight, on some soil. The next morning you may find woodlice and insects, such as beetles, sheltering under it. You may also find slugs and ants.

Keeping insects

Cover that lets air in.

Try keeping insects for a few days in a jar or a box to see how they behave. Put in a little damp soil or sand and bits of the plant on which you find the insects, so that they have the correct food to eat.

Magnifying glass for examining insects more closely.

Greenfly

If you watch Greenfly in July, you might see them give birth to live young. Put a ladybird in a jar together with the Greenfly and watch how they kick out at it to avoid being attacked and eaten.

Snails and other small animals

You have a very good chance of seeing all the animals on these pages in a garden, although they usually hide away among plants and under stones or bark during the day and in dry weather. This is because none of them has a waterproof skin, which means they are in danger of drying out and dying. They mostly come out to feed at night or after rain.

Not all slugs and snails are harmful to garden flowers and crops. Leave a few dead plants around the garden, and they will usually feed on these instead.

Garden Snail

Snails

Snails have long tentacles with eyes at their tips. When disturbed, the snail withdraws its tentacles.

In winter and in dry weather, snails hide away, often in cracks in walls or under stones. They retreat into their shells and seal the opening with layers of mucus that hardens as it dries.

Snails leave a silvery trail of mucus.

Most snails found in the garden feed on plants. Some snails damage growing plants, but most prefer dead and decaying leaves. They feed by filing off bits of leaf with rows of tiny teeth on their tongue.

During the day, some kinds of snail cluster together in a sheltered spot. After each feeding trip, at night or after rain, they usually return to the same place, by following their own trail of slimy mucus.

If you find a group of snails, mark their shells carefully with a waterproof felt tip pen. Check each day to see if the marked snails are still there. Snails may live in the same spot for several years.

Lots of legs

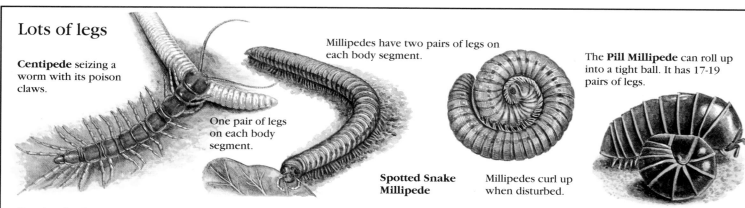

Centipede seizing a worm with its poison claws.

One pair of legs on each body segment.

Millipedes have two pairs of legs on each body segment.

The **Pill Millipede** can roll up into a tight ball. It has 17-19 pairs of legs.

Spotted Snake Millipede

Millipedes curl up when disturbed.

Centipedes have one pair of legs on each segment of their bodies. Centipedes move fast and hunt insects, spiders and worms, killing them with their poison claws.

Millipedes live in the soil, under stones and bark, and in compost and leaf litter. They feed mainly on rotting plants. Most, like the Spotted Snake Millipede, look rather like centipedes, but you can

tell the difference by checking the number of legs on each body segment. Each body segment has four legs. The Pill Millipede looks like a woodlouse, but it has more legs.

The snail's enemy

Song Thrush

Thrush's "anvil"

In dry weather, when earthworms are scarce, Song Thrushes eat snails. They hammer the snails against a stone to break the shells. Pieces of shell are left around the stone or "anvil".

Release the snail after a day or two.

Coloured paper

Droppings

To see how snails eat, keep one for a couple of days and feed it on damp, coloured paper. You will soon see thin patches appear on the paper where the snail has rasped at it with its tongue. The snail's droppings will be the same colour as the paper.

Slugs

Great Grey Slug

Hole for breathing.

This slug has a ridge or "keel" on its body.

Slugs do not have a shell to retreat into, so in cold and dry weather they burrow deep into the soil. They protect themselves from enemies by producing an unpleasant tasting mucus.

Mating

Brown-lipped Snails

Love dart

Eggs

In spring and summer you may find snails mating in the garden. During courtship, which can last several hours, the two snails crawl over each other. They then fire a chalky "love dart" into each other's skin. Soon after mating, each snail lays its round, white eggs in a hole that it has made in the ground. Three or four weeks later, the eggs hatch out into tiny snails. These will slowly grow into adults.

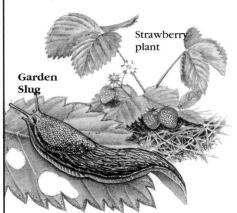

Strawberry plant

Garden Slug

Some slugs, like this Garden Slug will feed on growing plants. To find them, put straw or rhubarb leaves around the plant. The slugs shelter there during the day, when you can remove them.

Woodlice

Woodlouse

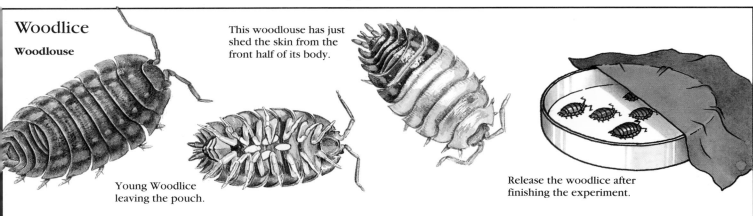

This woodlouse has just shed the skin from the front half of its body.

Young Woodlice leaving the pouch.

Release the woodlice after finishing the experiment.

Woodlice are common in most gardens and are very easy to spot. They feed on dead plants. Female Woodlice carry their young in a pouch under their bodies. When the young hatch, they stay under their mother's body until they are ready to live on their own. Woodlice shed their skin, moulting several times as they grow. They have seven pairs of legs.

Woodlice like dark, damp places. If you put a few on one side of a dish and then cover the other side of the dish with a cloth, you will see that they soon move to the darkened side.

Spiders

Spiders are some of the most interesting small animals in the garden. They are also very useful, as they feed on some of the insects that damage plants.

Most spiders spin webs to catch insects, but a few catch their prey without the help of webs. Almost all spiders kill their prey by biting it with poison fangs, and then feed by sucking out the body juices.

Look for spiders' webs early in the morning, especially in the autumn when dew or frost sparkles on the delicate threads and shows them up very clearly.

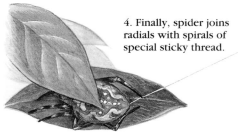

Garden Spider hiding under leaves, attached to its web by a thread.

Different kinds of spiders spin different kinds of webs. Some build orb webs like the one above. Spiders usually spin a new web each day as webs are easily destroyed by the weather.

Orb web

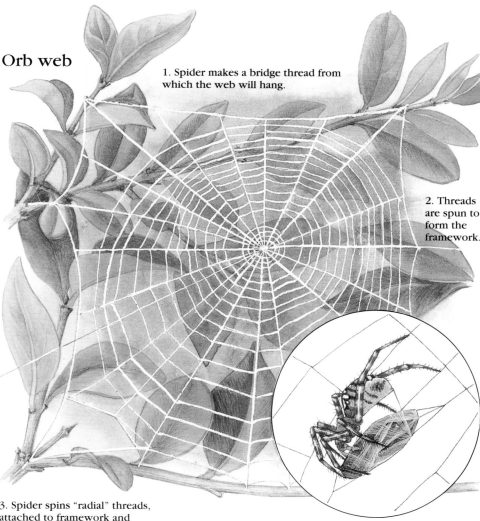

1. Spider makes a bridge thread from which the web will hang.

2. Threads are spun to form the framework.

4. Finally, spider joins radials with spirals of special sticky thread.

3. Spider spins "radial" threads, attached to framework and centre of web.

Sometimes spiders bind up a fly in thread before eating it.

They can also lose their stickiness in dusty conditions or by drying out in the sun. The spider may sit in its web or hide under leaves, joined to its web by a single thread.

When an insect gets caught in the web, it struggles and the thread vibrates. The spider then comes out of hiding and attacks. It often binds up its prey in thread before feeding on it.

Sheet web

House Spider

House Spiders spin their sheet webs or "cobwebs" in the corners of sheds and houses. Their webs are not sticky, but insects get tangled up and trapped in the close network of threads.

Tube web

Wall Spider

Tripwire thread

This spider often spins its tube-shaped web in cracks in walls. When an insect stumbles over a tripwire thread, the spider rushes out to catch it and drag it down the tube.

Money Spiders

Money Spider

Large numbers of these tiny spiders may cover the lawn with their delicate webs. Air currents often catch the webs and the tiny spider can be lifted up and carried several miles.

Watching spiders

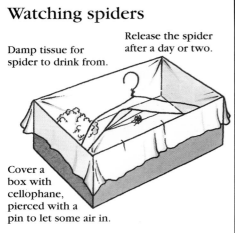

Release the spider after a day or two.

Damp tissue for spider to drink from.

Cover a box with cellophane, pierced with a pin to let some air in.

Catch a spider (a good place to look is on or near a web you find in the garden), and put it in a box with a bent coat-hanger like this. Watch the spider spin a new web, using the hanger as a support.

Spiders without webs

Crab Spiders can run sideways. They wait for insects to come near, and then seize them with their front legs.

This fierce-looking **Hunting Spider** hunts at night for insects on the ground. Look for it during the day under stones or logs.

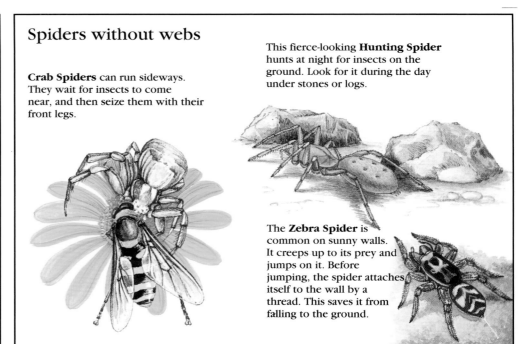

The **Zebra Spider** is common on sunny walls. It creeps up to its prey and jumps on it. Before jumping, the spider attaches itself to the wall by a thread. This saves it from falling to the ground.

How the Garden Spider breeds

Female

Male

Escape thread

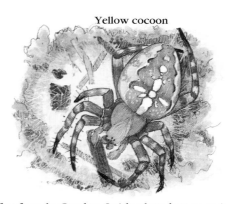

Yellow cocoon

Mating can be very dangerous for the male Garden Spider as there is always a chance that the female, which is bigger and stronger than the male, may attack him and eat him. When a male Garden Spider finds a female, he approaches her carefully, always ready to escape on a special thread that he has spun. The female may chase him away several times before allowing him to mate with her. Afterwards, the male makes a quick getaway in case he is attacked.

The female Garden Spider lays her eggs in autumn. She spins a cocoon of yellow thread around them, which she disguises with bits of bark and dust. Soon after, she dies. The young spiders hatch the following spring.

Wolf Spiders

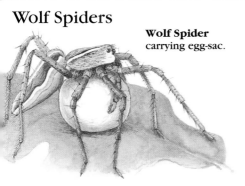

Wolf Spider carrying egg-sac.

Nursery tent

Egg-sac

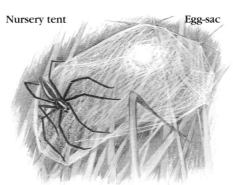

Like all spiders, Wolf Spiders spin special threads around their eggs. Instead of hiding them in a safe place, though the female carries the egg-sac with her wherever she goes.

One kind of Wolf Spider spins a tent around her egg-sac when the eggs are ready to hatch. She stays near it, and tears the tent open when the young are ready to live on their own.

Moulting

Garden Spider

Old skin

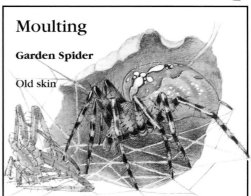

When a spider hatches out from an egg, it is very small. As it grows, it sheds its skin several times until it reaches adult size. You may find old skins on webs.

Birds

Most gardens are visited by a variety of birds all the year round. You can attract birds to your garden by putting out food and water, especially in winter, when food is scarce in the countryside. If there are trees or shrubs to provide cover, birds may even build their nests in gardens. If you find a nest, never disturb it or the parent birds may abandon it.

Watch birds quietly and make notes to help you identify them. Notice their size, shape, colour and any special markings.

The **Green Woodpecker** visits gardens and looks for ants on the lawn.

Nuthatch

The **Blackbird** can often be seen singing from a tree top or a chimney stack.

Greenfinch

The **Nuthatch** hops up and down tree trunks in search of insects to eat.

The **Treecreeper** looks for insects in bark. It circles tree trunks, always moving upwards from the base.

The **Great Tit** is larger than the Blue Tit and has a black cap.

The **Bullfinch** eats seeds but also feeds on the buds of fruit trees and bushes.

The **Wren** is a tiny bird with a short, up-turned tail. It flies back and forth in straight lines and never keeps still for long.

The **Pied Wagtail** hunts insects on lawns. Its tail bobs up and down.

House Sparrows take dust baths in dry soil to help clean their feathers.

The **Hedge Accentor** feeds on insects and seeds. It stays near the cover of hedges and shrubs.

A male **Robin** often claims a garden as his territory. He keeps all other Robins out except for his mate.

The **Chaffinch** feeds on the ground and mostly eats small seeds.

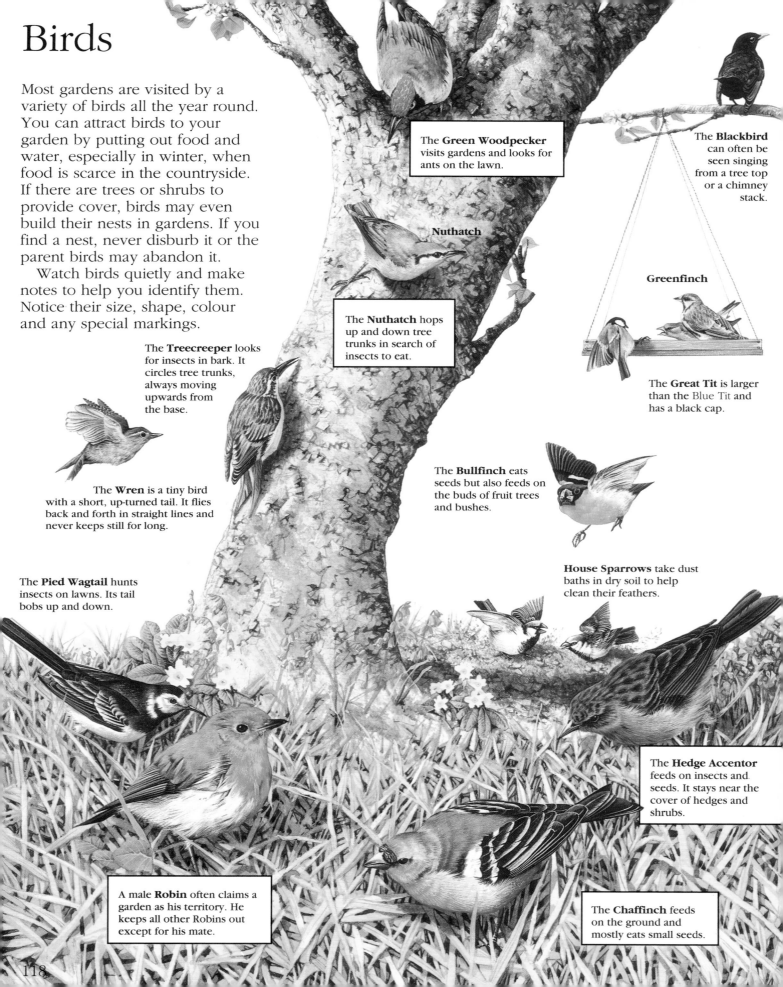

Collared Dove

Greenfinches and **Blue Tits** are common visitors to gardens when food is put out for them. (See page 105.)

Blue Tits

The **Goldfinch** feeds on plant seeds, but attacks Dandelion flowers in spring.

The birds on these pages are not to scale.

Spot the difference

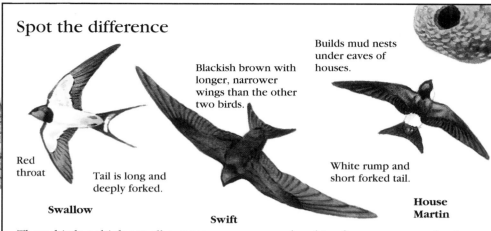

Red throat

Tail is long and deeply forked.

Swallow

Blackish brown with longer, narrower wings than the other two birds.

Swift

Builds mud nests under eaves of houses.

White rump and short forked tail.

House Martin

These birds, which are all summer visitors to Britain, look rather similar. The pictures will help you to identify them. All three catch insects while flying, but they feed at different heights. The Swallows feeds near the ground and is often seen swooping low over water. The House Martin's flight is less swooping and it feeds higher than the Swallow. The Swift feeds much higher in the air than the other two birds.

Catching insects

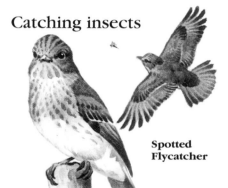

Spotted Flycatcher

The Spotted Flycatcher, another summer visitor, sits on a tree or post and waits for insects to pass nearby. It flies off to catch its prey, then returns to its perch.

Anting

Mistle Thrush covered with ants.

Some birds rub ants on their feathers or allow ants to crawl over them. They probably do this because a liquid from the ants helps to clean their feathers and rid them of mites.

Roosting

At night, many birds gather together in large numbers for warmth and safety. The tree or building they settle on for the night is called a "roost". Birds may fly many miles each evening to the same roost. In Britain, it is quite common to see thousands of Starlings roosting together often in the middle of towns.

Ponds & trees

Ponds and trees attract all kinds of wildlife. Many insects will live in or on the water, and frogs and toads may breed there. Birds will come to drink and bathe, and hunt for insects, especially if you put a stone for them to perch on.

As more and more farm ponds are being drained, valuable water habitats are lost. Garden ponds can help to replace them. Trees attract all kinds of wildlife too. Choose a tree in your garden, or in a park, and count how many different kinds of creatures you can spot.

Making a pond

Pond should be at least 1 m long, 70 cm wide and 40 cm deep.

Thick layer of newspaper or sand.

It is quite easy to make a small pond in the garden. Start by digging a hole with gently sloping sides. Then make a shallow shelf around the edge for border plants. Smooth the sides and bottom, and remove any sharp stones.

Place sand or a thick layer of newspaper over the sides and bottom of the hole. Line the pond with strong polythene, which you can buy at a garden centre. Weight the edge of the plastic down with stones.

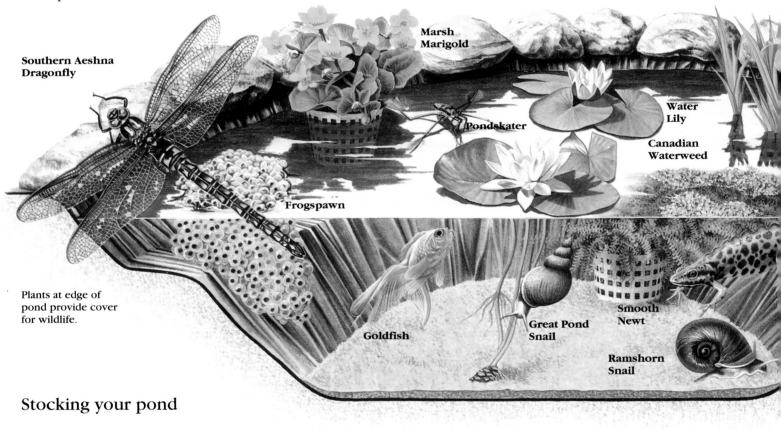

Southern Aeshna Dragonfly

Marsh Marigold

Pondskater

Water Lily

Canadian Waterweed

Frogspawn

Plants at edge of pond provide cover for wildlife.

Goldfish

Great Pond Snail

Smooth Newt

Ramshorn Snail

Stocking your pond

Fill the pond with fresh water and buy some water plants from a garden centre. Plants, such as Canadian Waterweed, are important as they provide oxygen, which fish and other animals need to breathe. Floating plants, such as Water Lilies, provide shade from the sun.

Stock the pond with fish and snails.

Other animals, especially insects, will visit the pond to feed and breed. Some insects, such as dragonflies, start life in ponds but leave the water when fully grown. The adults return to water to lay their eggs. Look out for other winged insects hunting for food around the pond. Frogs, toads and newts spend most of their adult life

on land. You may find them hiding in damp corners in your garden. In spring, they go to ponds to mate and lay their jelly-covered eggs, called spawn. Frogspawn is laid in clusters and toadspawn is laid in strings. When the tadpoles hatch, they stay in the water until their lungs and legs develop. Then they can survive on dry land.

This picture gives you an idea of the kind of wildlife you may find on a tree. You won't find all these things together, as shown here.

Trees provide food and shelter for many different kinds of animals. No matter what size or type a tree is, birds and all sorts of insects and small creatures will use it.

Trees in Britain are either broadleaved, with wide flat leaves, or conifers, with needle-like leaves.

Squirrels live in trees and are active by day. They feed on tree seeds and nuts. You are more likely to see Grey Squirrels in Britain, but on the continent you will only see Red Squirrels.

Many birds nest and roost in trees.

If you find an oak tree, look inside the galls for insect larvae.

Look for caterpillars on leaves and twigs.

Yellow Flag

Common Frog

Water Boatman

Put some stones on shelf for animals to climb onto, and for birds to perch on.

Climbing plants, such as Ivy and Honeysuckle, grow up tree trunks. They provide food shelter for animals.

Bracket fungi grow on tree trunks.

Some moths rest on tree trunks during the day. Beetles and other insects live in cracks and behind loose bark.

If you leave fallen leaves on the ground around trees, insects will hide and feed there. Birds will then come to hunt for the insects.

Fungi may grow among dead leaves in autumn.

If you have a fruit tree, leave a few of the fruits on the ground to attract butterflies and other insects that feed on the juice of fruit.

The wildlife on these pages is not drawn to scale.

121

The garden at night

Many animals (called nocturnal animals) are active only at night. Some come out at dusk, others emerge later and move around until dawn. Go into your garden at these times, with a torch covered in red tissue paper, to see what you can find.

Some nocturnal animals are noisy, so listen carefully and you may hear a grunting Hedgehog or a croaking Toad.

The flowers of some plants, such as Honeysuckle, produce a strong scent at dusk to attract the feeding moths.

The wildlife on these pages is not drawn to scale.

The **Tawny Owl** is the most common owl in gardens. It hunts at night for mice and other small animals, and may even attack birds while they roost.

The **Common Toad** hunts at night for insects and slugs. It always returns to the same place, usually a hole in the ground, to hide during the day.

The **Hedgehog** is a noisy animal and grunts as it hunts for food at night. If you spot one, you can encourage it to return by putting out a saucer of water and some cat or dog food.

The **Green Lacewing** lives on trees and bushes. The larvae and adults feed on aphids.

The **Wood Mouse** comes out only when it is very dark. It feeds mainly on seeds and berries and will climb bushes to reach fruit.

The male **Dark Bush-cricket** chirps loudly on summer evenings to attract female crickets.

Ground Beetles hunt for slugs and other small creatures at night.

Glow-worms are beetles. On summer nights, the glow produced by the wingless females attracts the winged males flying above.

At night, moths use the moon's light as a guide to fly in a straight line. They do this by keeping the moon's light on the same side of their body. Put a bright light in the garden at night which will attract moths, and then watch how they react. As they pass nearby, the moths are confused by the light and try to use it to steer by. Keeping the light on the same side of their body, they fly in a circle, getting closer to the light until finally they fly into it.

Bats are active at dusk and just before sunrise. They feed on insects.

Pipistrelle Bat (above)

Long-eared Bat (below)

Foxes hunt at night for small animals and birds. They may visit gardens to scavenge for food in dustbins. They have a strong, musty smell.

Some beetles fly at dusk. They are often attracted to lights and may crash into windows.

The **Common Shrew** needs to eat its own weight in food every day. It spends most of its time hunting for food in hedgerows and long grass and only comes out into the open at night.

Elephant Hawk Moth drinks **Honey suckle** nectar. **Heart and Dart Moth** on **Evening Primrose**. **Silver-Y Moth** on **Night Scented Stock**. **Burnished Brass Moth** on **Valerian**.

Visitors to the garden

The different kinds of animals and plants that will visit or live in your garden depend partly on what kind of garden you have (see page 100), and partly on the type of countryside near to it. On these pages you will find some of the animals and plants that live in woods, farmland, moors and by the sea, and that may visit or grow in gardens near to their natural habitats.

Birds, mammals and insects will visit gardens in their search for food and shelter. Wild plants grow when their seeds are blown into gardens by the wind. They may also be carried in on the fur of animals, or left behind in animals' droppings.

Near woodland

Redstart

Roe Deer

Cockchafer Beetle

14-spot Ladybird

Primrose

Gatekeeper or Hedge Brown Butterfly

Ringlet Butterfly

Near the sea

Herring Gulls

Yellow Wagtail

Burnet Rose

Sea Pink

Short-winged Conehead (a Bush-cricket)

Sand Wasp

Near fields and meadows

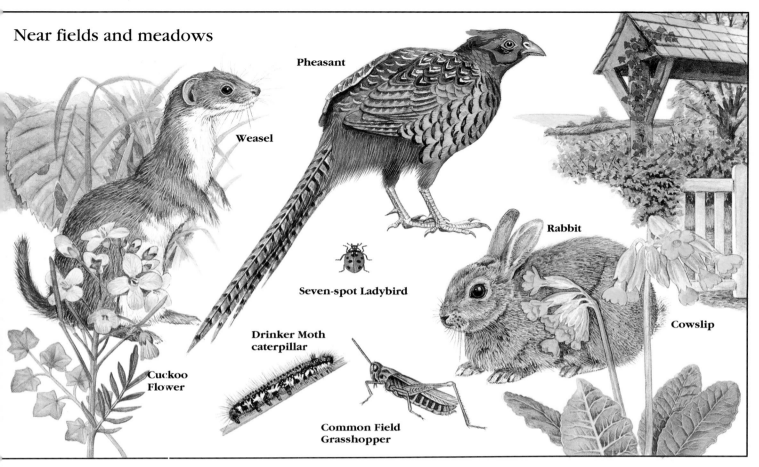

Weasel

Pheasant

Seven-spot Ladybird

Rabbit

Cowslip

Drinker Moth caterpillar

Cuckoo Flower

Common Field Grasshopper

Near heaths and moors

Oak Eggar Moth

Harebell

Gorse

Adder

Grayling Butterfly

Emperor Moth caterpillar

Heather

More wildlife in the garden

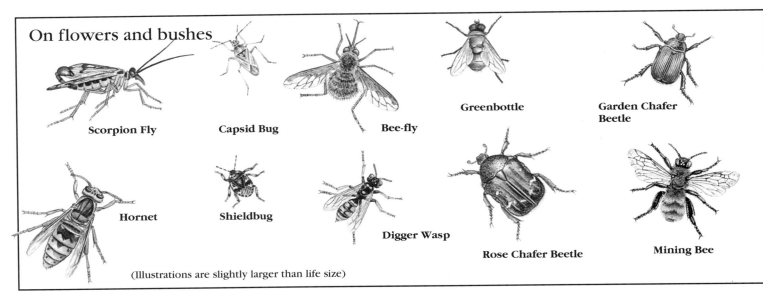

On flowers and bushes

Scorpion Fly

Capsid Bug

Bee-fly

Greenbottle

Garden Chafer Beetle

Hornet

Shieldbug

Digger Wasp

Rose Chafer Beetle

Mining Bee

(Illustrations are slightly larger than life size)

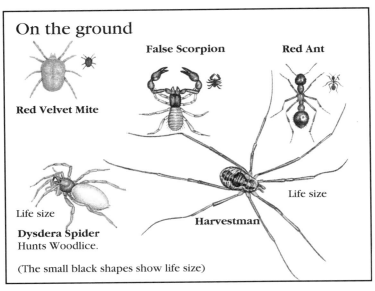

On the ground

Red Velvet Mite

False Scorpion

Red Ant

Dysdera Spider
Hunts Woodlice.

Life size

Harvestman

Life size

(The small black shapes show life size)

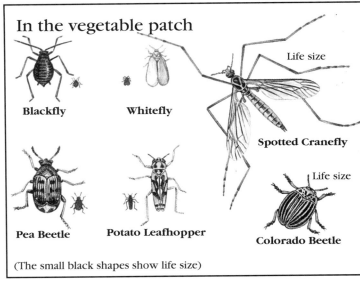

In the vegetable patch

Blackfly

Whitefly

Life size

Spotted Cranefly

Pea Beetle

Potato Leafhopper

Life size

Colorado Beetle

(The small black shapes show life size)

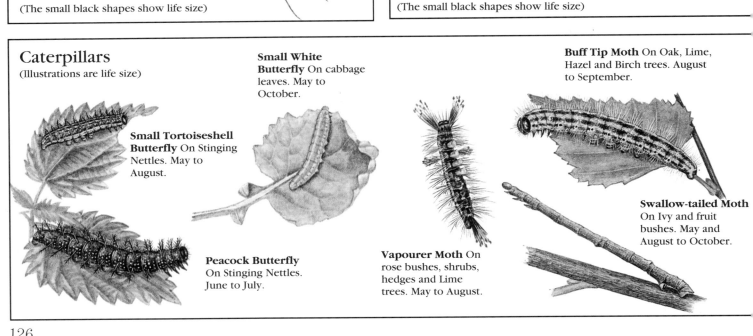

Caterpillars
(Illustrations are life size)

Small White Butterfly On cabbage leaves. May to October.

Buff Tip Moth On Oak, Lime, Hazel and Birch trees. August to September.

Small Tortoiseshell Butterfly On Stinging Nettles. May to August.

Peacock Butterfly On Stinging Nettles. June to July.

Vapourer Moth On rose bushes, shrubs, hedges and Lime trees. May to August.

Swallow-tailed Moth On Ivy and fruit bushes. May and August to October.

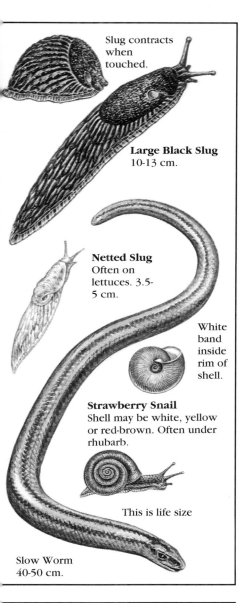

Slug contracts when touched.

Large Black Slug 10-13 cm.

Netted Slug Often on lettuces. 3.5-5 cm.

White band inside rim of shell.

Strawberry Snail Shell may be white, yellow or red-brown. Often under rhubarb.

This is life size

Slow Worm 40-50 cm.

Magpie Moth On fruit bushes. May to June.

Elephant Hawk Moth On Rosebay Willowherb. July to August.

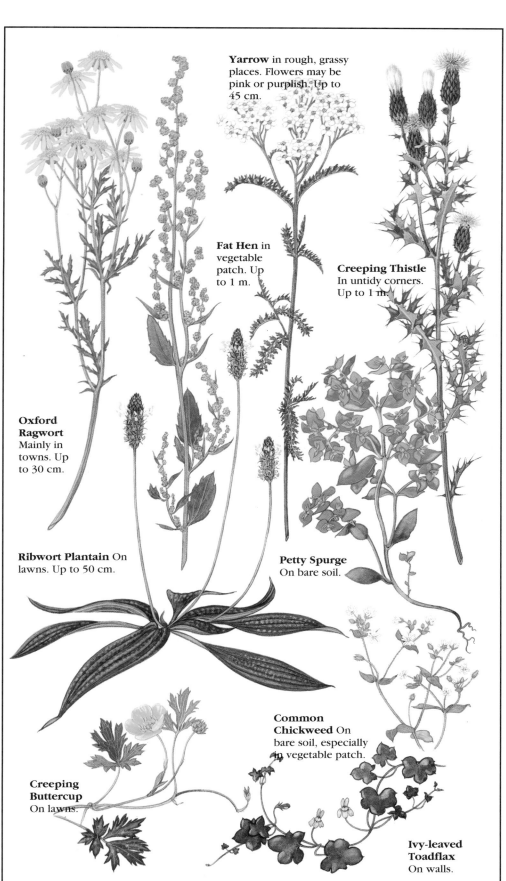

Yarrow in rough, grassy places. Flowers may be pink or purplish. Up to 45 cm.

Fat Hen in vegetable patch. Up to 1 m.

Creeping Thistle In untidy corners. Up to 1 m.

Oxford Ragwort Mainly in towns. Up to 30 cm.

Ribwort Plantain On lawns. Up to 50 cm.

Petty Spurge On bare soil.

Common Chickweed On bare soil, especially in vegetable patch.

Creeping Buttercup On lawns.

Ivy-leaved Toadflax On walls.

Water flowers

The flowers on these pages can be found in or near ponds and streams.

Bankside flowers

Many different kinds of plants and flowers grow in the soft, damp soil along the banks of ponds. The flowers that grow there are often brightly coloured, with large leaves and strong roots.

Meadowsweet

Meadowsweet grows in ponds, streams, marshes, water meadows, and also near ditches at the side of the road. It has clusters of sweet-smelling flowers on tall stems.

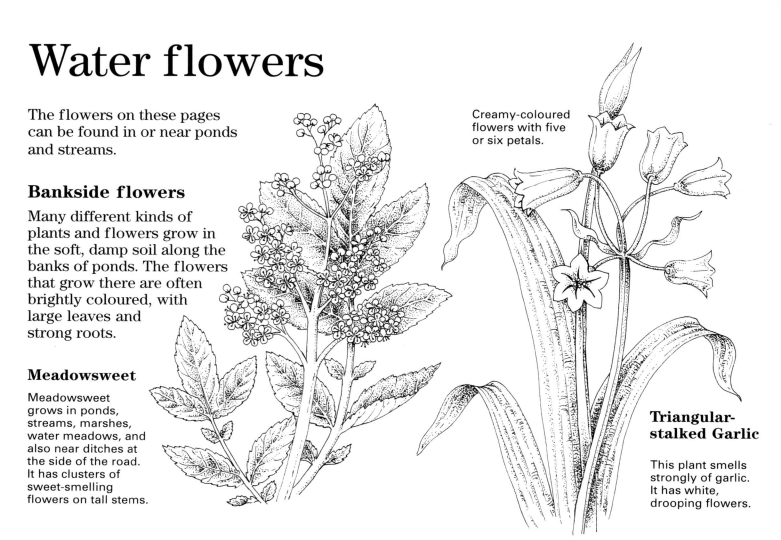

Creamy-coloured flowers with five or six petals.

Triangular-stalked Garlic

This plant smells strongly of garlic. It has white, drooping flowers.

Floating flowers

These flowers grow near the centre of ponds. The roots float freely in the water.

Floating water plantain

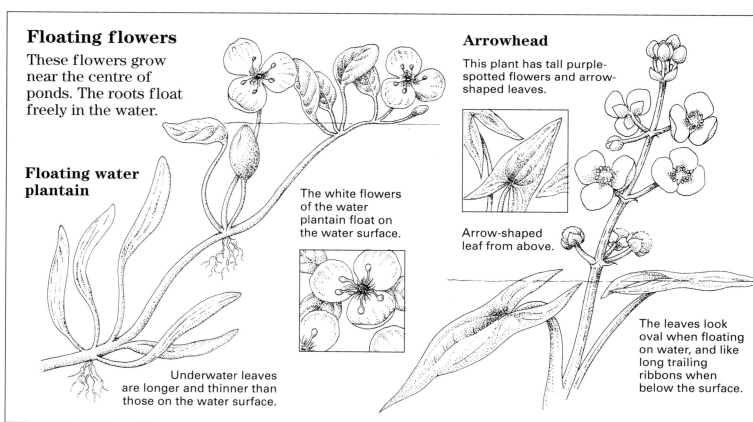

The white flowers of the water plantain float on the water surface.

Underwater leaves are longer and thinner than those on the water surface.

Arrowhead

This plant has tall purple-spotted flowers and arrow-shaped leaves.

Arrow-shaped leaf from above.

The leaves look oval when floating on water, and like long trailing ribbons when below the surface.

Rooted flowers

These flowers grow in fairly shallow water near the edges of ponds. The plants have their roots in the mud and the leaves either float or stand out of the water. Plants are usually tall with long underground stems, called rhizomes.

Marsh Calla

This plant grows in swamps, reed beds, muddy ditches and ponds. The flowers are white and the whole plant is poisonous.

Leathery, heart-shaped leaves.

Water Crowfoot

The flowers of the Water Crowfoot are white with a yellow centre. The roots are anchored in the mud at the bottom of streams.

Some leaves float on the water surface.

Frogbit

The white flowers float above the surface in spring. The shiny round leaves grow in clusters.

Underwater flowers

These flowers grow underwater in the deepest parts of ponds. The roots are anchored in the mud.

Water Soldier

These are found under water except when in flower. Then, the long, jagged leaves show above the surface.

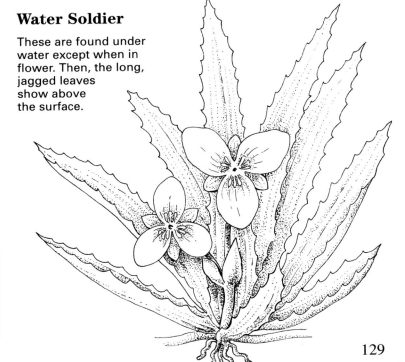

Bumble bee

Forester moth

Chalk hill blue butterfly

Insects are almost everywhere. You will find them in the garden, under the bark of trees, on walls and inside your home. This part of the book tells you all about common European insects. You will discover how tiny caterpillars turn into adult butterflies, which insects live around ponds, and how grasshoppers sing. This part of the book also shows you how to keep insects and make notes about them.

Wherever possible, the insects have been drawn life size. Where lengths are given, they refer to the length of the insect from the tip of its abdomen to its head, not including the antennae. When the wing span is given, this is a measurement from wing-tip to wing-tip.

In the other parts of this book the species names of animals and birds have capital letters. But many insects are commonly known by their family names, which do not have capital letters. Therefore, insect names in this part of the book are written without capital letters.

Seven-spot ladybird

Common blue butterfly

Peacock butterfly

INSECT WATCHING

Contents

Becoming an insect watcher	132	Insects and flowers	150
Differences to spot	134	Ants and bees	152
Breeding, growing and changing	136	Collecting and keeping insects	154
Insects in the garden	138	Common insects to spot	
Insects in a tree	140	Butterflies, beetles, dragonflies	156
Pond insects	142	Moths	157
Insect senses	144	Bugs, flies, etc.	158
Watching insects move	146	Bees, fleas, lice, etc.	159
Watching insects feed	148	Spiders and their webs	160

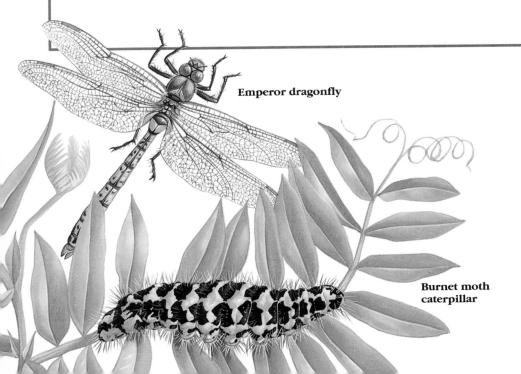

Emperor dragonfly

Burnet moth
caterpillar

Becoming an insect watcher

It is easy to become an insect watcher because it is never difficult to find insects. You can spot them in most places. Look first at as many types as you can, to learn how they are different from other animals. Later you may want to study one or two types in more detail.

There are more different types of insects (called species) than all the different kinds of mammals, fish, birds and reptiles put together. People are still discovering many new species and finding out more about those already known.

What is an insect?

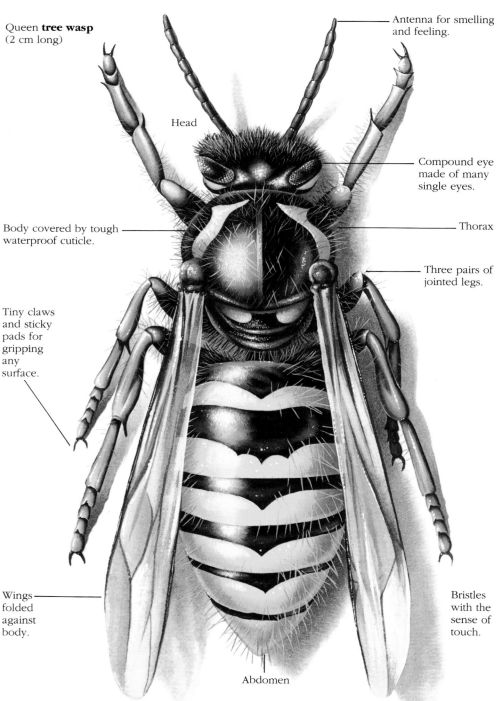

Queen **tree wasp** (2 cm long)

Antenna for smelling and feeling.

Head

Compound eye made of many single eyes.

Body covered by tough waterproof cuticle.

Thorax

Three pairs of jointed legs.

Tiny claws and sticky pads for gripping any surface.

Wings folded against body.

Bristles with the sense of touch.

Abdomen

These are not insects

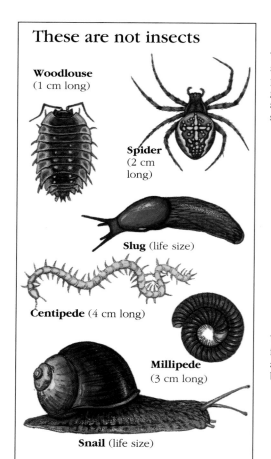

Woodlouse (1 cm long)

Spider (2 cm long)

Slug (life size)

Centipede (4 cm long)

Millipede (3 cm long)

Snail (life size)

Only insects have three body parts and three pairs of legs. Slugs and snails have no legs. Spiders have eight legs. The bodies of millipedes, centipedes and woodlice have lots of parts, called segments. Most of these segments have legs on them.

All adult insects have three parts to their bodies. These are: a head, a thorax (middle) and an abdomen (lower part). On their heads they have a pair of antennae, used mainly for smelling and feeling. Most insects have a pair of large eyes made up of many tiny eyes. At some time in their lives all insects will have three pairs of jointed legs attached to the thorax. Some insect legs may have a special job to do. For example, they may have a tiny pocket for collecting pollen. Others may be flat with hairs to help the insect swim. Apart from birds and bats, insects are the only other kind of animal that can fly properly.

What you need

These are some of the things it is useful to have if you want to be an insect watcher. You will need a good pocket lens and a field notebook for recording what you see. Choose a lens which magnifies 8 or 10 times. It is a good idea to fix it on some string round your neck, to keep it handy. You may not need all the things shown. This will depend on where you want to look for insects.

If you have a pocket-size book on insects, carry it with you and indentify the insects as you spot them.

Heron Meadow July 12th
2 pm
Sunny

Cinnabar caterpillars on leaves and stem of Ragwort.
Colour - yellow and black stripes

Heron Meadow
Cinnabar caterpillars on Ragwort.
gate
bush
Ants nest under stones

Spiral-bound notebook (see right).

A butterfly net may be useful. Stalk the insect slowly and quietly. Do not harm it and do not keep it captive for long.

Lay a white sheet under a bush. Gently knock the bush with a stick. The sheet will catch falling insects.

Trowel

A small trowel is useful for digging up earth. Sieve the soil to find insects.

Mark an area with string (about 1 m square). Count the insects you find there. Now count insects in another area the same size. Compare the results.

Take a bag with pockets to carry your equipment in.

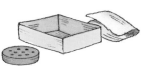

Carry insects in screw-top jars or boxes lined with paper or moss.

Keeping a notebook

It is best to use a spiral-bound notebook for your notes. Then you can tear off pages and keep together all the notes you have made at different times on a particular insect. Make rough notes when you are actually watching the insect. Make more careful ones later. Write down the date and the time when you saw the insect and what the weather was like. Try to describe the insect and the plant you found it on as fully as possible. If you want to return to an insect, draw a map to guide you.

Quick sketches

Make quick sketches of the insects you find. When you get home, look them up and try to identify them.

Head   Thorax   Abdomen

Draw three ovals for the head, thorax and abdomen.

Draw the insect's legs and antennae in position.

Draw in the wings, if the insect has any.

Add any special markings or colours if you have time.

Differences to spot

It is not always easy to tell one insect from another. Some flies look very like bees, while many bugs look like beetles. There are lots of different species of insect - many more than a million in the world.

When you are taking notes on an insect you have found, try to make a habit of asking yourself several questions. Does it have wings? How many pairs of wings? Does the insect have hard wing-cases? The charts on these pages show some of the insects which have these features.

This is not a scientific method of grouping (or classifying) insects, but it will help you to sort them out in your mind. Take notes on anything else that you notice about the insect. Does it have antennae? How long are they? Does the body have hairs on it? If so, then where? If it is an insect larva, does it have legs, and how many?

Make notes on the colours and patterns that you can see on the insect. Remember that insects change colour and shape as they grow into adults, and that the male of a species is sometimes a different colour from the female.

Quick check list

When you find an insect, look first to see whether it has wings. If it does, how many are there?

If it has one pair of wings, look at chart A.

If it has hard wing-cases, look at chart B.

If it has no wings, look at chart C.

If it has two pairs of wings, look at chart D.

A Insects with one pair of wings

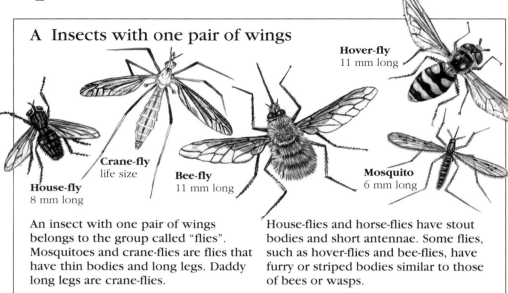

Hover-fly
11 mm long

Crane-fly
life size

Bee-fly
11 mm long

House-fly
8 mm long

Mosquito
6 mm long

An insect with one pair of wings belongs to the group called "flies". Mosquitoes and crane-flies are flies that have thin bodies and long legs. Daddy long legs are crane-flies.

House-flies and horse-flies have stout bodies and short antennae. Some flies, such as hover-flies and bee-flies, have furry or striped bodies similar to those of bees or wasps.

B Insects with hard wing-cases

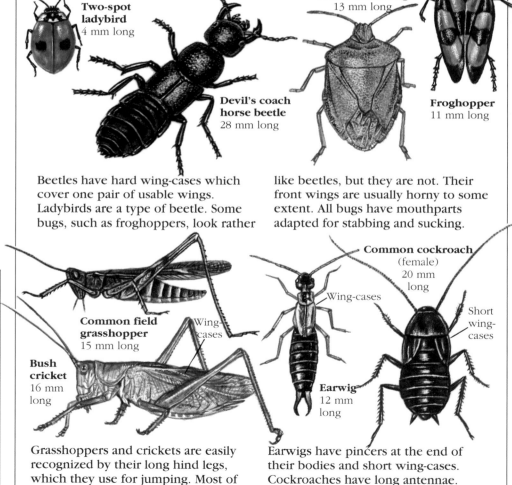

Wing-cases

Two-spot ladybird
4 mm long

Green shield bug
13 mm long

Devil's coach horse beetle
28 mm long

Froghopper
11 mm long

Beetles have hard wing-cases which cover one pair of usable wings. Ladybirds are a type of beetle. Some bugs, such as froghoppers, look rather like beetles, but they are not. Their front wings are usually horny to some extent. All bugs have mouthparts adapted for stabbing and sucking.

Common cockroach
(female)
20 mm long

Short wing-cases

Common field grasshopper
15 mm long

Wing-cases

Bush cricket
16 mm long

Wing-cases

Earwig
12 mm long

Grasshoppers and crickets are easily recognized by their long hind legs, which they use for jumping. Most of them have one pair of wings, covered with horny wing-cases.

Earwigs have pincers at the end of their bodies and short wing-cases. Cockroaches have long antennae. Female cockroaches often do not have wings. Males tend to have short wings.

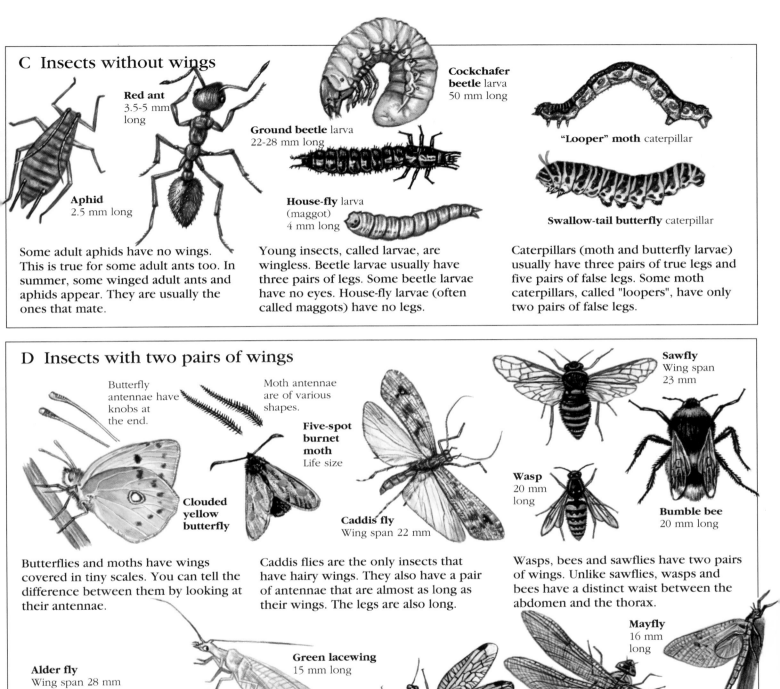

C Insects without wings

Red ant
3.5-5 mm
long

Aphid
2.5 mm long

Cockchafer beetle larva
50 mm long

Ground beetle larva
22-28 mm long

House-fly larva
(maggot)
4 mm long

"Looper" moth caterpillar

Swallow-tail butterfly caterpillar

Some adult aphids have no wings. This is true for some adult ants too. In summer, some winged adult ants and aphids appear. They are usually the ones that mate.

Young insects, called larvae, are wingless. Beetle larvae usually have three pairs of legs. Some beetle larvae have no eyes. House-fly larvae (often called maggots) have no legs.

Caterpillars (moth and butterfly larvae) usually have three pairs of true legs and five pairs of false legs. Some moth caterpillars, called "loopers", have only two pairs of false legs.

D Insects with two pairs of wings

Butterfly antennae have knobs at the end.

Moth antennae are of various shapes.

Five-spot burnet moth
Life size

Clouded yellow butterfly

Caddis fly
Wing span 22 mm

Sawfly
Wing span
23 mm

Wasp
20 mm
long

Bumble bee
20 mm long

Butterflies and moths have wings covered in tiny scales. You can tell the difference between them by looking at their antennae.

Caddis flies are the only insects that have hairy wings. They also have a pair of antennae that are almost as long as their wings. The legs are also long.

Wasps, bees and sawflies have two pairs of wings. Unlike sawflies, wasps and bees have a distinct waist between the abdomen and the thorax.

Alder fly
Wing span 28 mm

Green lacewing
15 mm long

Snake fly
Wing span 26 mm

Mayfly
16 mm
long

Scorpion fly
Wing span 26 mm

Emperor dragonfly
72 mm long

Alder flies, snake flies, and lacewings all have two pairs of wings that are both similar in size. Lacewings have translucent wings.

Snake flies can raise their head up, so that it looks like a snake about to strike. You can recognize a male scorpion fly by its up-turned tail.

Dragonflies have long, thin bodies and long wings. Mayflies have two or three long threads at the end of the abdomen and, usually, small hind wings.

Breeding, growing and changing

Most insects hatch from eggs. After they have hatched, they go through different stages of growth before becoming adults. Some young insects change shape completely before they are adult. Others just get bigger.

Insects such as crickets, earwigs, grasshoppers and bugs, hatch from the eggs looking like small adults. They have no wings when they hatch and are called nymphs. They moult several times, growing bigger each time. The nymph has small wing buds which expand into wings at the last moult.

Other insects change so much that when they hatch they do not look at all like the adults they will become.

The young of these types of insect, such as butterflies, moths, beetles, flies, ants and bees, are called larvae. A caterpillar is the larva of a moth or butterfly. Larvae moult several times as they grow.

When these larvae have grown to a certain size, they shed their skin for the last time and become pupae. Pupae do not feed and usually do not move. Inside the pupa, the body of the young insect slowly changes into an adult.

When the adult is ready to emerge, the pupal skin splits and the adult struggles out. It does not grow after this.

All insects have a soft skin at first, but this hardens and then cannot stretch. As they grow, insects have to change their skin by moulting.

A new skin grows under the old one. The old skin splits and the insect wriggles out, covered in its new, larger skin. Once the insect has become adult, it does not grow any more.

Dragonflies

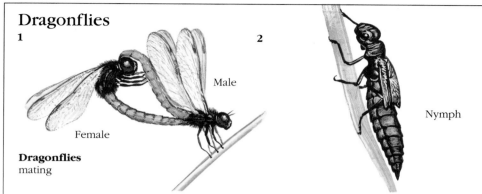

1 **Dragonflies** mating

2 Nymph

These dragonflies are mating. The male holds on to the neck of the female. The female lays her eggs either straight on the water or on a water plant. Nymphs hatch from the eggs.

Dragonfly nymphs live in the water for two years or more. When they moult, they change colour to blend in with their surroundings. They crawl onto a stem before they moult into an adult.

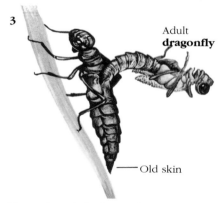

3 Adult **dragonfly** — Old skin

4 Adult **dragonfly** — Old skin

Here, the adult dragonfly is emerging from the nymph. The skin of the nymph has split and first the head and then the thorax of the adult appear. The old skin still clings to the stem.

After a short rest, the adult dragonfly pulls its abdomen out of the old skin. Then it rests on the stem by hanging from its legs, while its body gains shape and the wings expand.

Grasshoppers

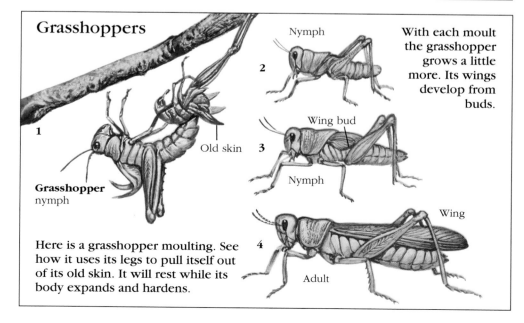

1 **Grasshopper** nymph — Old skin

2 Nymph

3 Wing bud — Nymph

4 Wing — Adult

With each moult the grasshopper grows a little more. Its wings develop from buds.

Here is a grasshopper moulting. See how it uses its legs to pull itself out of its old skin. It will rest while its body expands and hardens.

Mating

The adults of all types of insects mate with other insects of the same species. Then the females lay their eggs. Some are laid on stems, some are laid in or on the ground, and some in water.

Usually the eggs are laid on or near food that the larvae can feed on. The bluebottle eggs in the picture below have been laid on a dead animal. The larvae will feed on the animal when they hatch.

Lacewings lay their eggs on the end of a stalk that is made with special gum from the abdomen. It is thought that this method protects the eggs from ants that like to eat them.

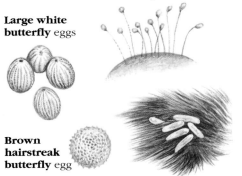

Lacewing eggs on stalks made of gum by female.

Large white butterfly eggs

Brown hairstreak butterfly egg

Bluebottle eggs

Female insects lay their eggs either singly, like the brown hairstreak butterfly, or in clusters, like the bluebottle and lacewing. A few insects leave the eggs once they are laid.

Gnats

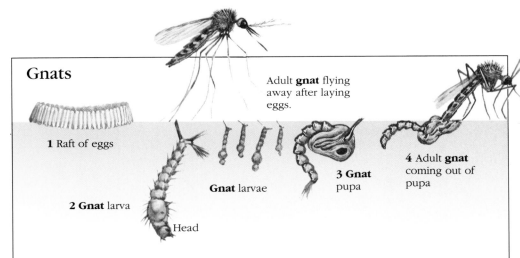

Adult **gnat** flying away after laying eggs.

1 Raft of eggs

2 Gnat larva

Head

Gnat larvae

3 Gnat pupa

4 Adult **gnat** coming out of pupa

Gnats lay their eggs in groups, which float like a raft on the water's surface (1). The larvae (2) hatch out, and hang from the surface, breathing air through a siphon. Each larva turns into a pupa (3), which also lives near the surface. When the adult has formed inside the pupa, the skin splits and it crawls out (4).

Butterflies

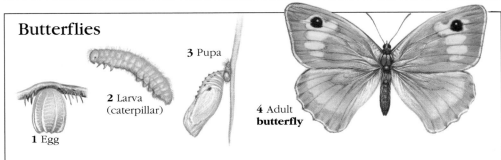

1 Egg

2 Larva (caterpillar)

3 Pupa

4 Adult **butterfly**

The meadow brown butterfly lays a single egg on grass (1). The caterpillar (2) hatches and spends the winter in this form. Early the next summer, it turns into a pupa (3).

Inside the pupa, or chrysalis, the body of the caterpillar breaks down and then becomes the body of the butterfly. This takes about four weeks. Then the pupa splits, and the adult emerges. It rests while its crumpled wings spread out and dry. Then it is ready to fly (4).

Stag beetles

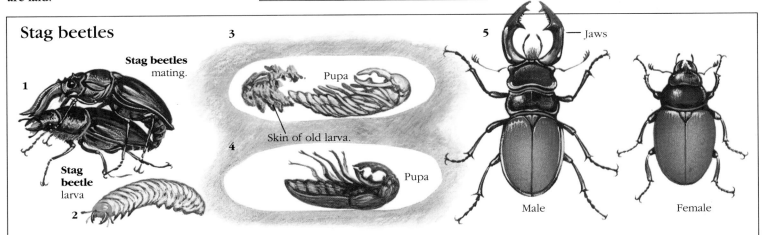

1

Stag beetles mating.

Stag beetle larva

2

3

Pupa

Skin of old larva.

4

Pupa

5

Jaws

Male

Female

After mating (1), the female stag beetle lays her eggs in the holes of rotten trees. The young larva (2) lives for three years, burrowing through the tree's soft wood. Then, the larva stops feeding, makes a pupal cell in the wood and becomes a pupa (3). It lies on its back to protect the newly-formed limbs until they harden (4). Then it emerges as an adult beetle (5). The males have large jaws that they use for fighting and to attract the females.

Insects in the garden

A good place to start a study of insects is your own garden. If you do not have a garden then look in a park or open green space. Make a chart of the insects you find there each month. Look under stones, on the bark of trees, on plants and grass, and among dead leaves. It is even worth looking in a garden shed.

Some insects spend the winter without moving or feeding. This is called hibernation. Make a note of where you find hibernating insects, but never disturb them.

1 On tree trunks

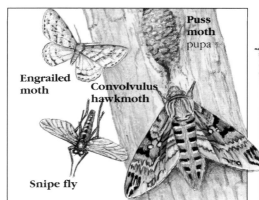

Moths, especially ones that are the colour of bark, rest on trees. In winter, look for pupae in bark crevices.

2 Under bark

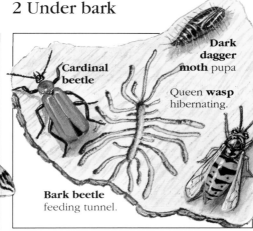

Queen wasps and beetles sometimes hibernate under loose bark. Look for bark beetle tunnels in the bark.

6 In wood piles

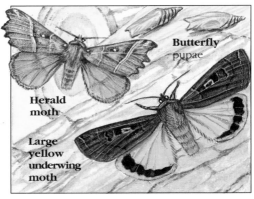

These insects hibernate in sheltered spots like wood piles in winter. Take great care not to disturb them.

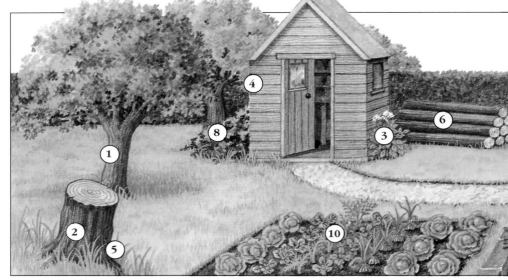

7 On walls

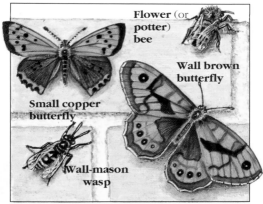

These insects can often be found on walls where they like to settle, particularly if the walls face the sun.

8 In the rubbish heap

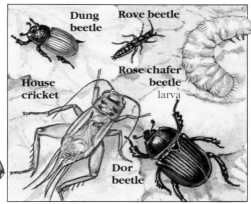

These insects feed on waste matter, such as animal droppings. You are most likely to find them in a rubbish heap.

9 Under stones

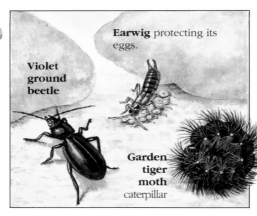

Lift up large stones and you will probably discover these insects. They like to live in dark, damp places.

3 On leaves and stems

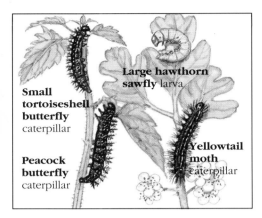

Small tortoiseshell butterfly caterpillar

Large hawthorn sawfly larva

Peacock butterfly caterpillar

Yellowtail moth caterpillar

Most caterpillars feed on leaves. Spot them in spring and summer, particularly on hedges and bushes.

4 Houses and sheds

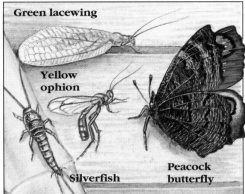

Green lacewing

Yellow ophion

Silverfish

Peacock butterfly

If you search a shed in winter, you may find a peacock butterfly or a green lacewing hibernating.

5 On grasses

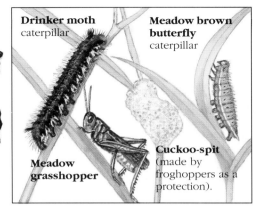

Drinker moth caterpillar

Meadow brown butterfly caterpillar

Meadow grasshopper

Cuckoo-spit (made by froghoppers as a protection).

Search carefully for insects on grasses. Many of them are green and blend in with surroundings, so are difficult to see.

The insect watcher's code

When looking for insects remember the insect watcher's code.

Always replace logs and stones exactly as you found them. They are often the homes of insects.

Search carefully and try not to damage flowers and twigs, and never peel the bark off trees.

You have a better chance of finding insects if you move slowly and quietly.

You can discover a lot just by waiting and watching.

10 In the soil

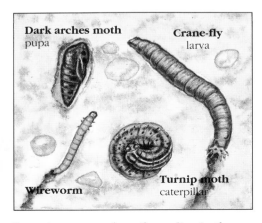

Dark arches moth pupa

Crane-fly larva

Wireworm

Turnip moth caterpillar

Some insects, such as these, live in the soil. You will have to dig to find them. The larvae feed on roots.

11 On flowers

Silver-washed fritillary

Hornet

In summer, you will see insects such as these feeding on the nectar and pollen of flowers.

12 On the ground

Devil's coach horse beetle

Ground beetle

Black ant

Watch ants and beetles scuttling over the ground in summer. See if you can follow them and spot where they go.

Insects in a tree

Thousands of different types of insect live in and on trees. You can make a study of the insects you find on one type of tree. The tree on this page is a common oak.

Try to choose a tree that stands on its own away from other trees. Make a note of how many kinds of insect you spot, where you find them on the tree and what the season is. See if you can identify them and discover some facts about them.

Is there a connection between the kinds of insect you find and the leaves, flowers or fruits on the tree? Compare the kinds of insect you find on your tree with those on other types of tree. Make a note of the differences and see if you can discover why each type of tree is better suited to certain insects.

Moth caterpillars

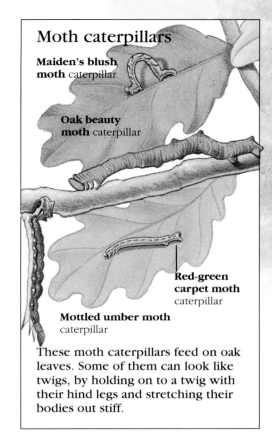

Maiden's blush moth caterpillar

Oak beauty moth caterpillar

Red-green carpet moth caterpillar

Mottled umber moth caterpillar

These moth caterpillars feed on oak leaves. Some of them can look like twigs, by holding on to a twig with their hind legs and stretching their bodies out stiff.

Greenfly

Greenfly
Look for leaves with yellow patches. These patches are caused by greenfly feeding.

Moths

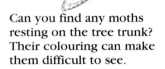

Goat moth   **Leopard moth**

Can you find any moths resting on the tree trunk? Their colouring can make them difficult to see.

Weevils

Nut weevil

In autumn, look for acorns with holes in them. These are where weevils have laid eggs. The female bores a tunnel into the acorn with her long nose and then places the egg at the end of it. The weevil larva feeds on the acorn.

Bark beetles

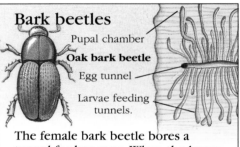

Pupal chamber

Oak bark beetle

Egg tunnel

Larvae feeding tunnels.

The female bark beetle bores a tunnel for her eggs. When the larvae hatch they bore tunnels at right angles to the main tunnel. They make a pupal chamber at the end, from which they emerge as adults.

Dig the soil a few metres from the tree and see what insects you can find there.

Look at rotting tree stumps as well as living trees. Note the different insects you find on each.

Green oak-roller

Green oak-roller moth

If disturbed, the caterpillar can lower itself on a silken thread.

The caterpillar hides and feeds inside an oak leaf, which it rolls over and binds with silk.

Carrion beetles

This four-spot carrion beetle feeds on green oak-roller moth caterpillars.

Beetles

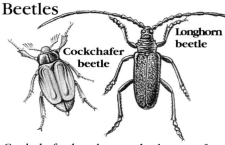

Cockchafer beetle

Longhorn beetle

Cockchafer beetles eat the leaves of trees and other plants. Longhorn beetles lay their eggs in crevices in the bark.

Feeding

Common goldeneye lacewing

10-spot ladybird

Lacewings and ladybirds feed on aphids such as greenfly that live on oak trees.

Bugs

Capsid bug

There are many types of capsid bug. Some like to live on oak trees. They feed on the sap of the leaves, or on young acorns.

Watch for birds eating insects on trees.

Look in the leaf litter on the ground beneath the tree for larvae and pupae.

Oak apple galls

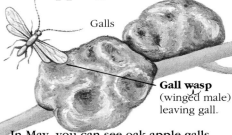

Galls

Gall wasp (winged male) leaving gall.

In May, you can see oak apple galls like these. They are made by gall wasp larvae. The adult wasps emerge in mid-summer.

Moth larva

Common swift moth caterpillars feed on the young roots of trees, and other plants. They pupate in the soil.

Beetle larva

Cockchafer larvae live in the soil for at least three years. They feed on the roots of trees and are very destructive to young trees.

Gall wasps

Gall

Gall wasp (wingless female)

Gall wasps lay their eggs in oak roots. Galls form with larvae inside. Wingless females emerge and crawl up the tree to lay their eggs in the buds, which swell into oak apples.

Pond insects

The best time of year to spot all these pond insects is in early summer. This is the time when the dragonflies and other flying insects change from being nymphs, larvae and pupae living in the water, to adults.

Look in different places around the pond. Watch the insects that fly over the pond and those that are on the surface. Search among the water weeds and use your net to find insects in the water.

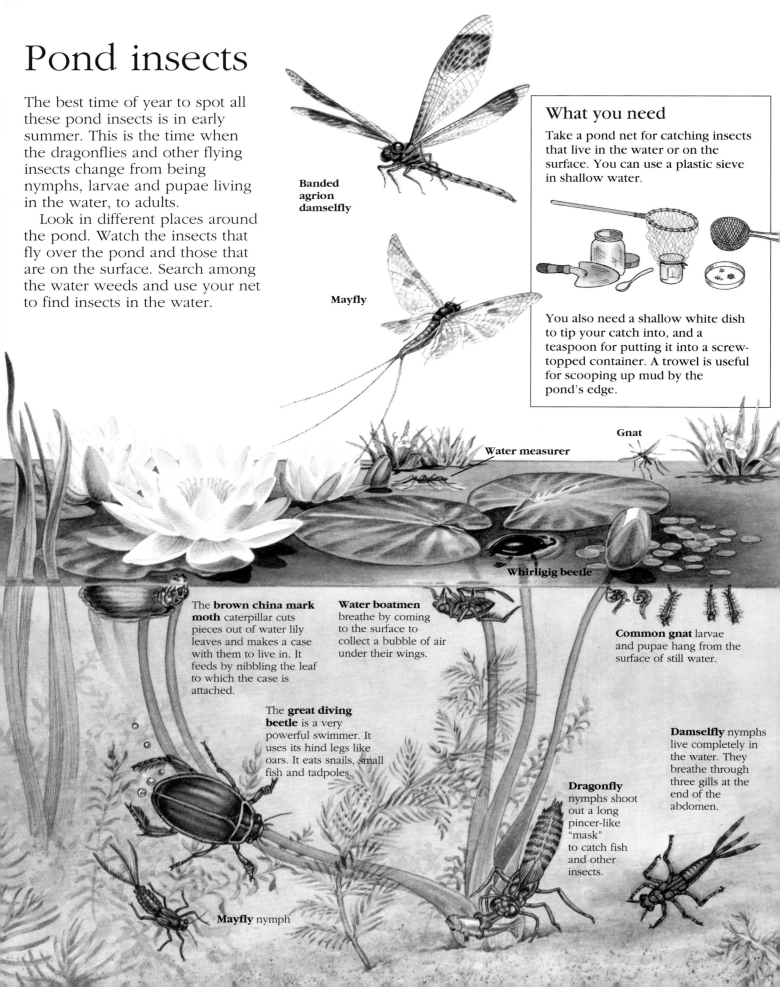

Banded agrion damselfly

Mayfly

What you need

Take a pond net for catching insects that live in the water or on the surface. You can use a plastic sieve in shallow water.

You also need a shallow white dish to tip your catch into, and a teaspoon for putting it into a screw-topped container. A trowel is useful for scooping up mud by the pond's edge.

Gnat

Water measurer

Whirligig beetle

The **brown china mark moth** caterpillar cuts pieces out of water lily leaves and makes a case with them to live in. It feeds by nibbling the leaf to which the case is attached.

Water boatmen breathe by coming to the surface to collect a bubble of air under their wings.

Common gnat larvae and pupae hang from the surface of still water.

The **great diving beetle** is a very powerful swimmer. It uses its hind legs like oars. It eats snails, small fish and tadpoles.

Damselfly nymphs live completely in the water. They breathe through three gills at the end of the abdomen.

Dragonfly nymphs shoot out a long pincer-like "mask" to catch fish and other insects.

Mayfly nymph

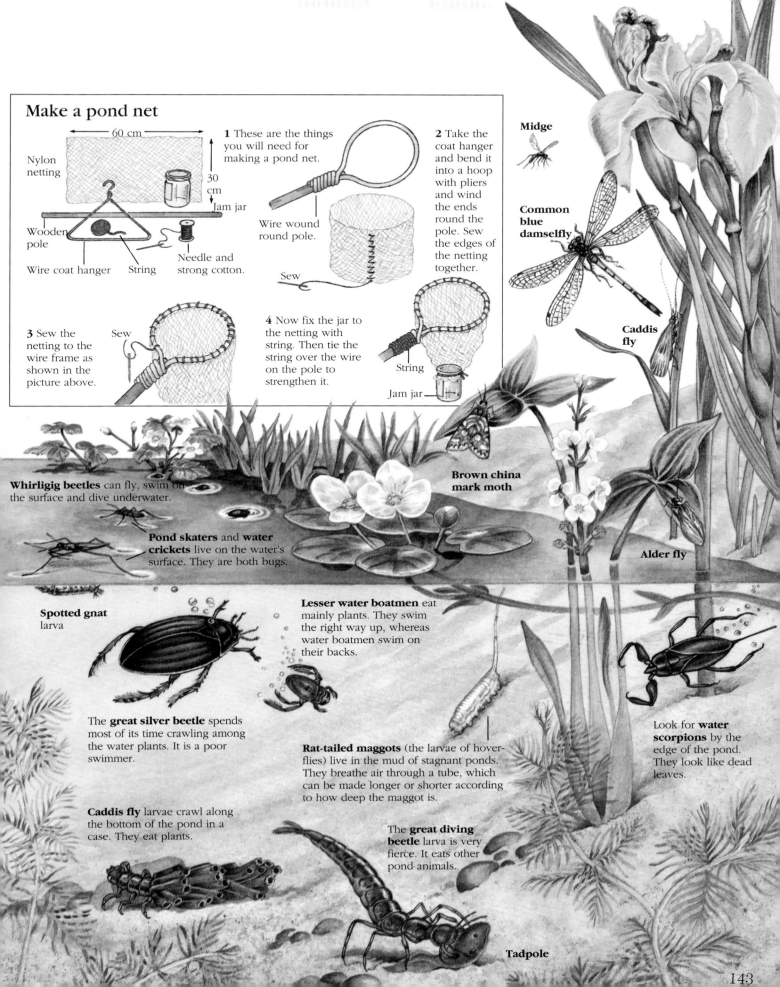

Make a pond net

1 These are the things you will need for making a pond net.

60 cm

Nylon netting

30 cm

Jam jar

Wooden pole

Wire coat hanger   String   Needle and strong cotton.

Wire wound round pole.

Sew

2 Take the coat hanger and bend it into a hoop with pliers and wind the ends round the pole. Sew the edges of the netting together.

3 Sew the netting to the wire frame as shown in the picture above.

Sew

4 Now fix the jar to the netting with string. Then tie the string over the wire on the pole to strengthen it.

String

Jam jar

Midge

Common blue damselfly

Caddis fly

Brown china mark moth

Alder fly

Whirligig beetles can fly, swim on the surface and dive underwater.

Pond skaters and **water crickets** live on the water's surface. They are both bugs.

Spotted gnat larva

Lesser water boatmen eat mainly plants. They swim the right way up, whereas water boatmen swim on their backs.

The **great silver beetle** spends most of its time crawling among the water plants. It is a poor swimmer.

Rat-tailed maggots (the larvae of hover-flies) live in the mud of stagnant ponds. They breathe air through a tube, which can be made longer or shorter according to how deep the maggot is.

Look for **water scorpions** by the edge of the pond. They look like dead leaves.

Caddis fly larvae crawl along the bottom of the pond in a case. They eat plants.

The **great diving beetle** larva is very fierce. It eats other pond animals.

Tadpole

143

Insect senses

Insects do not sense things in the same way that we do. They do not have a nose for smelling. However, insects can feel, smell and taste with their antennae. Some can also taste with their feet. The hairs on an insect's body help it to feel.

Most insects have hairs on their bodies. These hairs are stiff and they are connected to nerve cells. The insect can feel every movement of the hairs.

Simple eyes

The antennae are an important sense organ. They are sensitive to heat and damp, as well as being used for smelling and tasting. Only parts of the bluebottle's antennae are shown. The main parts are in front of the head.

Compound eye

Bluebottle (or **blow-fly**)

Insects have two kinds of eyes - simple eyes, called ocelli, and compound eyes. The compound eyes are made up of thousands of separate lenses. Insects do not focus their eyes in the same way that we do. They can, however, detect even the slightest movement. Some insects can see forwards, backwards, and downwards all at the same time.

Some insects, such as butterflies, bees and bluebottles, can taste with their feet. When they land on something sweet, they immediately put out their proboscis and start feeding.

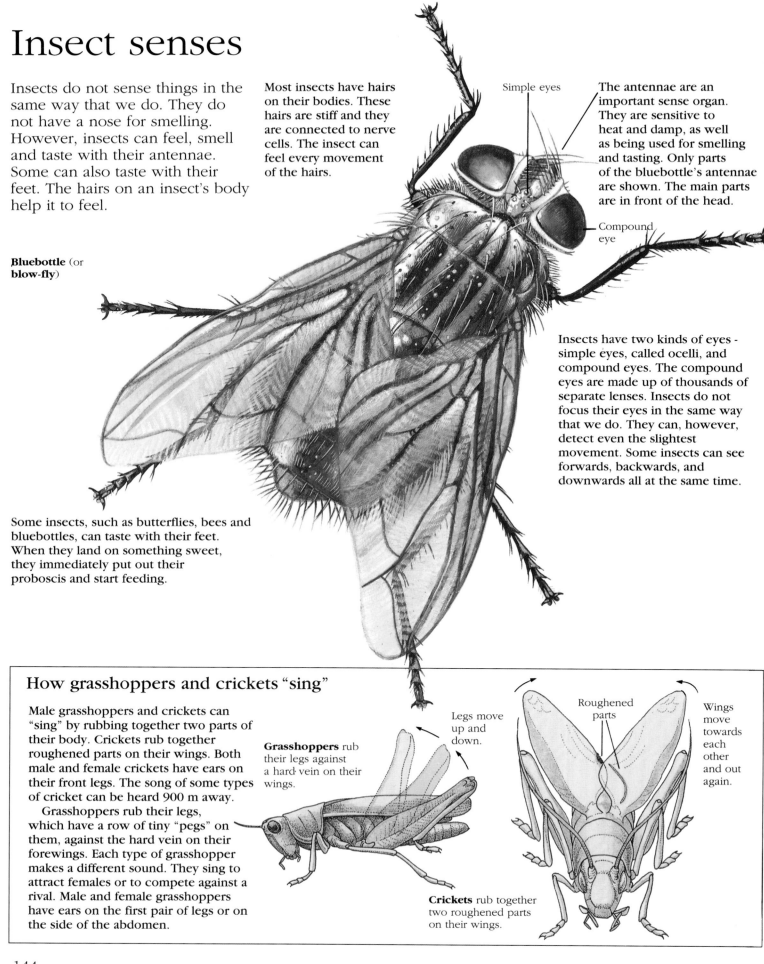

How grasshoppers and crickets "sing"

Male grasshoppers and crickets can "sing" by rubbing together two parts of their body. Crickets rub together roughened parts on their wings. Both male and female crickets have ears on their front legs. The song of some types of cricket can be heard 900 m away.

Grasshoppers rub their legs, which have a row of tiny "pegs" on them, against the hard vein on their forewings. Each type of grasshopper makes a different sound. They sing to attract females or to compete against a rival. Male and female grasshoppers have ears on the first pair of legs or on the side of the abdomen.

Grasshoppers rub their legs against a hard vein on their wings.

Legs move up and down.

Roughened parts

Wings move towards each other and out again.

Crickets rub together two roughened parts on their wings.

Antennae

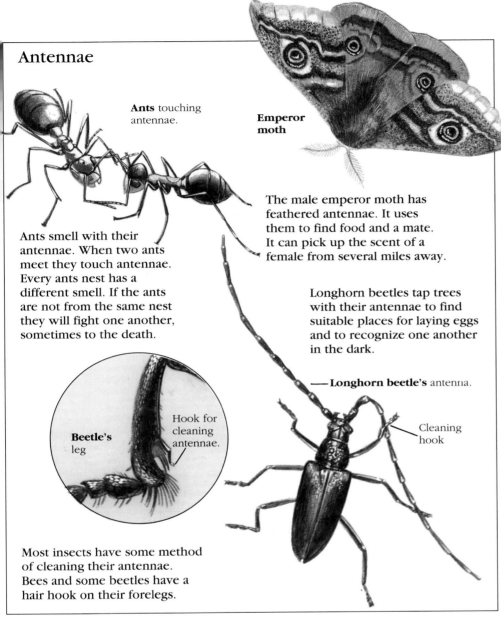

Ants touching antennae.

Emperor moth

Ants smell with their antennae. When two ants meet they touch antennae. Every ants nest has a different smell. If the ants are not from the same nest they will fight one another, sometimes to the death.

The male emperor moth has feathered antennae. It uses them to find food and a mate. It can pick up the scent of a female from several miles away.

Longhorn beetles tap trees with their antennae to find suitable places for laying eggs and to recognize one another in the dark.

— **Longhorn beetle's** antenna.

Beetle's leg

Hook for cleaning antennae.

Cleaning hook

Most insects have some method of cleaning their antennae. Bees and some beetles have a hair hook on their forelegs.

Hairs and feelers

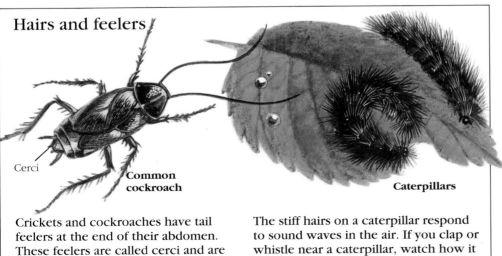

Cerci

Common cockroach

Caterpillars

Crickets and cockroaches have tail feelers at the end of their abdomen. These feelers are called cerci and are sensitive to touch.

The stiff hairs on a caterpillar respond to sound waves in the air. If you clap or whistle near a caterpillar, watch how it curls up or suddenly "freezes".

Things to do

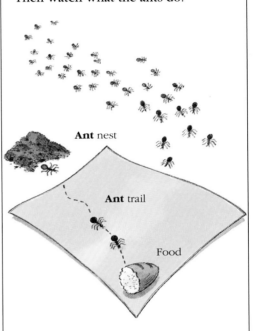

Ants can leave a scent trail. They press their bodies on the ground, leaving a smell for others to follow. If you find a trail, rub part of it out. Then watch what the ants do.

Ant nest

Ant trail

Food

Put a piece of paper near an ant nest and cover it with food. Watch several ants find the food. Then move the food to another part of the paper.

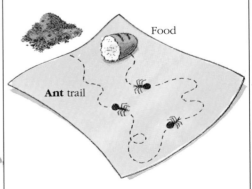

Food

Ant trail

Watch the ants coming from the nest. Do they go straight to the food? Or do they go first to where the food was before you moved it? Can you give a reason for what they do?

Watching insects move

Many insects have their own particular way of moving. If you learn to recognize these different movements, then you will be able to identify the insects more easily. Insects that walk or run usually have long, thin legs. Insects that dig, such as dor beetles, have forelegs that are shorter but stronger than the other two pairs. Insects that jump or swim often have specially developed hind-legs. Compare the way different insects fly. Wasps, flies and bees flap their wings faster than butterflies when they fly.

Flying

Look at the different shapes of insects' wings, and watch how fast or slowly they fly. Look to see if they have one pair of wings or two.

Halteres

Flies have only one pair of wings. Instead of hind wings they have two knobs, called halteres. These help the insect to balance.

When a **beetle** flies it holds up its stiff wing-cases, to let its wings move easily. When it lands it folds its wings back under the wing-cases.

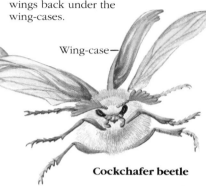

Wing-case

Cockchafer beetle

Jumping

Grasshopper jumping

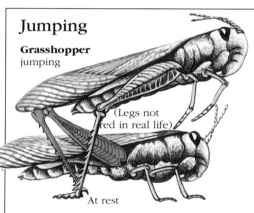

(Legs not ...ed in real life)

At rest

The grasshopper's powerful, long back legs with their strong thighs help it to leap. As it straightens its legs, the grasshopper is propelled into the air.

Swimming

Water boatman

Hairs

Some underwater swimmers have flattened hind legs, fringed with long hairs. They use these legs like oars, moving them both together.

Walking on water

Pond skater

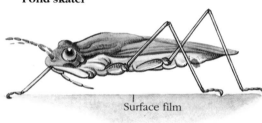

Surface film

Heavy objects break the surface film on water and sink. A pond skater is light and has long spread-out legs. It walks on the surface without breaking the film.

Digging

Mole cricket burrowing

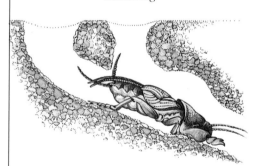

Insects that burrow often have short, wide front legs. These legs are flattened and can have teeth, which helps the insect dig into the soil.

How caterpillars move

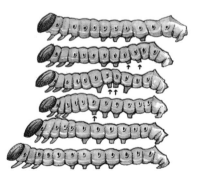

Caterpillars have three pairs of walking legs and up to five pairs of false legs. All caterpillars, except "loopers", walk by moving each pair of false legs in turn.

Looper caterpillars

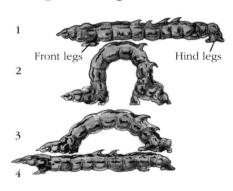

1

Front legs   Hind legs

2

3

4

A "looper" caterpillar moves forward by bringing forward its hind legs (1, 2) causing the body to arch, and then stretching out its front legs (3, 4).

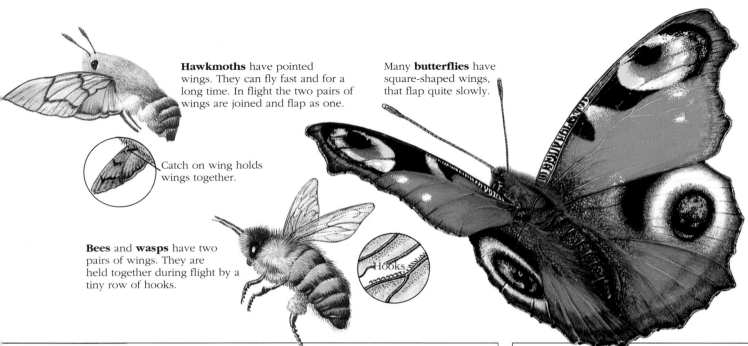

Hawkmoths have pointed wings. They can fly fast and for a long time. In flight the two pairs of wings are joined and flap as one.

Many **butterflies** have square-shaped wings, that flap quite slowly.

Catch on wing holds wings together.

Bees and **wasps** have two pairs of wings. They are held together during flight by a tiny row of hooks.

Hooks

Walking on land

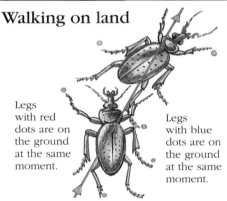

Legs with red dots are on the ground at the same moment.

Legs with blue dots are on the ground at the same moment.

Insects that walk often have long thin legs, which are all alike. They walk by moving three legs at a time and balancing on the other three.

How click beetles click

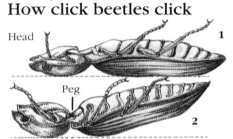

Head

1

Peg

2

If a click beetle falls on its back (1), it arches its body until only its head and tail touch the ground. A peg on its thorax makes it double up (2). Its wing-cases hit the ground and the beetle is thrown into the air, with a "clicking" sound.

How insects move

Find out what happens when different insects meet water, other insects or things in their way. Put down twigs, stones or some paper. Note down what you see.

See whether insects move at the same speed on different kinds of surface. Compare how they move on soil, grass and wood.

Smoke the top side of a plate over a candle. Be very careful and do not hold the plate over the flame for too long as it may crack. When it has cooled, put the plate on the ground and watch insects move over it. Look at the different tracks made in the soot with a pocket lens and see what patterns each insect makes.

How flies walk upside down

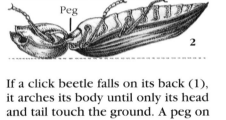

Close-up of foot.

House-fly

House-flies have sticky, hairy pads on their feet. Because the fly is so light, the grip of the pads is strong enough to hold it on almost any surface.

How springtails jump

1 At rest

2 Jumping

Fork

3 Landing

Springtails cannot fly, but they can jump. Their forked tail, which folds under the body, flicks down on the ground and throws the insect forward.

Watching insects feed

Insects feed on almost every kind of animal and plant. Some insects, such as cockroaches, will eat almost anything, but most insects feed only on one particular kind of food. There are insects that feed on cork, paper, clothes, ink, cigarettes, carpets, flour - and even shoe-polish.

The diet of an insect may change at different stages in its life. Most insects eat either plants or animals. However, some insects eat only animals when they are larvae and eat only plants when they are adults, or vice versa.

Insects that eat plants are called herbivores. More than half of all insects eat plants. Some feed on the leaves, flowers or seeds of plants, others bite the roots or suck the sap from inside plant stems. Some insects feed on nectar and pollen. You can find out more about this on page 150.

Some insects feed on animals smaller than themselves, or suck the blood from larger ones, sometimes after paralyzing or killing them. Female mosquitoes and horse-flies usually need to have a meal of mammal's blood before they can produce eggs. Many insects feed inside the bodies of other animals, and live there all the time. They are called parasites.

Some insects are called scavengers. They eat any decaying material that they find in the soil, such as animals that are already dead, and rotting plants. They also feed on the dung of animals. Flea larvae eat the droppings of adult fleas, as well as dirt and the skin fragments that come from the animal they are living on.

Plant feeders

Leaf eaters

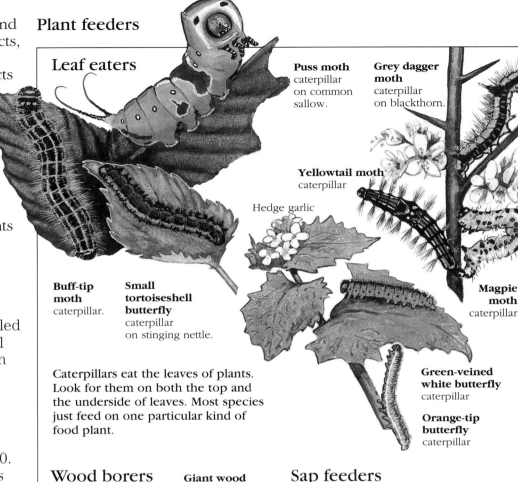

Puss moth caterpillar on common sallow.

Grey dagger moth caterpillar on blackthorn.

Yellowtail moth caterpillar

Hedge garlic

Buff-tip moth caterpillar.

Small tortoiseshell butterfly caterpillar on stinging nettle.

Magpie moth caterpillar

Green-veined white butterfly caterpillar

Orange-tip butterfly caterpillar

Caterpillars eat the leaves of plants. Look for them on both the top and the underside of leaves. Most species just feed on one particular kind of food plant.

Wood borers

Giant wood wasp

Wood wasps lay their eggs in pine trees. The larvae eat the soft wood.

Sap feeders

Bugs, such as greenfly, pierce leaves and plant stems and suck the sap inside.

Piercing tube

Greenfly

Leaf miners

Blotch mine caterpillars eat around themselves.

Serpentine mine caterpillars move forward as they eat.

Caterpillars of tiny moths and flies tunnel between the two surfaces of a leaf and eat the tissues inside.

Seed eaters

Nut weevil

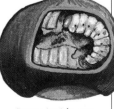

Larva inside nut.

The female nut weevil bores a hole in newly formed hazel nuts and acorns and lays an egg. The grub hatches and feeds on the nut. The nut falls to the ground and the larva eats its way out and pupates in the soil.

Insect mouthparts

Insects either suck liquids, or bite and chew solid food. Insects that suck have a hollow tube, called a proboscis. Bees, butterflies and moths suck nectar from inside flowers. Bugs can pierce plant stems and suck the sap inside. Mosquitoes pierce the skin of animals or humans and suck their blood.

Insects that bite and chew have three different pairs of mouthparts - a large pair called mandibles, a smaller pair called maxillae and a third pair which are joined together to form a kind of lower lip.

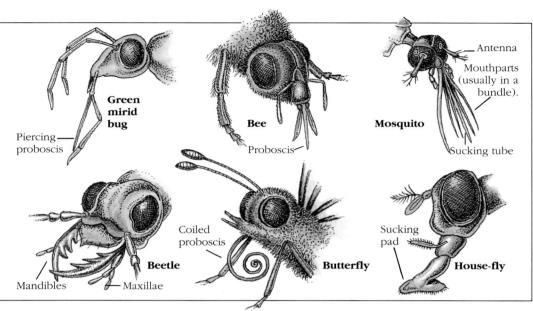

Green mirid bug
Piercing proboscis

Bee
Proboscis

Mosquito
Antenna
Mouthparts (usually in a bundle).
Sucking tube

Beetle
Mandibles
Maxillae

Coiled proboscis
Butterfly

Sucking pad
House-fly

Animal feeders

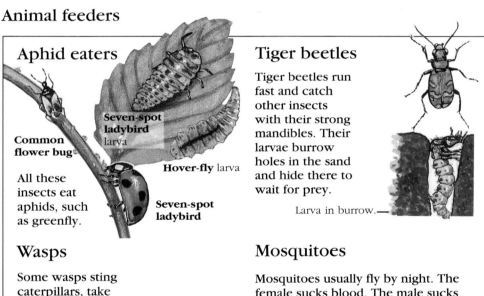

Aphid eaters

Common flower bug

All these insects eat aphids, such as greenfly.

Seven-spot ladybird larva

Hover-fly larva

Seven-spot ladybird

Wasps

Some wasps sting caterpillars, take them to their nest and lay eggs upon them.

Red-banded sand wasp

Dragonflies

Some dragonflies are often called "hawkers" because they fly so fast and overpower other insects.

Tiger beetles

Tiger beetles run fast and catch other insects with their strong mandibles. Their larvae burrow holes in the sand and hide there to wait for prey.

Larva in burrow.

Mosquitoes

Mosquitoes usually fly by night. The female sucks blood. The male sucks nectar from flowers.

Skin

Robber-flies

Robber-flies pounce on insects in the air and suck them dry.

Scavengers

Blow-flies

Blow-flies lay their eggs on meat. The larvae (maggots) eat the meat when they hatch.

Bluebottle (Blow-fly)

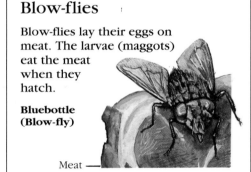

Meat

Dor beetles

Balls of dung.

Eggs

Dor beetles dig tunnels under cow dung. The female lays her eggs in chambers. The larvae feed on balls of dung.

Burying beetles

Burying beetles dig a hole and pull dead animals underground. They lay their eggs near the corpse.

Insects and flowers

Many insects visit flowers for food. Moths and butterflies feed on nectar, a sweet liquid found inside most flowers. Bees collect pollen, the yellow dust inside flowers, as well as nectar.

Flowers do not need the nectar they produce, except to attract insects. The insects help the flowers to make new seeds. Most insects that visit flowers are hairy. When they feed on a flower the hairs become dusted with pollen from the ripe stamens (the male parts inside a flower). Then the insects visit other flowers of the same species, and some of the sticky pollen may be accidentally brushed off onto the stigmas (the female parts of the flower).

This is called pollination. New seeds start to grow only when a flower has been pollinated.

Flowers that attract insects usually have a strong scent and can be brightly coloured. Insects do not see colours as we do. Flowers that look one colour to us, such as the yellow tormentil, appear white with dark centres to an insect.

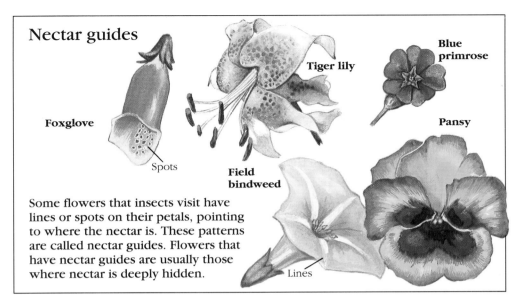

Nectar guides

Foxglove

Spots

Tiger lily

Blue primrose

Pansy

Field bindweed

Lines

Some flowers that insects visit have lines or spots on their petals, pointing to where the nectar is. These patterns are called nectar guides. Flowers that have nectar guides are usually those where nectar is deeply hidden.

Adult bees feed only on nectar. Wasps feed on sweet liquids, such as from a ripe plum, as well as on nectar. Bees make honey from the nectar they gather. Bee larvae feed on pollen mixed with the honey. Young queen bees are fed on a richer type of this food, called royal jelly. Wasp larvae have a few meals of nectar and then feed on insects captured and brought to them by the adults.

Wasp

Michaelmas daisy

Common blue butterfly

Look for drone-flies on hogweed and wild carrot.

Drone-fly

Hogweed

Pollination

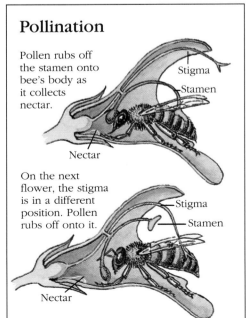

Pollen rubs off the stamen onto bee's body as it collects nectar.

Stigma

Stamen

Nectar

On the next flower, the stigma is in a different position. Pollen rubs off onto it.

Stigma

Stamen

Nectar

Feeding on flowers

Garden chafer beetle

Beetles have mouthparts that bite and chew. Nectar feeding beetles cannot suck nectar like bees. This means they only feed on flowers where the nectar is easy to get at.

Hover fly

Proboscis

Some flies that suck nectar look like bees. They have a hairy body and their tongue, called a proboscis, is longer than that of other flies. Look for them on wide-open flowers.

Long proboscis

Hawkmoth

Most moths fly at dusk or at night. They are attracted to pale-coloured flowers that can be seen easily in the dark. Nectar is stored deep inside the flower, so a moth must have a long proboscis.

Watch how a butterfly extends its long proboscis into a flower, as soon as it lands. Butterflies feed from bright, scented flowers.

Large skipper butterfly

Bumble bee

Proboscis

Bees only gather nectar from one species of flower at a time. Watch this for yourself. Follow a single bee from flower to flower. Can you identify the type of flower it visits? Make a list of the different types of flower that bees visit.

Pollen on legs.

Honey bee

Honey bees collect nectar and pollen. Nectar is sucked up through the proboscis. Pollen is packed on the hind legs and held there by stiff bristles. This pollen can help to make seeds in the next flower the bee visits.

Make a butterfly garden

Try growing some of these plants to attract butterflies. Butterflies feed on flowers, and some lay eggs on weeds such as nettles. Keep a monthly record of the kinds of flowers that different insects visit. Note the shape and colour of each flower and whether it has a strong scent. Find out which flowers seem to attract most insects.

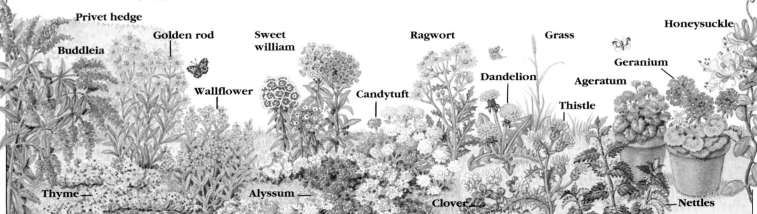

Privet hedge

Buddleia

Golden rod

Sweet william

Ragwort

Grass

Honeysuckle

Wallflower

Candytuft

Dandelion

Geranium

Ageratum

Thistle

Thyme

Alyssum

Clover

Nettles

Ants and bees

Ants and bees are "social" insects. This means that they live in colonies of sometimes thousands of insects. The food and work in the colony is shared.

In each colony there is a queen, who is the only egg-laying female. Then there are the males, called drones, whose only job is to mate with the queen. The third type of insect are undeveloped females. These are called workers and they do all the work in the colony. Each worker has a particular task, either to collect food and to care for the eggs and larvae, or to guard the nest.

An ant nest

Ants make their nests by burrowing in sand or soil. Some worker ants have the special job of building and repairing the nest. A gland in the ant's jaw produces a sticky liquid which can help to "cement" the nest together. Ant nests are made up of a network of chambers and passages. The queen has her own chamber and there are separate chambers for eggs, larvae and pupae. Other chambers are used for storing food or for rubbish. The entrance of the nest is closed at night, during rain or when it is very cold. In winter, the worker ants make the nest go deeper below ground.

How ants are born

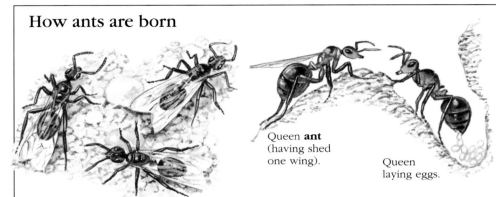

Queen **ant** (having shed one wing).

Queen laying eggs.

In warm summer weather, the winged males and queens leave the nest on a mating flight. After mating, the males die. The queen flies to the ground.

Each queen starts a new nest. She rubs or bites off her wings. Then she finds, or makes, a space in the soil where she can lay her first batch of eggs.

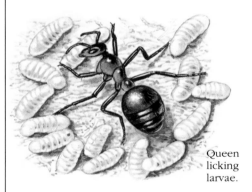

Queen licking larvae.

Worker ants picking up larvae.

The queen feeds the larvae with her own saliva. Later they become worker ants and take over the job of looking after the nest and the eggs.

Now the queen does nothing but lay more eggs. Workers feed the larvae and lick them clean. They cut the pupae open to let the new ants climb out.

Queen in chamber.   Worker and larvae.

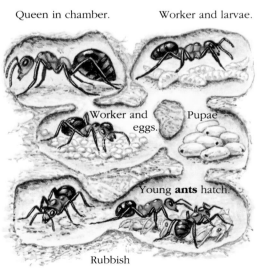

Worker and eggs.   Pupae

Young **ants** hatch.

Rubbish

Food

Ants carrying **insect**.

Ant milking **aphids**.   **Aphids**

Some ants go out collecting small insects, worms and other food. Others lick the sweet honeydew that aphids on nearby plants produce.

Defence and cleaning

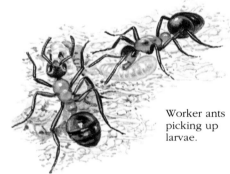

Ant in defence position, about to squirt poison.

Jaws

Worker moving rubbish.

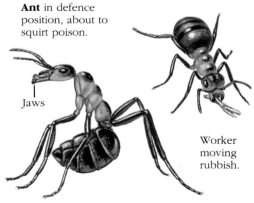

Worker ants guard the nest. Ants keep their nest very clean, moving rubbish out of the nest or into special chambers. Some ants can squirt poison at an enemy.

Honey bees

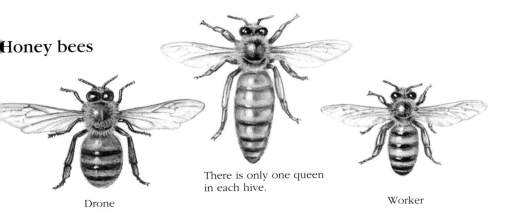

Drone

There is only one queen in each hive.

Worker

These are three different kinds of honey bee that you will find in a bee hive. The only honey bees you will see flying around are the workers. The others stay only in the hive.

The workers do all the jobs. Young workers clean out cells, then as they get older, they feed the larvae, build new cells and make honey. Later they collect nectar and pollen.

The honeycomb

This is what the inside of a honey bee's comb looks like. It is made of six-sided wax cells. Those near the outside are for breeding drones and for storing honey. Those in the middle are brood cells for worker bees. Pollen is packed in cells next to the brood cells. Queen bee larvae have special cells.

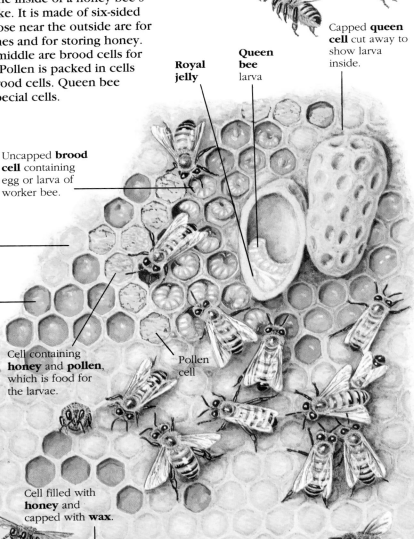

Royal jelly

Queen bee larva

Capped **queen cell** cut away to show larva inside.

Uncapped **brood cell** containing egg or larva of worker bee.

Brood cell, capped, with larva inside.

Uncapped **honey cell.**

Cell containing **honey** and **pollen,** which is food for the larvae.

Pollen cell

Cell filled with **honey** and capped with **wax**.

How a bee grows

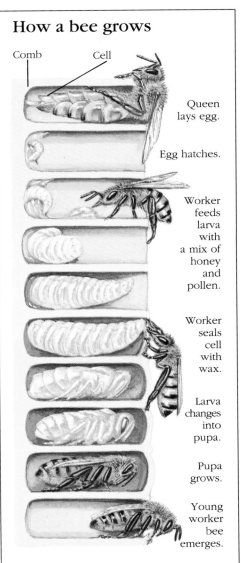

Comb   Cell

Queen lays egg.

Egg hatches.

Worker feeds larva with a mix of honey and pollen.

Worker seals cell with wax.

Larva changes into pupa.

Pupa grows.

Young worker bee emerges.

The queen lays one egg in each cell. After three days the eggs hatch. The worker bees feed the larvae on a mixture of honey and pollen. Queen bee larvae are fed on a rich mixture of honey and pollen and some other substances, called royal jelly.

After six days the larvae are large and fat and fill their cells. Worker bees seal the cells with wax made in the bodies of the bees. Inside the cells the larvae pupate. Two weeks later the young bees eat through the seal of wax and emerge fully grown. Before the young worker bees fly from the hive, they sometimes have the special job of keeping the air fresh in the hive by fanning their wings.

Collecting and keeping insects

When you find an insect, out in the garden or in some other place, put it in a small tin. Also place in the tin a piece of the plant on which you found the insect. The plant will give the insect some food and help you to identify it.

Number each tin. Write the numbers in your notebook and, against each one, write a description of the insect and where you found it. Was it in a dry or damp place, a sunny or a shady place?

If you want to keep your insects, when you get home you must put them in a place that is as similar as possible to their natural surroundings. You will need containers that are big enough to hold sufficient food and give the insects some room to move around. It is best to use glass or clear plastic containers, then you can see what is happening inside.

It is usually a good idea to put some sand or soil at the bottom, with a stone and some plants. Keep the containers in a cool place away from the sunlight, but not in a draught.

Make sure you have a good supply of fresh food and change it each day. Most caterpillars have their own particular food plant and will not eat anything else. There is no point in collecting them unless you can give them the right food supply.

Look at the insects in your "zoo" every day and record any changes that you see. You could keep a note of how much caterpillars eat and their length, or describe what happens to them when they pupate. See if you can spot different types of behaviour in different types of caterpillars. Watch how they move and eat.

Collecting crawling insects

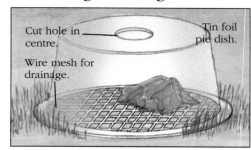

Cut hole in centre. Tin foil pie dish. Wire mesh for drainage.

Try making a trap like this. Put bait, such as a piece of meat, in the trap to attract insects. A good place to put the trap is at the bottom of a hedge.

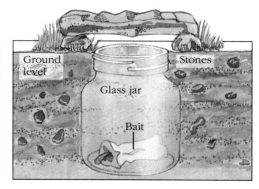

Ground level. Stones. Glass jar. Bait.

You could also make a pitfall trap. Try different baits, such as jam, raw meat, fruit or beer. Keep a record of the insects that are attracted by each bait.

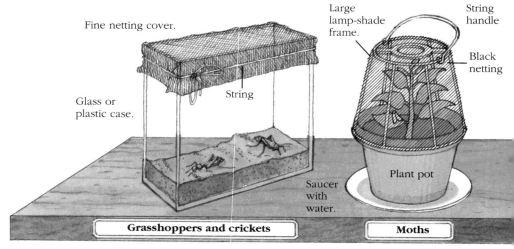

Fine netting cover. Glass or plastic case. String. Large lamp-shade frame. String handle. Black netting. Saucer with water. Plant pot.

Grasshoppers and crickets | **Moths**

In late summer, you may find crickets and grasshoppers. Keep them in a large glass case or jar with sand in the bottom. Put in fresh grass every other day.

Make a moth cage. Keep it out of the sun and in hot weather spray it with water. If you want the moths to breed, put in the right plant for the larvae to feed on.

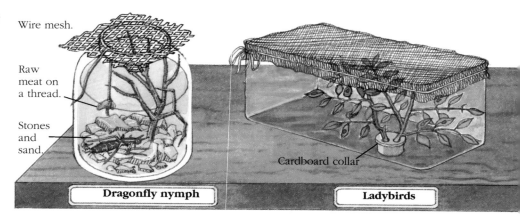

Wire mesh. Raw meat on a thread. Stones and sand. Cardboard collar.

Dragonfly nymph | **Ladybirds**

Keep a dragonfly nymph on its own in a large jam jar and feed it on raw meat. Put in an upright stick for the nymph to cling to when it sheds its skin.

Keep ladybirds in a large case to give them room to fly. They feed on greenfly, often found on rose shoots. Cut off the whole shoot and keep it in water.

Sugaring

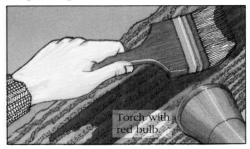

Torch with red bulb.

You can attract moths by "sugaring". Paint tree trunks or posts at dusk with a mixture of black treacle and rum or beer. Warm, still evenings are best.

Lights

Light-traps are used to catch insects. Other lights, such as from a lamp, also attract them. How many can you find that are attracted to light in this way.

Remember

It is easy to collect insects, but remember that they are very fragile. Handle them as little as possible and do not collect more than you need to study.

If you keep the insects for a few days to study, make sure you supply them with a piece of the plant on which you found them.

Never collect a rare or protected species.

Once you have finished looking at them, take the insects back to the place where you found them. Let flying insects go at dusk so that birds or cats do not attack and kill them.

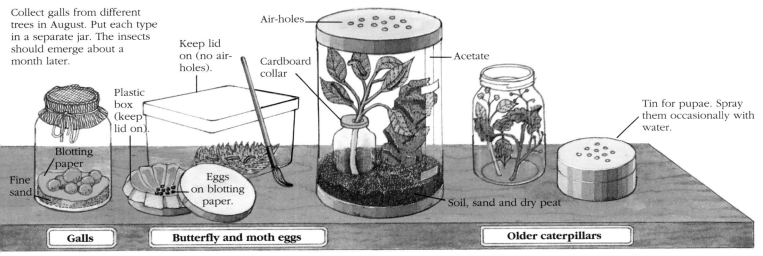

Collect galls from different trees in August. Put each type in a separate jar. The insects should emerge about a month later.

Keep lid on (no air-holes).

Plastic box (keep lid on).

Air-holes

Cardboard collar

Acetate

Blotting paper

Fine sand

Eggs on blotting paper.

Soil, sand and dry peat

Tin for pupae. Spray them occasionally with water.

Galls

Butterfly and moth eggs

Older caterpillars

Collect butterfly or moth eggs in small boxes. When the caterpillars hatch, put them in another box and give them a new leaf of their food plant each day.

To make a container for older caterpillars, roll up some acetate and fix it with sticky tape. Put one half of a tin on one end and its lid on the other end.

If you find a caterpillar whose food you do not know, collect several plants. Put them with the caterpillar in a jar. Look after a few hours to see which it eats.

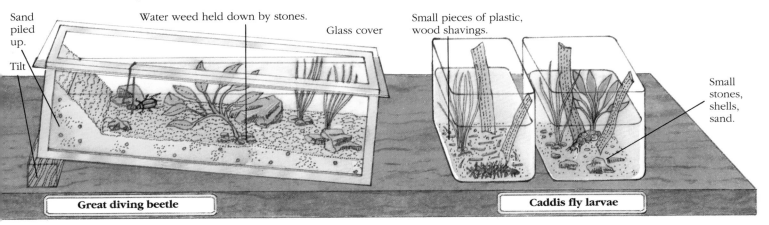

Sand piled up.

Tilt

Water weed held down by stones.

Glass cover

Small pieces of plastic, wood shavings.

Small stones, shells, sand.

Great diving beetle

Caddis fly larvae

Great diving beetles and water boatmen are very fierce, so keep each one on its own. Feed them on maggots or raw meat attached to a thread, and change daily.

See how caddis fly larvae make their protective cases. Collect several caddis flies and carefully remove the larvae from their cases by prodding them with

the blunt end of a pin. Put them in separate aquariums with different materials in each, and watch what happens. Feed them on water weed.

Common insects to spot

Butterflies

Red admiral May to June and July to September.

Speckled wood April to June and August to September.

Orange-tip May to June.

Small white May to June and July to August.

Green-veined white May to June and August to September.

Underside of wing.

Common blue May to June and August to September.

Large white May to August.

Wall May to June and August to September.

Meadow brown Mid-June to September.

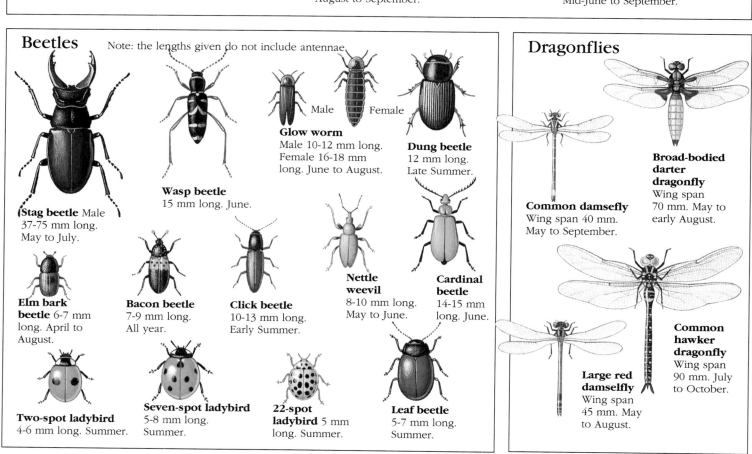

Beetles

Note: the lengths given do not include antennae.

Stag beetle Male 37-75 mm long. May to July.

Wasp beetle 15 mm long. June.

Glow worm Male 10-12 mm long. Female 16-18 mm long. June to August. Male Female

Dung beetle 12 mm long. Late Summer.

Elm bark beetle 6-7 mm long. April to August.

Bacon beetle 7-9 mm long. All year.

Click beetle 10-13 mm long. Early Summer.

Nettle weevil 8-10 mm long. May to June.

Cardinal beetle 14-15 mm long. June.

Two-spot ladybird 4-6 mm long. Summer.

Seven-spot ladybird 5-8 mm long. Summer.

22-spot ladybird 5 mm long. Summer.

Leaf beetle 5-7 mm long. Summer.

Dragonflies

Common damsefly Wing span 40 mm. May to September.

Broad-bodied darter dragonfly Wing span 70 mm. May to early August.

Large red damselfly Wing span 45 mm. May to August.

Common hawker dragonfly Wing span 90 mm. July to October.

Each caption tells you the time of year you are most likely to see the insect. The butterflies and moths are drawn life size. The beetles and dragonflies are not.

Moths

Eyed hawkmoth May to July.

Scalloped oak July to August.

Buff-tip July to August.

Yellowtail July to August.

Small magpie May to mid-July.

Angle shades May to October.

Magpie July to mid-August.

Vapourer Late August to October.

Blood-vein May to September.

Silver-Y Migratory (June to October).

Burnished brass June to September.

Puss moth (male) May to June.

Poplar hawkmoth May to August.

Pale tussock May to June.

Brimstone May to June and August to September.

Female

Male

Dot June to August.

Lackey July to August.

Herald Early spring to autumn.

Ghost swift June to July.

Drinker June to mid-August.

Six-spot burnet Late June to mid-August.

Remember, if you cannot see the insect you want to identify on these pages, turn to the page earlier in the book which deals with the kind of place where you found the insect.

More common insects to spot

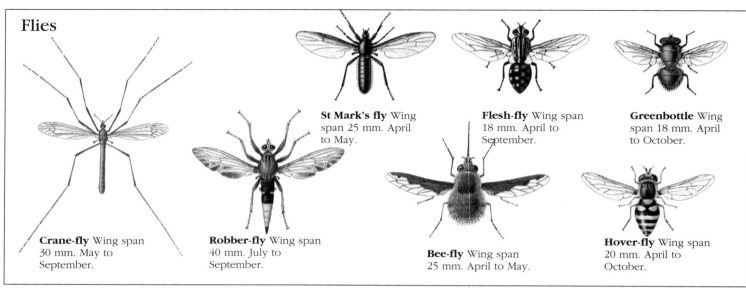

Flies

St Mark's fly Wing span 25 mm. April to May.

Flesh-fly Wing span 18 mm. April to September.

Greenbottle Wing span 18 mm. April to October.

Crane-fly Wing span 30 mm. May to September.

Robber-fly Wing span 40 mm. July to September.

Bee-fly Wing span 25 mm. April to May.

Hover-fly Wing span 20 mm. April to October.

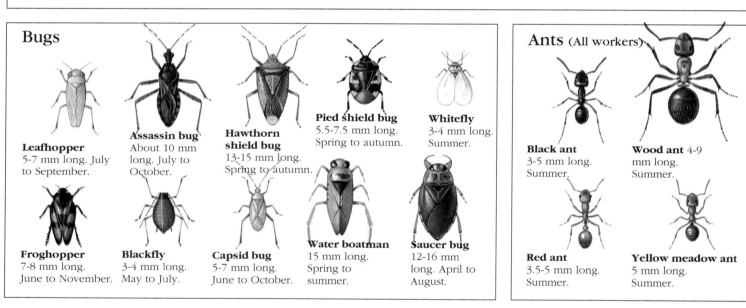

Bugs

Leafhopper 5-7 mm long. July to September.

Assassin bug About 10 mm long. July to October.

Hawthorn shield bug 13-15 mm long. Spring to autumn.

Pied shield bug 5.5-7.5 mm long. Spring to autumn.

Whitefly 3-4 mm long. Summer.

Froghopper 7-8 mm long. June to November.

Blackfly 3-4 mm long. May to July.

Capsid bug 5-7 mm long. June to October.

Water boatman 15 mm long. Spring to summer.

Saucer bug 12-16 mm long. April to August.

Ants (All workers)

Black ant 3-5 mm long. Summer.

Wood ant 4-9 mm long. Summer.

Red ant 3.5-5 mm long. Summer.

Yellow meadow ant 5 mm long. Summer.

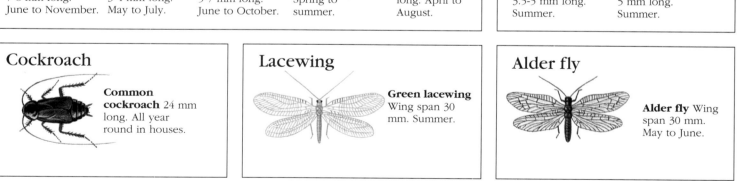

Cockroach

Common cockroach 24 mm long. All year round in houses.

Lacewing

Green lacewing Wing span 30 mm. Summer.

Alder fly

Alder fly Wing span 30 mm. May to June.

Earwig

Common earwig About 16 mm long. All year, especially summer.

Scorpion fly

Common scorpion fly Wing span 30 mm. May to July.

Snake fly

Snake fly Wing span 28 mm. May to July.

Each caption tells you the time of year you are most likely to see the insect. The lengths given do not include antennae.

Mayfly

Green drake mayfly Wing span 25 mm. April to September.

Flea

Cat flea 2-3 mm long. All year round.

Grasshoppers and crickets

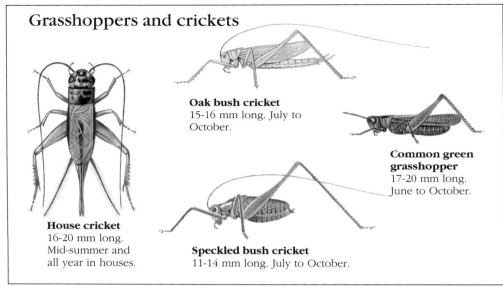

Oak bush cricket 15-16 mm long. July to October.

Common green grasshopper 17-20 mm long. June to October.

House cricket 16-20 mm long. Mid-summer and all year in houses.

Speckled bush cricket 11-14 mm long. July to October.

Thrip

Onion thrip 2 mm long. Summer.

Bristle tail

Silverfish 10 mm long. All year round.

Springtail

Water springtail 2 mm long.

Louse

Book louse 2.5 mm long.

Wasps

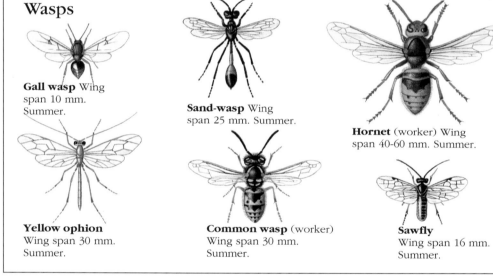

Gall wasp Wing span 10 mm. Summer.

Sand-wasp Wing span 25 mm. Summer.

Hornet (worker) Wing span 40-60 mm. Summer.

Yellow ophion Wing span 30 mm. Summer.

Common wasp (worker) Wing span 30 mm. Summer.

Sawfly Wing span 16 mm. Summer.

Caddis fly

Caddis fly Wing span 35 mm. May to October.

Stonefly

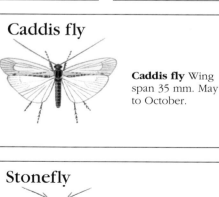

Stonefly Wing span 20 mm. Summer.

Bees (All workers)

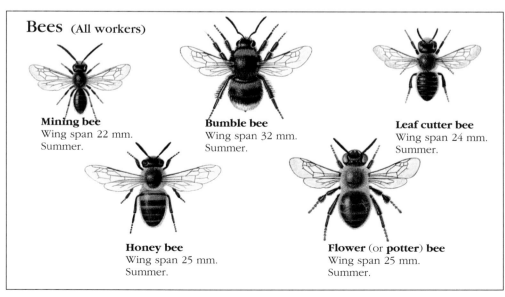

Mining bee Wing span 22 mm. Summer.

Bumble bee Wing span 32 mm. Summer.

Leaf cutter bee Wing span 24 mm. Summer.

Honey bee Wing span 25 mm. Summer.

Flower (or **potter**) **bee** Wing span 25 mm. Summer.

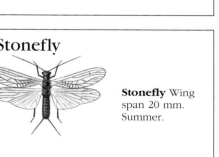

Remember, if you cannot see the insect you want to identify on these pages, turn to the page earlier in the book which deals with the kind of place where you found the insect. 159

Spiders and their webs

This page shows you some of the interesting things you may see if you go spider-watching. Look for spiders' webs in the early morning when they are covered with frost or dew.

Spiders in bushes can be caught like insects, but in a wood or field, drag a strong bag through the plants and tip the contents out onto a white sheet.

If you want to study spiders closely, have a jam-jar ready to keep them in. Put them back where you found them afterwards.

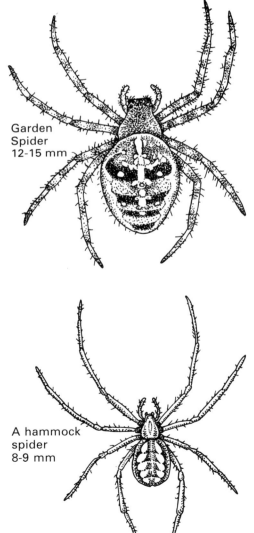

Garden
Spider
12-15 mm

A hammock
spider
8-9 mm

The sizes given are body lengths.

Orb web

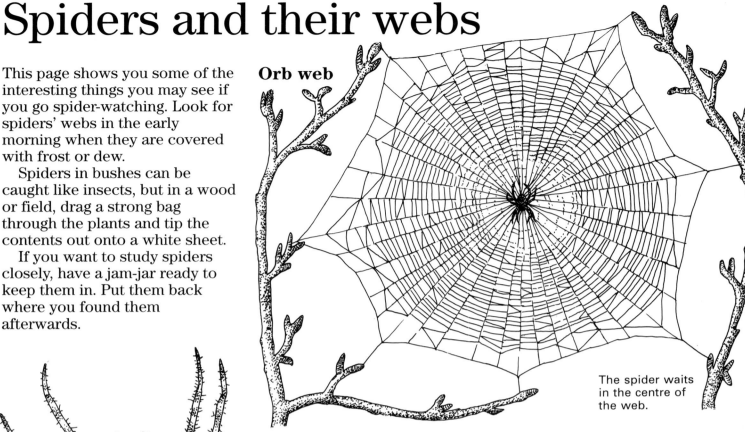

The spider waits in the centre of the web.

This is the orb web of a Garden Spider. You will find it hard to see unless it is covered with dew or frost. Flying insects which bump into the web get caught in the sticky threads.

The spider waiting in the middle feels the vibrations of any trapped insects. It will rush out and paralyse the prey with its poison fangs and then take the insect back to the centre of the web to eat.

Hammock web

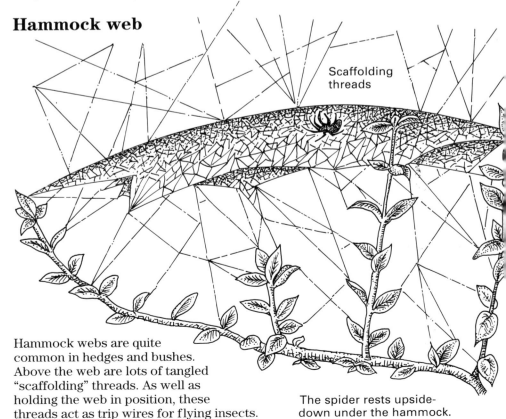

Scaffolding
threads

Hammock webs are quite common in hedges and bushes. Above the web are lots of tangled "scaffolding" threads. As well as holding the web in position, these threads act as trip wires for flying insects.

The spider rests upside-down under the hammock.

Sheet web

This is a sheet web made by a house spider. House spiders live behind pictures and in the corners of rooms and sheds. They hide in a silken tube at the corner of the sheet web.

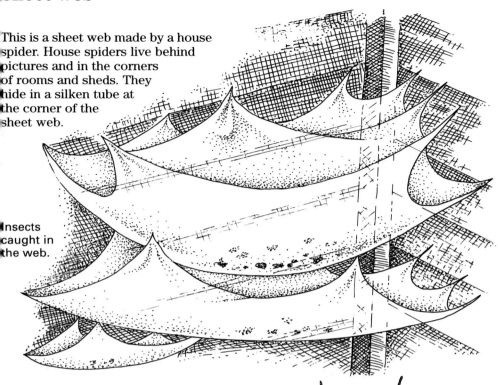

Insects caught in the web.

Spiders and their young

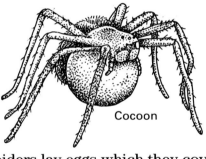

Cocoon

Spiders lay eggs which they cover with a cocoon of threads. This hunting spider carries her cocoon with her.

A hunting spider 11-13 mm

Underwater web

Look in ponds for the Water Spider. To study it properly you will have to keep it in an aquarium for a while.

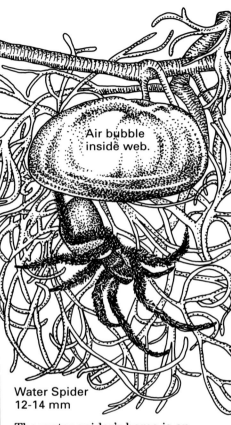

Air bubble inside web.

Water Spider 12-14 mm

The water spider's home is an underwater web attached to water weed. It is rounded and filled with air. The spider fills it by bringing down bubbles of air with its hind legs. It lives inside the bubble, swimming out to catch any passing water insects.

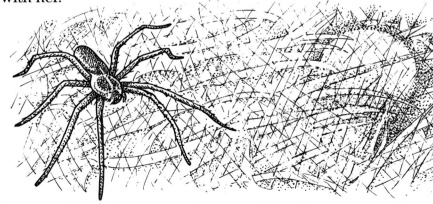

Baby spiders

Some spiders spin a protective tent over the cocoon. The spiders hatch inside this "nursery tent" while the mother stands guard.

When the young spiders are ready to live on their own, the mother spider tears open the web to set them free.

Some spiders that do not have nursery webs carry their young on their backs until the baby spiders can fend for themselves.

The fresh water of ponds and streams is a home or hunting ground for many living creatures and plants.

There you will spot the common birds, fish, insects, mammals, plants and amphibians of Europe, all described in this part of the book.

As you turn these pages, you will discover how water animals and plants live and how to collect wild specimens and keep them at home for study.

To identify your fresh-water wildlife, turn to the pages which deal with the kind of animal or plant you have seen. If you can't find a picture of it there, turn to the section called *More freshwater life you can spot* and you may find a picture of it there.

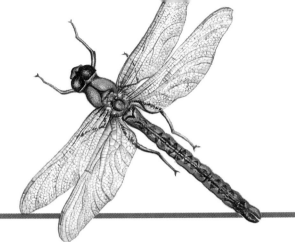

The Usborne Nature Trail Book of
PONDS & STREAMS

Contents

How to start	164	Fish	182
Living together	166	Frogs, toads and newts	184
Pollution	167	Keeping amphibians	186
Plants of ponds and streams	168	Other water animals	187
How water plants grow	170	More freshwater life you can spot	
Watching water birds	172	Fish and plants	188
Birds - mating and nesting	174	Amphibians and reptiles	189
Watching water insects	176	Water insects and their young	190
How insects grow	178	Birds	191
Mammals	180	Index	192

How to start

The best time to study streams and ponds is in the spring and summer, when the plants are flowering and the animals are most active. Winter can be a good time to spot birds though.

Always move slowly and quietly and be careful your shadow does not disturb fish. You will find more wildlife near the bank, where there is more plant cover.

Freshwater life can be found in lakes, rivers, ditches and canals, as well. You may even find plants and insects in rainwater tubs.

Be responsible!

Plants and animals live in harmony with each other and their surroundings. If you remove many plants and animals then you will upset the balance and threaten the survival of some of those that are left behind (see page 167). If you destroy their surroundings (their habitat), you will threaten their survival as well. Never leave litter behind when you leave.

What to take

Clean jam jars

Empty margarine pot for putting animals in and watching them.

Magnifying glass

Fishing net with small mesh.

Binoculars

Safety first

Never go into the water if you cannot swim and only go into shallow water. Do not wade rivers or deep streams. There may be strong currents. Always take a friend or adult with you. If you do fall in and get wet, go straight home to change you clothes and get dry - unless of course it is a very hot sunny day.

A pond survey

With some friends, make a map of your pond, showing where you found certain plants and animals. Note down the types of things going on around the pond and what it is used for, such as boating and fishing, or if cattle drink there. How do all these activities affect the pond? Check for signs of pollution, such as litter and oil.

Note down the animals you see. Record every kind of plant you can see. Look for insects on the plants.

What to look for

Even a small pond or stream can have many plants and animals, if it is not too shaded or polluted. Here are some of the plants you should look for and their hiding places.

Damselfly

Look under water plants for eggs an small animals.

Great Diving Beetle

In a stream, look under stones for worms, insects and leeches. In a pond, the gaps beneath stones tend to get silted up, so you will not find much wildlife beneath them.

Mayfly nymph

Do's and don'ts

Do test water depth with a long pole before wading in.

Do replace stones and logs exactly as you found them.

Don't handle anything you catch. Put it straight into a dish or jar.

Don't use logs or stones as stepping-stones without testing them first.

Do put animals and plants back into the pond as soon as possible.

Don't stamp your feet or move quickly. This will frighten animals.

Don't take too many animals or whole plants. Part of a plant will be enough to identify it.

Don't smash ice on ponds in winter. This will disturb animals living there.

Do keep jars with specimens in the shade, to keep the water cool.

Even a small pond or stream can have many plants and animals, if it is not too shaded or polluted. Here are some of the plants you should look for and their hiding places.

Remember, wading a pond is very difficult because of the depth of soft mud and rotting leaves at the bottom.

Sweep the net in two or three different spots near the bank and further away from the bank.

Test the water depth with a pole hanging from string or tape held across the pond.

After sweeping the net in the water, put its contents in a pot of clean water and wait for the mud to settle.

Sieving the water with an old tea strainer separates the water animals and plants from the mud. When you have identified the wildlife, put it back.

Measure the distance across the pond and around the pond. Draw the shape on a large sheet of paper. Add the names of plants and animals where you found them.

Look along banks for flowers, reeds and grasses.

The **Pond Skater** skims and jumps over the surface.

Look among reeds for birds' nests. Do not disturb them.

Moorhen chick

Look on the surface for insects, birds and plants.

Look for holes in the banks where animals live.

Look in the water for fish, plants and insects.

Stickleback

Great Crested Newt

Water Shrew

Great Pond Snail

Look on the bottom for animals with shells.

The **Water Spider** lives under the water in an air bubble.

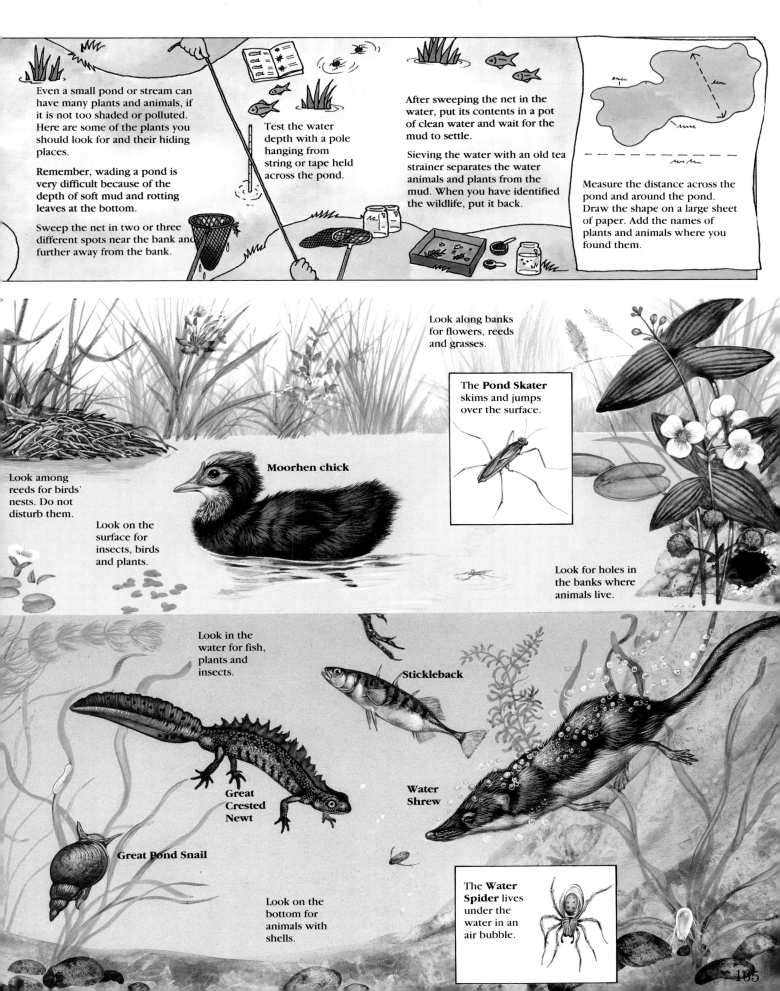

105

Living together

In a thriving pond there is a balance of different kinds of animals and plants, so that there is enough food for them all to survive. It is important not to disturb this balance.

How plants help

Animals need a gas called oxygen to survive. Water animals can get oxygen from the surface and some from the water itself. Oxygen in the water comes from the water plants.

Plants need sunlight to make food and produce their oxygen.

Canadian Pondweed

Try this experiment. Put some Canadian Pondweed in water and leave it in the sun. Oxygen bubbles will soon appear.

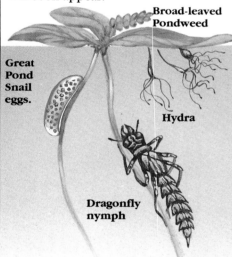

Broad-leaved Pondweed

Great Pond Snail eggs.

Hydra

Dragonfly nymph

Plants can provide animals with shade and shelter from enemies. They act as a support for eggs, such as those of the Great Pond Snail. Some tiny animals cling on to plants, such as the Hydra, which catch prey swimming by. Insects, such as the Dragonfly, use plant stems to climb out of the water when they are ready to become adults.

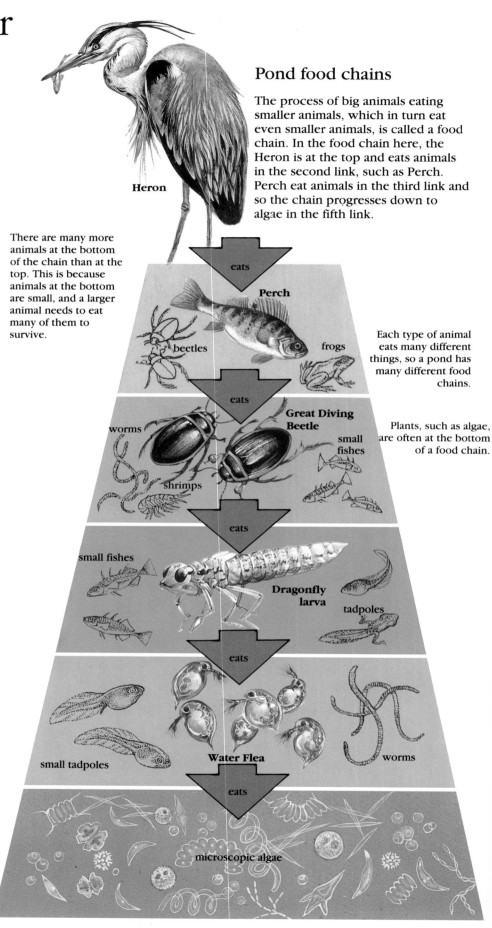

Pond food chains

The process of big animals eating smaller animals, which in turn eat even smaller animals, is called a food chain. In the food chain here, the Heron is at the top and eats animals in the second link, such as Perch. Perch eat animals in the third link and so the chain progresses down to algae in the fifth link.

Heron

There are many more animals at the bottom of the chain than at the top. This is because animals at the bottom are small, and a larger animal needs to eat many of them to survive.

eats

Perch

beetles

frogs

Each type of animal eats many different things, so a pond has many different food chains.

eats

worms

Great Diving Beetle

small fishes

shrimps

Plants, such as algae, are often at the bottom of a food chain.

eats

small fishes

Dragonfly larva

tadpoles

eats

small tadpoles

Water Flea

worms

eats

microscopic algae

Pollution

Human beings have a lot to answer for. Their pollution is a serious threat to the plants and animals living in the fresh water of rivers, ponds and streams. Here are some of the ways, not all man made though, that fresh water can become polluted. Phosphates from detergents in the home, such as those used to wash clothes, pass through sewage works and into fresh water. Phosphates

cause water plants to grow strongly. When they die, the plants are broken up by bacteria which use up all the oxygen in the water. Water animals need oxygen to live, so this lack of oxygen can kill them. Human sewage entering rivers is also broken up by bacteria which starve the rivers of oxygen. Another problem from sewage is that it can cause fungus to grow which kills off plants.

The stream is usually clear and unpolluted at its source.

Mining waste floats on the surface, blocking out the light which plants need to make food. Some pieces of waste settle into spaces in the river bed where animals live.

Burning fossil fuels, such as petrol in cars and coal in power stations, releases sulphur and nitrogen into the air. These two gases make the rain more acid. This acid rain falls into fresh water and can kill fish.

Poisons and chemical from factories are released into rivers. These can kill fish and make the water smell bad.

Farmers use fertilizers on their land to grow more crops Some of these chemicals are washed off the land by rain into fresh water, or seep through the ground into fresh water. Fertilizers can make water plants grow faster and bigger. The more decaying plants there are, the less oxygen there is for water animals to breath. Algae grows faster and bigger too. This can cause the water to become murky and so cut off light from water plants growing at the bottom.

Water sports, such as boating and water skiing can disturb animal and plant life and damage river banks.

Overhanging tress block out the light from water plants and stop them growing. Fallen leaves from the trees use up much oxygen as they rot by the activity of bacteria. This is not a man made problem, but it can be solved by humans cutting back the trees.

Rain running off large heaps of manure can poison fish.

Rubbish dumped into ponds poisons the water and kills pond life. Water birds can get trapped by rubbish, such as string and wire, and die.

Plants of ponds and streams

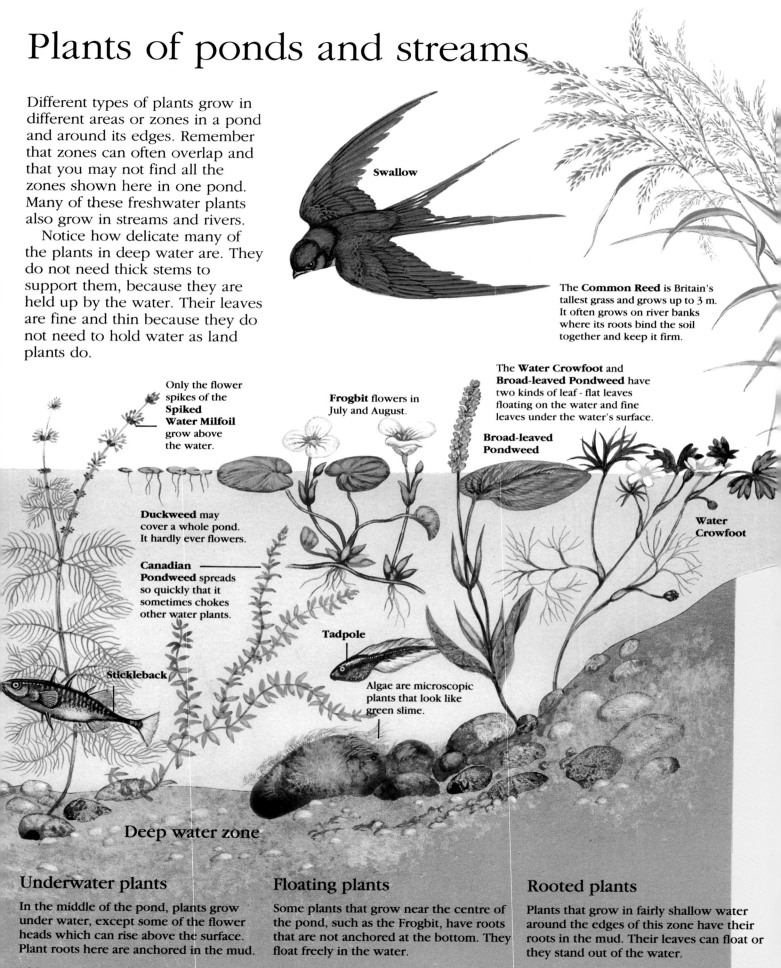

Different types of plants grow in different areas or zones in a pond and around its edges. Remember that zones can often overlap and that you may not find all the zones shown here in one pond. Many of these freshwater plants also grow in streams and rivers.

Notice how delicate many of the plants in deep water are. They do not need thick stems to support them, because they are held up by the water. Their leaves are fine and thin because they do not need to hold water as land plants do.

Swallow

The **Common Reed** is Britain's tallest grass and grows up to 3 m. It often grows on river banks where its roots bind the soil together and keep it firm.

Only the flower spikes of the **Spiked Water Milfoil** grow above the water.

Frogbit flowers in July and August.

The **Water Crowfoot** and **Broad-leaved Pondweed** have two kinds of leaf - flat leaves floating on the water and fine leaves under the water's surface.

Broad-leaved Pondweed

Duckweed may cover a whole pond. It hardly ever flowers.

Canadian Pondweed spreads so quickly that it sometimes chokes other water plants.

Water Crowfoot

Tadpole

Algae are microscopic plants that look like green slime.

Stickleback

Deep water zone

Underwater plants

In the middle of the pond, plants grow under water, except some of the flower heads which can rise above the surface. Plant roots here are anchored in the mud.

Floating plants

Some plants that grow near the centre of the pond, such as the Frogbit, have roots that are not anchored at the bottom. They float freely in the water.

Rooted plants

Plants that grow in fairly shallow water around the edges of this zone have their roots in the mud. Their leaves can float or they stand out of the water.

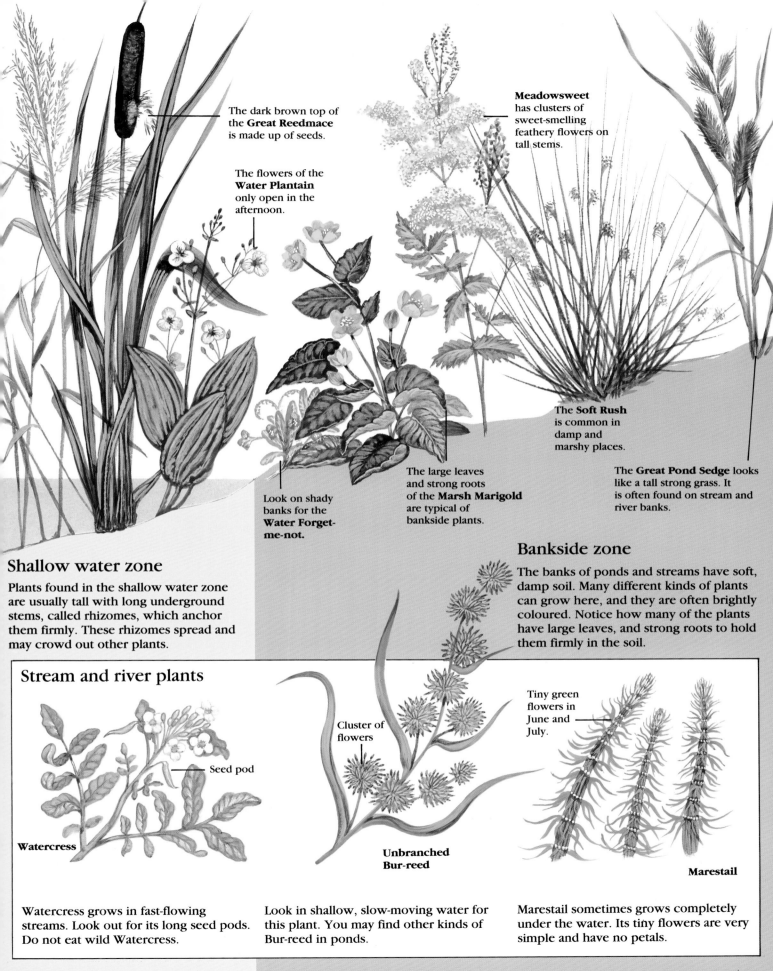

The dark brown top of the **Great Reedmace** is made up of seeds.

The flowers of the **Water Plantain** only open in the afternoon.

Meadowsweet has clusters of sweet-smelling feathery flowers on tall stems.

Look on shady banks for the **Water Forget-me-not.**

The large leaves and strong roots of the **Marsh Marigold** are typical of bankside plants.

The **Soft Rush** is common in damp and marshy places.

The **Great Pond Sedge** looks like a tall strong grass. It is often found on stream and river banks.

Shallow water zone

Plants found in the shallow water zone are usually tall with long underground stems, called rhizomes, which anchor them firmly. These rhizomes spread and may crowd out other plants.

Bankside zone

The banks of ponds and streams have soft, damp soil. Many different kinds of plants can grow here, and they are often brightly coloured. Notice how many of the plants have large leaves, and strong roots to hold them firmly in the soil.

Stream and river plants

Seed pod

Watercress

Cluster of flowers

Unbranched Bur-reed

Tiny green flowers in June and July.

Marestail

Watercress grows in fast-flowing streams. Look out for its long seed pods. Do not eat wild Watercress.

Look in shallow, slow-moving water for this plant. You may find other kinds of Bur-reed in ponds.

Marestail sometimes grows completely under the water. Its tiny flowers are very simple and have no petals.

How water plants grow

Many water plants grow from seeds. The seeds are formed after pollen from the male part of the flower (the stamen) reaches the female part (the ovary) of the same kind of plant. When the seeds are ripe, they scatter from the parent plant and can grow into new plants. Some water plants can also spread by sending out underground stems (rhizomes).

Some underwater plants do not spread by seed at all. Instead, new plants grow from winter buds or from pieces that break off the parent plant.

How pollen is scattered

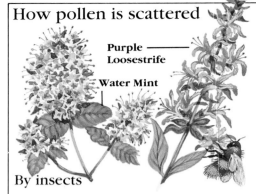

Purple Loosestrife

Water Mint

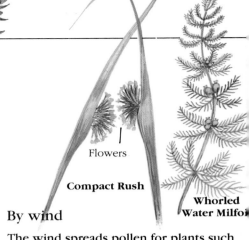

Flowers

Compact Rush

Whorled Water Milfoil

By insects

In some plants, pollen is spread by insects. The flowers' bright colours and scent attract the insects. The pollen rubs off on to their bodies and they carry it to other plants.

By wind

The wind spreads pollen for plants such as these. Their flowers are often small and dull. This is because they do not need to attract insects to spread the pollen.

How seeds are scattered

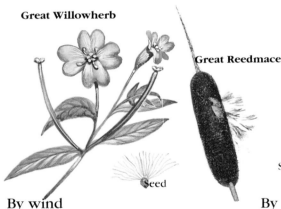

Great Willowherb

Great Reedmace

Seed

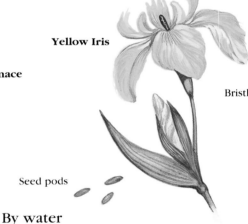

Yellow Iris

Seed pods

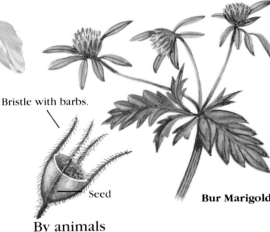

Bristle with barbs.

Seed

Bur Marigold

By wind

Some seeds are carried by the wind on a hairy parachute. Great Willowherb seeds may travel as faraway as 150 km.

By water

Some seeds, like the ones in these Yellow Iris pods, are carried by water. The pods open when softened by water.

By animals

Seeds with barbs, or hooks, catch on to the fur of animals or people's clothing, as they brush past. Later they drop off.

How Water Lilies grow

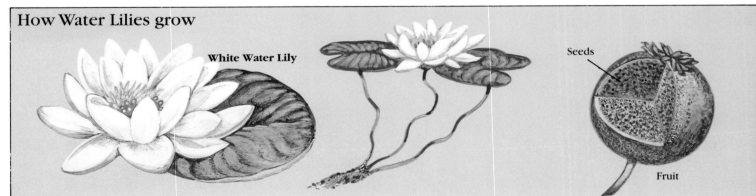

White Water Lily

Seeds

Fruit

Look in ponds for the White Water Lily. Its leaves and flowers float on the water's surface. At night, the flowers close and sometimes sink just below the surface until morning.

The plant is anchored to the bottom by stout rhizomes. The stalks grow at an angle. If the water level rises, the stalks can straighten up so that the flowers and leaves still float.

The flowers spread their pollen by insects. When the fruits are ripe, they sink to the bottom and release up to 2,000 seeds. The seeds float away. Some sink and grow into new plants.

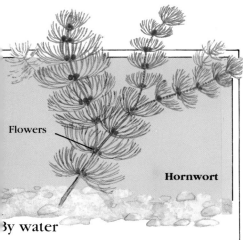

Flowers

Hornwort

By water

This plant flowers and spreads its pollen under the water. The male flowers release pollen into the water. Some of it settles on the female flowers and pollinates them.

Another way that water plants spread.

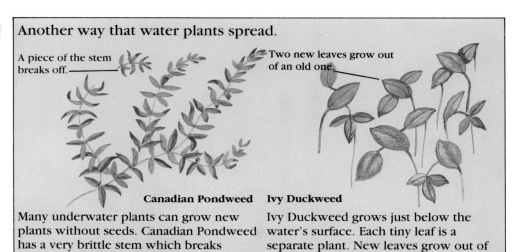

A piece of the stem breaks off.

Two new leaves grow out of an old one.

Canadian Pondweed

Ivy Duckweed

Many underwater plants can grow new plants without seeds. Canadian Pondweed has a very brittle stem which breaks easily. Each piece that breaks off grows into a new plant.

Ivy Duckweed grows just below the water's surface. Each tiny leaf is a separate plant. New leaves grow out of slits in the sides of old ones and then break away to become new plants.

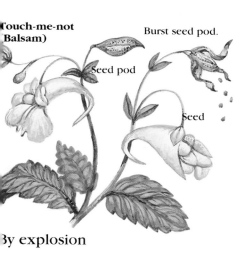

Touch-me-not (Balsam)

Burst seed pod.

Seed pod

Seed

By explosion

If anything touches the ripe seed pods of this plant, they burst open and scatter the seeds on the ground.

Watching a plant grow

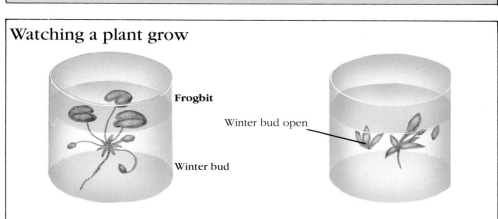

Frogbit

Winter bud

Winter bud open

Frogbit grows winter buds on underwater roots. Each bud contains a new plant and a store of food. When the buds are ripe, they break off and sink. In spring, when the stored food is used up, the buds float to the surface and grow into new plants. Collect some Frogbit in the autumn and watch how it grows. Place it in a jar of pond water and keep it cool.

In winter

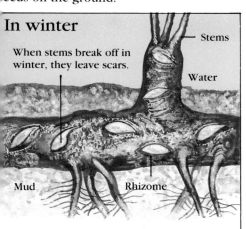

When stems break off in winter, they leave scars.

Stems

Water

Mud

Rhizome

In winter, plants such as the White Water Lily die down. They live off food stored in their rhizomes. In spring, new stems grow up from the rhizomes.

Insect-eating plants

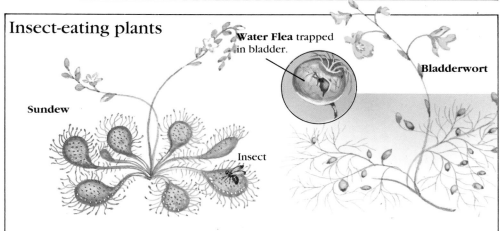

Water Flea trapped in bladder.

Bladderwort

Sundew

Insect

The Sundew grows in bogs and marshes where the soil is very poor. It gets food by trapping insects on its hairy leaves and digests them with special juices.

The Bladderwort is also an insect-eating plant. It catches its tiny prey in underwater bladders which are filled with air. Then it feeds on them.

Watching water birds

Birdwatching by ponds and streams is exciting because you can see so many different types. Some birds spend most of their lives on or by water. Others may come just to drink and bathe. In winter, you may spot sea birds as they shelter and search for food inland.

The best place to look for birds is by water surrounded by thick vegetation. Early in the morning is a good time to see them. In parks, some water birds are tame enough to be fed. Others are shy, so you must hide and wait quietly to see them. Keep a record of the birds you spot and their habits. If you find a nest, be sure not to disturb it.

Feeding

Watch the birds on or around a pond closely. Spot the different ways they feed and the shapes of their bills. Each bill is shaped to suit a different way of feeding. Time how long a diving duck can stay under the water.

Mallards are dabbling ducks. They feed near the surface and eat mostly plants. They also up-end to get food from deep water.

Tufted Ducks dive down 1 m or 2 m for water plants, insects and small fish.

Female   Male

Wigeon feed mainly on grasses and grain, cropped from fields. They also dabble in water.

The **Swift** feeds and even sleeps on the wing. It eats flies and beetles.

The **Shoveler** uses its wide bill to sieve food from water and mud.

The **Bittern** nests in reed beds where it is camouflaged well. It eats frogs, small fish and insects.

The **Teal** is Britain's smallest duck. It is a surface-feeder and eats mainly water plants and their seeds.

The **Moorhen** eats plants and small animals in the water as well as seeds and grain on land.

The **Kingfisher** dives for small fish and insects. It sometimes beats a fish against a branch to kill it. Then it swallows the fish head first, so that the fins and scales do not open and choke the bird.

Flocks in flight

Geese in V-shape.

Ducks in straight line.

Redshank

Common Sandpiper

Taking a count ·

Count the first ten birds in a flock. Then estimate how many sets of ten there might be altogether. Multiply your estimated figure by 10 to get the total number of birds.

Flight patterns

Different sorts of birds fly in different flock patterns. These patterns can help you to identify the birds. Many birds fly in a line or a'V-shape. See if you can spot other patterns.

Keeping together

Birds that fly in flocks usually have special markings for others to follow. They also call to each other so that they keep the flock together, especially after dark.

The **Greylag Goose** spends a lot of time on land. It crops the grass with its bill.

Looking after feathers

Goosander

Great Crested Grebe

Bathing

Water birds often bathe to keep clean. They flap their wings on the water and roll over to wet their bodies thoroughly. Then they shake themselves dry.

Oiling

Next, the birds rub oil over the feathers with their bills and heads. The oil comes from the preen glands near their tails. It keeps the feathers in good condition and waterproofs them.

Pintail

Preening

Finally, they fluff up their feathers, nibble each one and draw them through their bills. This cleans and oils the feathers even more, and settles them back into place.

How feathers work

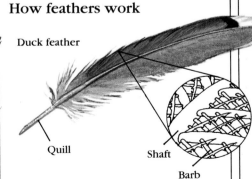

Duck feather

Quill

Shaft

Barb

The barbs on a bird's feather grow out of the shaft. They fit together very closely, rather like the teeth of a zip. This helps keep the bird's body dry and warm.

Birds - mating and nesting

Birds become very active in the spring when most of them breed. The male birds attract the females by showing off their bright feathers. Some develop crests and ruffs of feathers at this time. They also have special mating calls and can perform acrobatics in the air or on the water. Sometimes both male and female birds take part in these courtship displays.

After the female accepts the male as her mate, a nest is built. See if you can spot which materials each kind of bird collects for its nest.

Courtship

Great Crested Grebes start their courtship early in the year. Head-shaking (above) is a common display. The birds swim towards each other, calling and shaking their heads from side to side.

After head-shaking, the Grebes may "dance" together. First they dive to collect weed. Then they swim towards one another and rise out of the water, swaying their bills and paddling hard.

Fighting

This Mute Swan is puffing out its feathers. This makes the bird look bigger and helps to frighten away enemies. Some birds fight to defend their nest or territory.

This Greylag Goose is standing in a threat position and probably hissing to chase away other adult geese that dare to come too close to its nest or territory.

Coots fight with their claws, holding themselves up with their wings. Fights do not last very long, and usually only the males take part.

Nesting

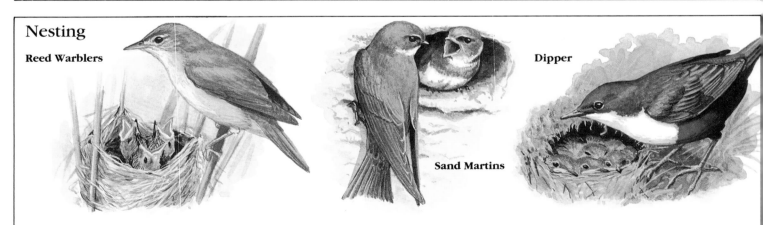

The Reed Warbler nests in reed beds. The grass nest is shaped like a deep basket, so that the eggs and young birds do not fall out, even in a strong wind.

Look for groups of Sand Martins nesting in mud or sand banks. Each nest is at the end of a tunnel, which the birds dig with their feet and bills.

The Dipper hides its nest in cracks in rocks near a stream, under a bridge or behind a waterfall. The cup-shaped nest is made of moss and grasses.

Female

Male

Kingfishers

Male

Female

Pochards

Male

Mallards

Female

During courtship, some male birds, such as the Kingfisher, offer the females a present of food. When the female has accepted her present, this means she is ready to mate.

The Mallard is a common duck, so you have a very good chance of seeing the male's striking courtship display. He dives, flaps his wings, sprays water from his bill, whistles and grunts. The female

attracts the male by jerking her head backwards and forwards. The male Pochard swims around the female and jerks his head backwards and forwards to attract her.

Looking after the young

Grey Herons

Some birds, such as the Grey Heron, are born helpless. They are blind, have no feathers, and cannot leave the nest for over a month. The young beg for food by pecking at their parents' bills.

Other types of young bird beg for food with loud cries or gaping beaks. Some birds, such as ducks and grebes, have feathers and can swim and feed a few hours after hatching.

Keeping the young safe

Little Grebes (or **Dabchicks**)

Little Grebe chicks can swim soon after they hatch. Sometimes they climb on to their parents' backs to keep safe from danger.

Little Ringed Plover

Like many birds that nest on the ground, the Little Ringed Plover moves away from the nest pretending to be hurt to divert an enemy from its young and eggs.

Watching water insects

When you visit a pond or stream, you will soon spot several different types of insects. Look in the air, on the water's surface and in the water itself. To help you to identify an insect, note down its colour, the shape and number of its wings, where you saw it, and any other details.

All adult insects have bodies with three parts, three pairs of legs, and usually a pair of antennae or feelers. Many have wings at some time in their lives.

Most insects breathe by taking in air through holes in their bodies. Many underwater insects carry a bubble of air on their bodies, which they collect at the surface.

A thin film on the water's surface stops an insect from sinking. See how this works by floating a needle on water.

Place some blotting paper on the surface of some water. Now place a needle on the blotting paper.

Watch the needle stay on the surface as the blotting paper soaks up water and sinks.

The **Water Boatman** swims and takes in air at the surface, upside down. It has a sharp bite when picked up.

Strong legs for swimming.

Above the water

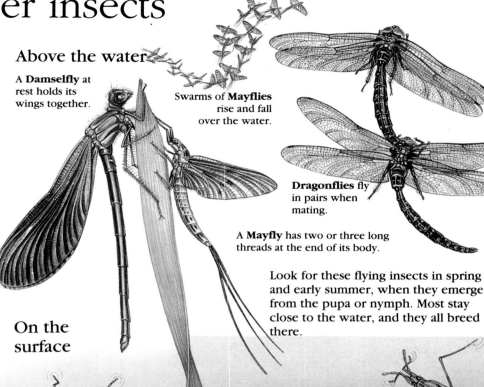

A **Damselfly** at rest holds its wings together.

Swarms of **Mayflies** rise and fall over the water.

Dragonflies fly in pairs when mating.

A **Mayfly** has two or three long threads at the end of its body.

Look for these flying insects in spring and early summer, when they emerge from the pupa or nymph. Most stay close to the water, and they all breed there.

On the surface

The **Water Measurer** moves slowly. The hairs on its body stop it from getting wet.

Tiny **Springtails** can jump 30 cm, using their hinged tails.

The **Pond Skater** slides rapidly over the surface. It can also jump.

Whirligig Beetles have one pair of eyes looking into the water, and another pair looking into the air. They whirl and spin while hunting for food.

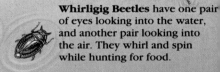

Notice the different ways that these insects move on the water's surface. They feed mostly on dead insects that fall on the water.

Under the water

Breathing tube

The antenna breaks the surface film of the water while it collects air.

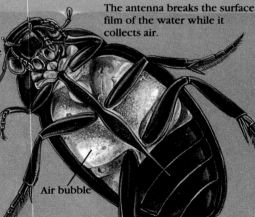

Air bubble

The **Water Scorpion** is not a real scorpion at all. It takes in air at the surface through a breathing tube. It stores air under its wing cases.

The **Great Silver Beetle** carries a bubble of air trapped by the hairs on its underside.

How insects feed

Young **Stickleback**

Great Diving Beetle

Many water beetles eat other animals. The Great Diving Beetle feeds on tadpoles, insects and small fish. Its prey can sometimes be larger than itself.

The front legs are used for catching prey.

Tadpole

Water Stick Insect

It hides among reed stems, waiting for prey. The front legs shoot out to catch animals, such as insects and tadpoles. Then it sucks out their juices.

The Lesser Water Boatman feeds on algae and rotting plants on the bottom. Unlike the Water Boatman, it swims with its right side up.

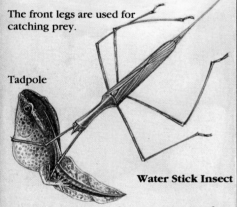

Lesser Water Boatman

Making an insect aquarium

This picture shows the things you will need to make an aquarium. Keep the aquarium near a window, but not in direct sunlight. If you use tap water, add some pond water and leave it for a few days before adding the animals. Do not fill it too deep and add snails to keep the sides from being covered in algae.

Nymphs and larvae

Feed nymphs and larvae on worms or tiny bits of raw meat. Remove uneaten pieces of meat or the water will become unpleasant.

Clean waterproof tank. (A plastic or glass bowl will do.)

Pond or tap water.

Twig for nymphs to climb on to.

Stones

Snail

Washed sand or gravel 5 cm deep.

Flying insects

To keep flying insects, such as beetles, put a lid or some fine netting over the aquarium to stop them from escaping.

Glass or plastic cover resting on small pieces of wood.

Leave a gap for air to get in.

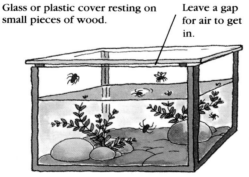

Feed beetles on worms or tiny bits of raw meat.

Tiny insects

Keep these insects in separate containers, or they will eat each other. Feed them on pieces of meat or worms.

Lid with air holes.

Margarine pot

Clear plastic cover with air holes.

Rubber band

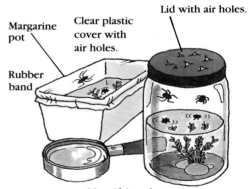

Magnifying glass

Fierce insects

Keep tiny insects in a jar or pot. Put in pond water, some mud and a few plants. Do not forget to make air holes in the clear plastic cover or the jar's lid.

Great Diving Beetle

Water Stick Insect

Water Scorpion

Water Boatman

Remember!

Only take a few insects from the water. Make sure they have the right food and enough room. Always return them to the pond or stream when you have finished studying them.

How insects grow

You can find some exciting insects in ponds and streams, even in polluted water. Most insects go through several stages of development from the egg to adult. (Follow the life cycle of the Caddis Fly in this section.) The early stages may last for years, but the adult may only live for a few hours or days.

Some water insects, such as water beetles, spend all their lives in the water. Others, such as the Alder Fly, leave the water when fully grown.

The Caddis Fly

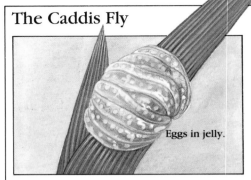

Eggs in jelly.

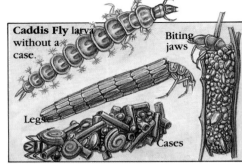

Caddis Fly larva without a case.

Biting jaws

Legs

Cases

Egg

The Caddis Fly begins its life in fresh water. The eggs are laid in jelly on plants or stones, either above or below the water's surface.

Larva

The larva hatches from the egg. Then it may make a protective case of shells, stones or leaves. The larva eats plants from the bottom of the pond.

Where insects lay eggs

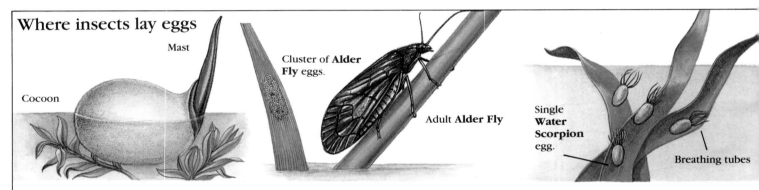

Mast

Cocoon

Cluster of **Alder Fly** eggs.

Adult **Alder Fly**

Single **Water Scorpion** egg.

Breathing tubes

On the water

The Great Silver Beetle lays its eggs in a silky cocoon on the surface of the water. The hollow "mast" of the cocoon allows air to reach the eggs.

Above the water

Look for insect eggs on water plants and stones above the water's surface. When the larvae hatch, they fall or crawl down into the water.

Below the water

Some insects lay their eggs under the water on plants or stones, or on the mud bottom. The Water Scorpion lays its eggs on plant stems.

Larvae and nymphs

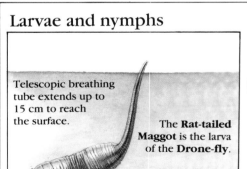

Telescopic breathing tube extends up to 15 cm to reach the surface.

The **Rat-tailed Maggot** is the larva of the **Drone-fly**.

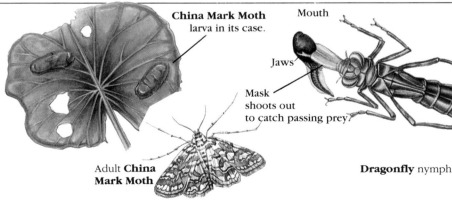

China Mark Moth larva in its case.

Mouth

Jaws

Mask shoots out to catch passing prey.

Adult **China Mark Moth**

Dragonfly nymph

Put some mud from a pond or stream into a dish. Add a little water and sieve it with an old tea strainer. See if you can spot the Rat-tailed Maggot and its breathing tube.

Look for small holes in the leaves of Water Lilies and Pondweed. Underneath the leaves, you may see this moth larva, which makes a case out of the leaves and also feeds on them.

A young dragonfly is called a nymph when it hatches from the egg. It has a strong pair of jaws fixed to a hinge, called a mask. See how the adult emerges from the nymph on page 19.

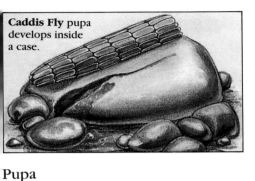

Caddis Fly pupa develops inside a case.

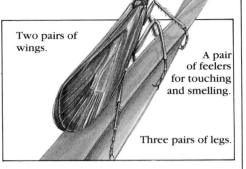

Two pairs of wings.

A pair of feelers for touching and smelling.

Three pairs of legs.

An underwater viewer

Place sealed end in water.

Use a large clean plastic sweet jar that you can see through. Remove the lid. Place the bottom of the jar in the water and look through the top.

Pupa

After about a year, the larva stops eating and changes into a pupa. Over a period of time, the pupa then slowly changes into an adult Caddis Fly.

Adult

When the adult is fully grown, the pupa leaves its case, if it has one, and moves to the surface. Then the adult splits out of its pupal skin and flies away.

A Dragonfly emerges

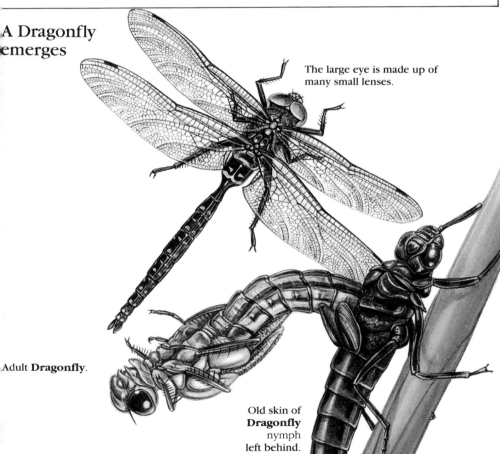

The large eye is made up of many small lenses.

Adult **Dragonfly**.

Old skin of **Dragonfly** nymph left behind.

Water surface

Adult Dragonflies emerge in summer. First, the brown nymph crawls out of the water and onto a plant stem. Then its skin splits down the back and the adult Dragonfly slowly pulls itself out, head first. It rests on the plant while its body hardens and the wings expand. Then it flies away. Dragonflies only live for about a month.

Watching Gnats grow

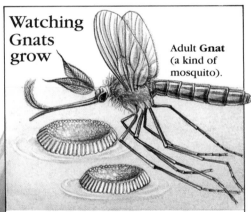

Adult **Gnat** (a kind of mosquito).

Egg rafts (about 5 mm long).

In early summer, look on the surface of still water for Gnat eggs, which look like tiny rafts. Keep some out of doors in a jar of pond water.

Small jar

Breathing tubes

Larva

Pupa

The larva changes into a pupa after about three weeks. The pupa develops into an adult. Then the pupal skin splits open and the adult flies away.

Mammals

Most mammals that live near fresh water are very shy and you will not see them often. All you hear is a plop as they jump into the water. Some only come out at night. They are called nocturnal mammals.

Mammals can hear well and have a good sense of smell. So if you go animal tracking, approach the water quietly, facing the wind. If you find animal tracks or feeding signs, try to identify them. Then you will know which animal you are following.

Spot the difference

Water Vole

Tiny ears

Blunt snout

Short, furry tail.

Brown Rat

Large ears

Pointed snout

Long, naked tail.

The Water Vole is often confused with the Brown Rat. They look rather alike and both are often seen swimming. Look at the differences carefully, so that you can tell them apart if you spot them. The Water Vole often swims under the water, but the Brown Rat keeps more to the surface of the water.

The **Harvest Mouse** has been driven out of cornfields by farm machinery. Nowadays it often sleeps in reed beds. This mouse is an expert climber and can hang by its tail. It comes out in the daytime.

This bat often flies over water in the daytime, hunting for insects. It can swim well too.

Daubenton's Bat

The **Brown Rat** prefers rivers and canals. Look for it at any time of day. It eats almost anything.

The **Water Shrew** sometimes leaps out of the water to catch insects. It also eats fish and frogs. You may see it walking on the bottom of streams, looking for food.

Look for plant stems which have been bitten off. These could be clues to the feeding spot of a **Water Vole**.

Holes in the bank, either above or below water, could be the entrance to a **Shrew's** or **Vole's** burrow.

Rare water mammals

Muskrat

Beaver

European Mink

The Muskrat is a large vole that lives in parts of Europe, but not in Britain. It swims fast and keeps near the surface of shallow, overgrown water.

A few Beavers survive in Europe, mostly in remote northern areas. They build their homes, called lodges, with branches or logs that they cut from trees.

Some Mink are wild. Others have escaped from fur farms. You might see one in a reed bed or by a river. They hunt and swim at night. They are very fierce.

Otter

Waterproof fur

When it dives for fish, it shuts its ears and nostrils.

Webbed toes for swimming.

Spraints

Its thick tail acts as a rudder.

The Otter is a shy, nocturnal animal. It lives in lonely places, and is well suited to life in the water. It eats fish, frogs and shellfish. Otter cubs are born in a tunnel,

called a holt, in a bank or among tree roots. They are very playful and make slides down the river bank in the mud or snow. You might see one of these

slides, or find Otter droppings, called spraints, on a rock or clump of grass. Otters often leave behind remains of fish they have eaten.

Tracks

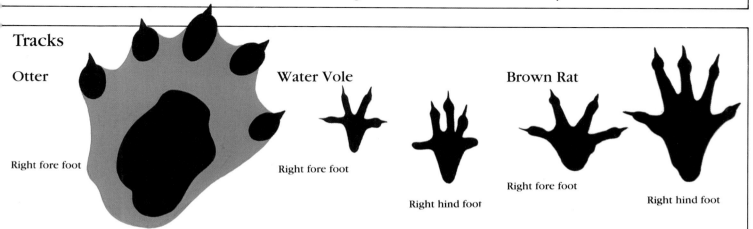

Otter

Right fore foot

Water Vole

Right fore foot

Right hind foot

Brown Rat

Right fore foot

Right hind foot

Look for animal tracks in firm mud or snow. The best time to look is in the morning, before the fresh tracks have been spoiled.

To help you identify them later, measure and draw the tracks, and the pattern, or trail, the tracks make together. Remember that you will not find a

complete track showing all of the animal's foot, very often. An Otter track, for instance, may not show the web, claw marks or even the fifth toe.

Fish

Some types of freshwater fish prefer still water and other types prefer moving water. Make a check-list to help you to identify the different types. What colour and shape are they? Do they have whiskers, or barbels, near the mouth? Do they live at the surface or on the bottom? How fast do they swim?

Most freshwater fish lay their eggs, called spawning, in shallow water. Look for eggs among water plants, and on the water's bottom. Young fish are called fry.

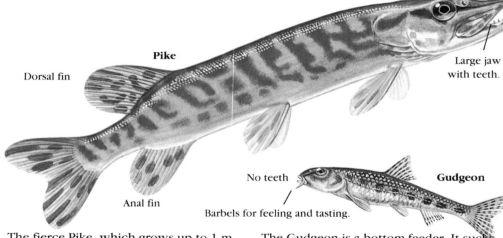

Pike

Dorsal fin

Anal fin

Large jaw with teeth.

No teeth

Barbels for feeling and tasting.

Gudgeon

The fierce Pike, which grows up to 1 m long, hunts frogs, young birds, fish, and even other Pike. It lurks in reeds, waiting for its prey, and then attacks with its sharp teeth.

The Gudgeon is a bottom-feeder. It sucks insect larvae, worms and shellfish into its mouth. There are no teeth in the mouth, but it has teeth in its throat which break up the food it swallows.

In a pond

Most pond fish are rounder and fatter than the slim, streamlined fish in moving water. They swim more slowly too.

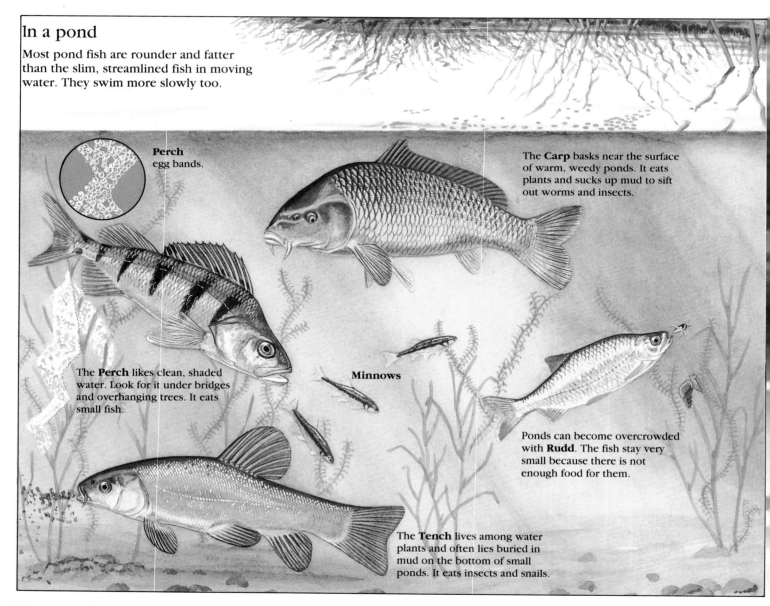

Perch egg bands.

The **Carp** basks near the surface of warm, weedy ponds. It eats plants and sucks up mud to sift out worms and insects.

Minnows

The **Perch** likes clean, shaded water. Look for it under bridges and overhanging trees. It eats small fish.

Ponds can become overcrowded with **Rudd**. The fish stay very small because there is not enough food for them.

The **Tench** lives among water plants and often lies buried in mud on the bottom of small ponds. It eats insects and snails.

Building a nest

Three-spined Stickleback

Male

The male has a red throat and belly in the breeding season.

Female

Male

Male

Look for the Three-spined Stickleback in ponds and ditches. In May, a male builds a nest where the female will lay her eggs. He glues bits of plants together with sticky threads from his body. The male "dances" to attract a female to the nest. When the female has laid her eggs, she leaves the nest. The male then fans the eggs with his fins to keep fresh water flowing over them. When the eggs hatch, the male guards the fry and chases away enemies. When one of the baby fish strays away from the nest, he follows it. Then, catching the fry in his mouth, he brings it back to the nest.

In a stream

The **Dace** is often found in large schools near the surface of the water.

The **Grayling** has a large dorsal fin. It eats insect larvae. It cannot live in polluted water.

The small **Minnow** often moves about in groups, called schools. It is eaten by other fish and by water birds.

Trout live in fast-flowing streams. Their dark spots act as a camouflage on the stony bottom.

The **Bullhead** hides under stones in the day. It comes out at night to feed on insect larvae and small shellfish.

Eels

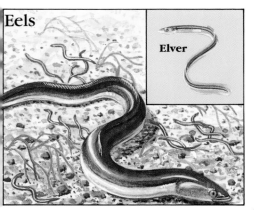

Elver

Eels live in fresh water until they are about ten years old. Then they move down the river into the sea, to breed and die. The young eels, called elvers, travel back to fresh water.

Salmon

Salmon spend some of their lives in the sea, but return to the rivers to breed. Often they go back to the river where they were born. The female lays up to 15,000 eggs on the river bottom.

Remember!

If you want to see fish, approach the water slowly and quietly. Keep your shadow off the water. Try feeding fish with bread or maggots.

Frogs, toads and newts

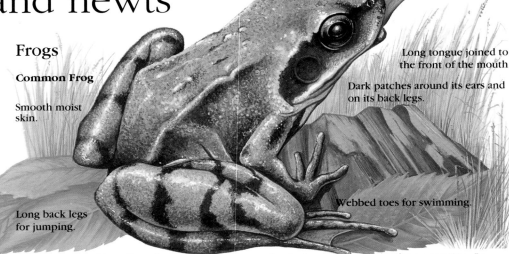

Frogs, toads and newts are born in water, but spend most of their adult life on land. These types of animals are called amphibians.

Young amphibians, called tadpoles, develop from eggs, called spawn. These are laid in the water. They breathe by taking in oxygen from the water through their gills. As they grow, their gills and tails disappear and lungs and legs develop. Newt tadpoles keep their tails. Eventually, they leave the water, but return in the spring to breed.

Frogs

Common Frog

Smooth moist skin.

Long back legs for jumping.

Long tongue joined to the front of the mouth.

Dark patches around its ears and on its back legs.

Webbed toes for swimming.

The Common Frog lives in damp grass and undergrowth. Its basic skin colour can change to match its surroundings. This helps it to hide from snakes, hedgehogs, rats and other enemies. In winter, the frog hibernates in the mud bottom of a ditch or pond. It shoots out its long tongue to catch flies.

How frogs breed

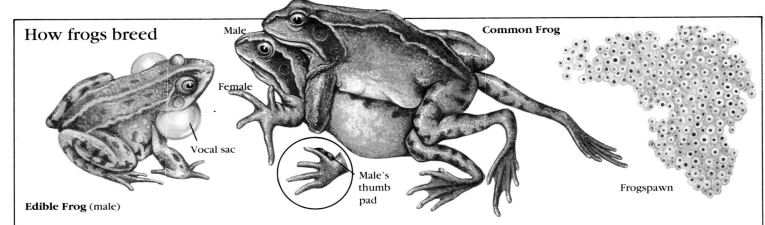

Male

Female

Vocal sac

Edible Frog (male)

Male's thumb pad

Common Frog

Frogspawn

Frogs breed in ponds. Male frogs croak to attract females. The male Edible Frog makes his croak sound louder by blowing up his vocal sacs.

When mating, the male frog holds on to the female with his spiky thumb pads. The female lays a clump of frogspawn in the water.

A clump of frogspawn contains up to 4,000 eggs. The jelly absorbs water and swells up and floats to the surface, where the sun warms the eggs.

How frogspawn develops

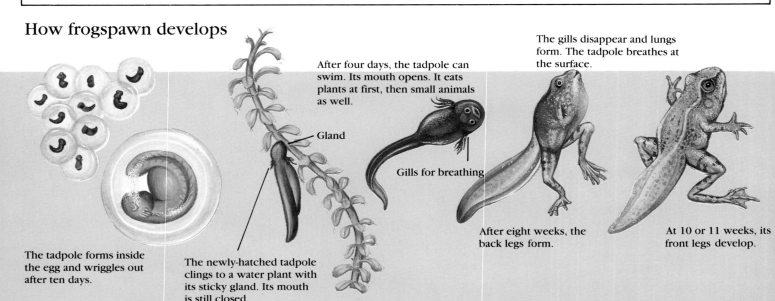

After four days, the tadpole can swim. Its mouth opens. It eats plants at first, then small animals as well.

The gills disappear and lungs form. The tadpole breathes at the surface.

Gland

Gills for breathing

The tadpole forms inside the egg and wriggles out after ten days.

The newly-hatched tadpole clings to a water plant with its sticky gland. Its mouth is still closed.

After eight weeks, the back legs form.

At 10 or 11 weeks, its front legs develop.

Toads

Common Toad

Dry, warty skin.

Toads have blunter faces and fatter bodies than frogs.

Poison on the skin helps to ward off enemies.

Old skin being eaten.

Short back legs for crawling.

During the day, the Common Toad hides in holes in the ground, but at night hunts for food. It grows a new skin several times in the summer. It scrapes off the old one and eats it. In winter, the toad hibernates in an old animal burrow.

Danger

Toad

Grass Snake

If a toad is threatened by a Grass Snake, it may blow itself up so that the snake cannot swallow it.

Toadspawn

Toadspawn

In spring, toads may travel for ten days to reach their breeding ponds. They mate like frogs, but lay eggs in ribbons about 2 m long.

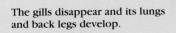

At 12 or 13 weeks, the tail disappears and the tiny frog, 1 cm long, is ready to leave the water. It will be fully grown in three years. Few tadpoles survive to this stage. Most are eaten by other pond creatures.

Newts

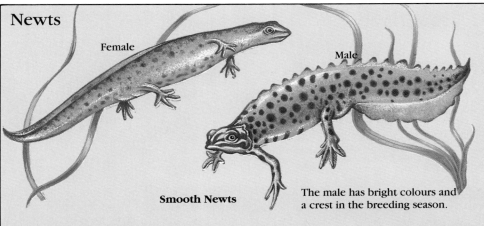

Female

Male

Smooth Newts

The male has bright colours and a crest in the breeding season.

Newts, like toads, spend most of their life on land, hiding by day and feeding at night. They look rather like lizards, but are not scaly.

Look for the newts in water, in spring. You might see the male Smooth Newt performing his courtship dance. He arches his back and flicks his tail.

Its front legs grow first. The tadpole eats water fleas and tiny worms.

A **newt** tadpole has three pairs of feathery gills for breathing.

Single egg on leaf.

The gills disappear and its lungs and back legs develop.

Newts lay their eggs singly, on water plants. The leaves are often bent over to protect the eggs. The tadpoles hatch after about two weeks. The young newts, called efts, leave the water in August. Some stay in the water until the next year.

Keeping amphibians

Frogspawn

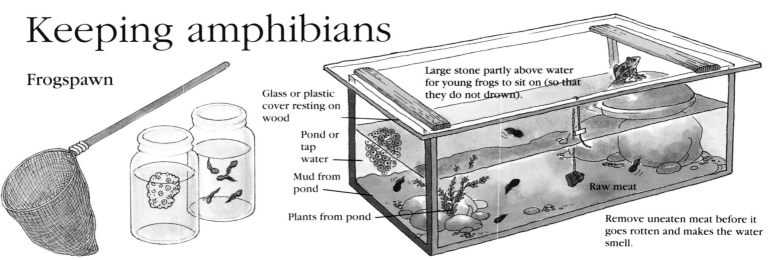

Large stone partly above water for young frogs to sit on (so that they do not drown).

Glass or plastic cover resting on wood

Pond or tap water

Mud from pond

Plants from pond

Raw meat

Remove uneaten meat before it goes rotten and makes the water smell.

Look in ponds in March and April. Use a net to collect frogspawn. Put a little in a jar of water and return the rest to the pond. If the eggs have already hatched, collect a few tadpoles to study instead.

Put the aquarium in a light place, but out of direct sunlight. Change the water as soon as it smells bad. When the frogs have grown, return them to the edge of the pond where you found the spawn.

Newly-hatched tadpoles will eat plants in the aquarium. After about a week, they will need raw meat too. Hang small pieces in the water, tied with thread, and replace them every two days.

Toads

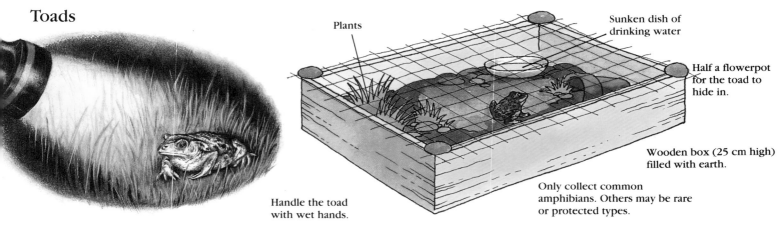

Plants

Sunken dish of drinking water

Half a flowerpot for the toad to hide in.

Wooden box (25 cm high) filled with earth.

Handle the toad with wet hands.

Only collect common amphibians. Others may be rare or protected types.

During the breeding season, visit ponds at night in March and April. When a male toad croaks, shine a torch at him, and he will freeze. Take him home in a wet plastic box with air holes.

Make a box like this and put netting over it to stop the toad jumping out. Keep it in the shade, either in the garden or indoors. Return it to the pond's edge, in the autumn, so it can hibernate.

Feed the toad twice a week with live earthworms, slugs and insects. Offer it small pieces of meat held in tweezers and move it about to make it look alive. Keep the dish filled with fresh water.

Newts

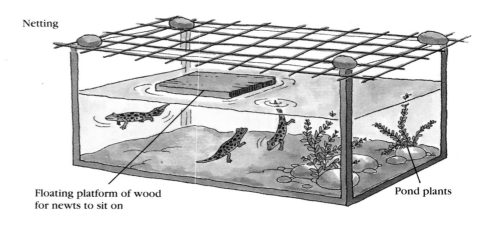

Stick for fishing rod

Cotton line

Matchstick float

Worm

Netting

Floating platform of wood for newts to sit on

Pond plants

In early spring, fish for newts or catch them in a net. When the newt bites the worm bait, pull the line in. Take it home in a jar with some pond water. Do not collect rare types of newt.

Keep newts in an aquarium in a light place, but not in direct sunlight. In August, take them back to the edge of the same pond, so that they can find a place to hibernate during the cold months.

Feed young newts and tadpoles on Water Fleas from the pond. Feed adult newts on earthworms and small bits of raw meat dropped into the water. Keep a diary as the young develop and grow.

Other water animals

Worms and leeches

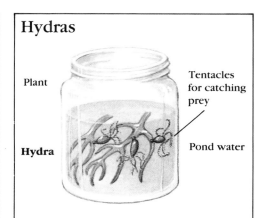

Suckers for holding on to prey

Tubifex Worms **Horse Leech**

There are many kinds of worms and leeches in fresh water. The Tubifex Worm lives head down in a tube of mud. Leeches swim about hunting for fish, frogs, insect larvae and snails.

Hydras

Plant

Tentacles for catching prey

Hydra

Pond water

These tiny plant-like animals contract into blobs when disturbed. Leave some water plants in water for an hour to see if there are any Hydras attached to them.

Spiders and mites

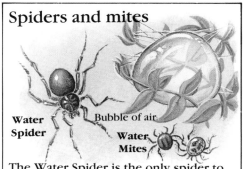

Water Spider

Bubble of air

Water Mites

The Water Spider is the only spider to live under water. It spins a web between plants, then fills it with air collected on its body from the surface. The spider can stay in this "diving bell" for a long time, without surfacing for air. Look for the tiny Water Mites which are related to the spider family.

Animals with shells

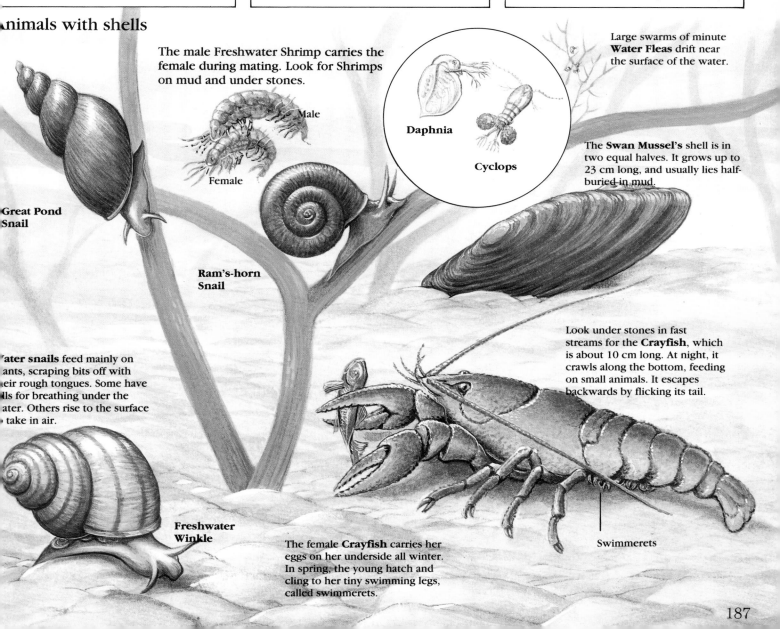

The male Freshwater Shrimp carries the female during mating. Look for Shrimps on mud and under stones.

Male

Female

Daphnia

Cyclops

Large swarms of minute **Water Fleas** drift near the surface of the water.

The **Swan Mussel's** shell is in two equal halves. It grows up to 23 cm long, and usually lies half-buried in mud.

Great Pond Snail

Ram's-horn Snail

Water snails feed mainly on plants, scraping bits off with their rough tongues. Some have gills for breathing under the water. Others rise to the surface to take in air.

Look under stones in fast streams for the **Crayfish**, which is about 10 cm long. At night, it crawls along the bottom, feeding on small animals. It escapes backwards by flicking its tail.

Freshwater Winkle

The female **Crayfish** carries her eggs on her underside all winter. In spring, the young hatch and cling to her tiny swimming legs, called swimmerets.

Swimmerets

More freshwater life you can spot

Fish

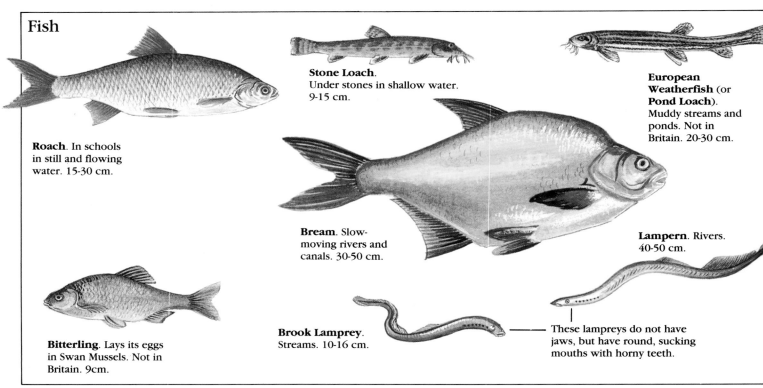

Stone Loach. Under stones in shallow water. 9-15 cm.

European Weatherfish (or **Pond Loach**). Muddy streams and ponds. Not in Britain. 20-30 cm.

Roach. In schools in still and flowing water. 15-30 cm.

Bream. Slow-moving rivers and canals. 30-50 cm.

Lampern. Rivers. 40-50 cm.

Brook Lamprey. Streams. 10-16 cm.

These lampreys do not have jaws, but have round, sucking mouths with horny teeth.

Bitterling. Lays its eggs in Swan Mussels. Not in Britain. 9cm.

Plants

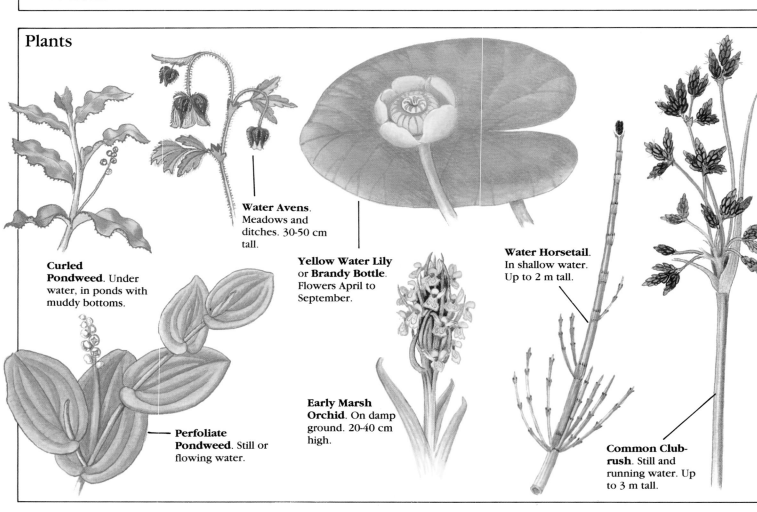

Water Avens. Meadows and ditches. 30-50 cm tall.

Curled Pondweed. Under water, in ponds with muddy bottoms.

Yellow Water Lily or **Brandy Bottle**. Flowers April to September.

Water Horsetail. In shallow water. Up to 2 m tall.

Perfoliate Pondweed. Still or flowing water.

Early Marsh Orchid. On damp ground. 20-40 cm high.

Common Club-rush. Still and running water. Up to 3 m tall.

If you cannot see the fish or plant you want to identify here, you may be able to find it earlier in this part of the book.

Toads

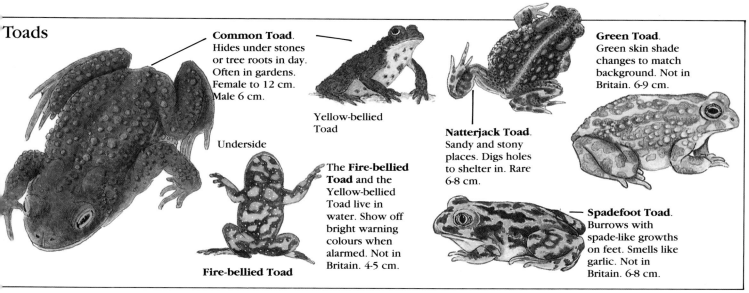

Common Toad. Hides under stones or tree roots in day. Often in gardens. Female to 12 cm. Male 6 cm.

Yellow-bellied Toad

Underside

The **Fire-bellied Toad** and the Yellow-bellied Toad live in water. Show off bright warning colours when alarmed. Not in Britain. 4-5 cm.

Fire-bellied Toad

Natterjack Toad. Sandy and stony places. Digs holes to shelter in. Rare 6-8 cm.

Green Toad. Green skin shade changes to match background. Not in Britain. 6-9 cm.

Spadefoot Toad. Burrows with spade-like growths on feet. Smells like garlic. Not in Britain. 6-8 cm.

Frogs

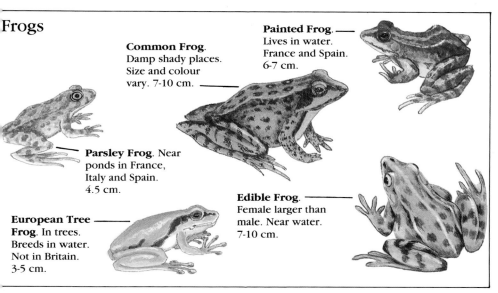

Common Frog. Damp shady places. Size and colour vary. 7-10 cm.

Painted Frog. Lives in water. France and Spain. 6-7 cm.

Parsley Frog. Near ponds in France, Italy and Spain. 4.5 cm.

Edible Frog. Female larger than male. Near water. 7-10 cm.

European Tree Frog. In trees. Breeds in water. Not in Britain. 3-5 cm.

Tortoise

European Pond Tortoise. Muddy ponds and marshes. Central and southern Europe. Up to 36 cm.

Newts

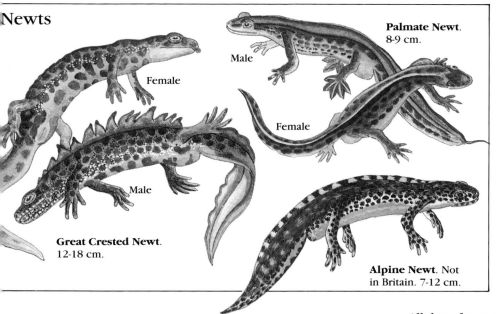

Female

Male

Female

Male

Palmate Newt. 8-9 cm.

Great Crested Newt. 12-18 cm.

Alpine Newt. Not in Britain. 7-12 cm.

Snakes

Viperine Snake. Often in water. Zigzag markings like **Adder**, but harmless. Southern Europe. 1 m.

Tesselated Snake. Very good swimmer. Central and southern Europe. 1.5 m.

Water insects and their young

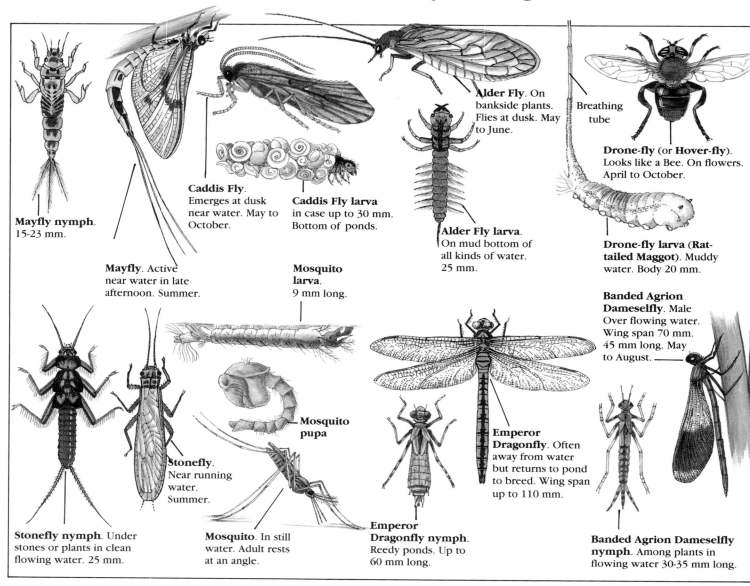

Mayfly nymph.
15-23 mm.

Mayfly. Active near water in late afternoon. Summer.

Caddis Fly. Emerges at dusk near water. May to October.

Caddis Fly larva in case up to 30 mm. Bottom of ponds.

Mosquito larva. 9 mm long.

Alder Fly. On bankside plants. Flies at dusk. May to June.

Alder Fly larva. On mud bottom of all kinds of water. 25 mm.

Breathing tube

Drone-fly (or Hover-fly). Looks like a Bee. On flowers. April to October.

Drone-fly larva (Rat-tailed Maggot). Muddy water. Body 20 mm.

Stonefly. Near running water. Summer.

Stonefly nymph. Under stones or plants in clean flowing water. 25 mm.

Mosquito pupa

Mosquito. In still water. Adult rests at an angle.

Emperor Dragonfly. Often away from water but returns to pond to breed. Wing span up to 110 mm.

Emperor Dragonfly nymph. Reedy ponds. Up to 60 mm long.

Banded Agrion Dameselfly. Male Over flowing water. Wing span 70 mm. 45 mm long. May to August.

Banded Agrion Dameselfly nymph. Among plants in flowing water 30-35 mm long.

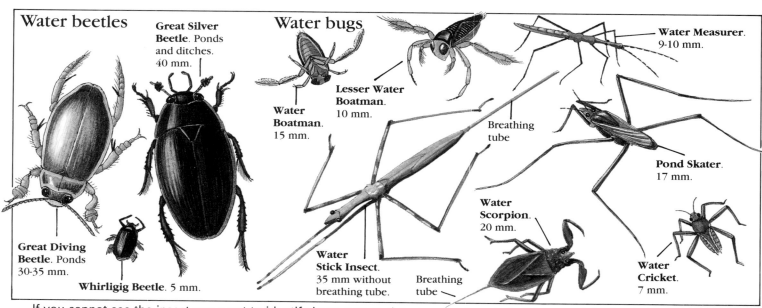

Water beetles

Great Silver Beetle. Ponds and ditches. 40 mm.

Great Diving Beetle. Ponds 30-35 mm.

Whirligig Beetle. 5 mm.

Water bugs

Water Boatman. 15 mm.

Lesser Water Boatman. 10 mm.

Water Measurer. 9-10 mm.

Breathing tube

Pond Skater. 17 mm.

Water Stick Insect. 35 mm without breathing tube.

Breathing tube

Water Scorpion. 20 mm.

Water Cricket. 7 mm.

If you cannot see the insect you want to identify here, turn to the pages on insects in this part of the book. You may be able to see a picture of it there.

Birds

Measurements are from beak to tip of tail.

Grey Heron. Nests in trees. Feeds in shallow water and marshes. 90 cm.

Osprey. Dives to catch fish in claws. Rare. A few breed in Scotland. 51-58 cm.

Mallard. Most common duck. Often in parks. 58 cm.

Female

Male

Chick

Great Crested Grebe. In lakes and reservoirs. Winters also on coast. 48 cm.

Winter

Summer

Female

Male

Teal. Europe's smallest duck. 35 cm.

Coot. Lives in flocks outside breeding season. Notice white mark on head. 38 cm.

Chick

Snipe. Hides among plants near water, where it feeds. Long bill for probing in mud. 27 cm.

Chick

Moorhen. Common in parks. Notice white flash under tail. 33 cm.

Water Rail. Hides in reed beds. 28 cm.

Spotted Crake. White spotted body. Feeds at water edge at dusk. Very secretive. 23 cm.

Summer

Winter

Black-headed Gull. Loses dark cap in winter. 35-38 cm.

Swallow. Summer visitor. Catches insects on the wing. 19 cm.

Yellow Wagtail. Lives in Britain. Blue-headed Wagtail in Central Europe. Other varieties in Europe (see below). 16.5 cm.

Yellow Wagtail

Pied wagtail

Female

Scandinavia

Blue headed wagtail

White Wagtail

Male

Grey Wagtail. Lives near fast-flowing streams. 18 cm.

Italy

Spain and France

White Wagtail. Lives in Europe. Pied Wagtail in Britain. 18 cm.

Reed Bunting. By rivers and in marshy places. 15 cm.

you cannot see the bird you want to identify here, turn to the pages earlier in the book on birds, and you may be able to see a

Index

Abdomen, 132
Acacia, False, 43, 49, 63
Accentor, Hedge, 118
Acid rain, 167
Aconite, Winter, 78
Acorn, 48, 49, 50
Adder, 125
Ageratum, 151
Agrimony, 75
Alder, Common, 43, 62
Algae, 166, 167, 168
Almond, 61
Alyssum, 151
Amphibians, 184-185, 186-187, 189
Anemone, Wood, 57, 66, 71, 85
Ant, 108, 112, 136, 139, 145, 152
   Black, 112, 139, 158
   Red, 135, 158
   Wood, 50, 158
   Worker, 112
   Yellow meadow, 158
Annual rings, 52
Antenna, 110, 112
Anthers, 73
Aphid, 54, 122, 135, 149, 152
Apple, 36, 50
   Crab, 47, 49, 61
Archangel, Yellow, 85
Arrowhead, 128
Arum, 78, 85
Ash, 40, 43, 49, 63
   Mountain, see
   Rowan
Assassin bug, 158
Aster, Sea, 86
Aubretia, 111
Avens, Water, 75, 81, 94, 188
Avocet, 22

Bacteria, 167
Badger, 57
Bark, 37, 38, 45, 52, 53, 54, 55
   Rubbings, 45
Bat, 123
   Daubenton's, 180
   Long-eared, 57, 123
   Pipistrelle, 27
Beaks, 18, 22, 23
Bearberry, Alpine, 90
Beaver, 181
Bedstraw, Lady's, 93
Beech, 38, 39, 40, 41, 43, 45, 62, 84
Bee, 36, 101, 104, 112, 113, 136, 144, 145, 146, 147, 149, 150, 152-153, 159
   Bumble, 101, 112, 130, 135, 151, 159
   Flower, 138, 159
   Honey, 151, 159
   Leaf cutter, 113, 159
   Mining, 126, 159
   Potter, see Flower
   Solitary, 104
Beetle, 59, 121, 123, 136, 145, 146, 149, 151, 156

Beetle (cont.)
   Bacon, 156
   Bark, 138
   Burying, 149
   Cardinal, 100, 138, 156
   Click, 103, 147, 156
   Cockchafer, 54, 103, 124, 135, 141, 146
   Colorado, 126
   Devil's Coach Horse, 105, 134, 139
   Dor, 138, 146, 149
   Dung, 138, 156
   Elm Bark, 54, 156
   Four-spot carrion, 141
   Garden Chafer, 126, 151
   Great diving, 142, 143, 155, 164, 166, 177, 190
   Great silver, 143, 176, 178, 190
   Greater Stag, 57
   Ground, 122, 135, 139
   Leaf, 156
   Longhorn, 141, 145
   Oak bark, 140
   Pea, 126
   Rose Chafer, 126, 138
   Rove, 138
   Stag, 137, 156
   Tiger, 149
   Timberman, 56
   Violet ground, 138
   Wasp, 113, 156
   Whirligig, 142, 143, 176, 190
Bilberry, 90
Bindweed, 108, 150
   Field, 94, 150
   Sea, 87
Birch, silver, 41, 44, 45, 62
Bird,
   Bath, 10
   Feeding, 105
   Nest, 104
   Table, 10, 105
Birds, 172-173, 174-175, 191
Bistort, Amphibious, 79
Bitterling, 188
Bittern, 172, 173
Blackbird, 7, 10, 11, 15, 28, 101, 118
Blackcap, 27
Blackcap, 27
Bladderwort, 171
   Great, 171
Bluebell, 57, 67, 71, 84
Box, 38
Bracken, 56
Bream, 188
Bristle tail, 159
Broadleaved trees, 37, 38, 40-44, 48, 49, 51, 53, 56, 57, 61-63
Bryony, 108
   White, 92
Buddleia, 111, 151
Buds, 36, 37, 39, 42-43
Bugle, 71, 85, 107
Bugloss, Viper's, 86, 95
Bugs, 136, 158

Bullfinch, 11, 29, 118
Bullhead, 183
Bunting, Reed, 4, 6, 191
Burdock,
   Greater, 82
   Lesser, 108
Bur-reed, Unbranched, 169
Buttercup, 68
   Bulbous, 93
   Creeping, 81
   Field, 70
Butterfly, 101, 110, 111, 136, 137, 144, 146, 147, 149, 150, 151, 155, 156
   Brimstone, 111
   Brown hairstreak, 137
   Chalk hill blue, 130
   Clouded yellow, 135
   Comma, 111
   Common blue, 130, 150, 156
   Gatekeeper, 124
   Grayling, 125
   Green-veined White, 111, 148, 156
   Hedge Brown, 124
   Holly Blue, 104
   Large skipper, 151
   Large White, 110, 137, 156
   Meadow Brown, 111, 137, 139, 156
   Orange-tip, 101, 148, 156
   Peacock, 104, 111, 126, 131, 139
   Red Admiral, 111, 156
   Ringlet, 124
   Silver-washed Fritillary, 139
   Small Copper, 111, 138
   Small Tortoiseshell, 110, 111, 126, 139, 148
   Small White, 111, 126, 156
   Speckled Wood, 57, 156
   Swallow-tail, 135
   Wall, 156
   Wall brown, 138
Butterwort,
   Common, 90
Buzzard, 24, 30

Cabbage, Wild, 93
Calla, Marsh, 129
Candytuft, 151
Calyx, 70
Cambium, 37, 52
Campion,
   Bladder, 92
   Moss, 91
   Red, 71, 94
   Sea, 87
   White, 89
Capsid Bug, 126, 141, 158
Carp, 182
Carrot, Wild, 150

Caterpillar, 103, 110, 111, 126-127, 131, 135, 136, 139, 140, 141, 145, 146, 148, 154, 155
   Green Tortrix, 54
   Looper, 135, 146
   Pine Looper, 54
   Sawfly, 54
   Tent, 54
Catkins, 43, 47
Cedar, 40, 48, 60
Celandine, Lesser, 85
Centipede, 101, 114, 132
Chaffinch, 3, 5, 10, 18, 29, 118
Chamomile, 89, 93
Cherry, 43, 46, 61, 49
Chestnut, 36, 39, 40, 41, 42, 63
   Sweet, 43, 49, 50, 61
Chickweed, 108
Chicory, 95
Chiffchaff, 18
Chlorophyll, 37, 40, 41
Chrysanthemum, 107
Cinquefoil, Creeping, 83
Clary, 80
Clematis, Wild, 82, 83
Cloudberry, 92
Clover, 106, 151
   Red, 80, 94
   White, 86, 88, 107
Cockroach, 134, 145, 148, 158
Common flower bug, 149
Coltsfoot, 83, 109
Columbine, 71, 95
Comfrey, Common, 80
Compost, 100, 101, 107, 108
Cones, 48
Conifer trees, 37, 39, 40, 48, 51, 56, 60
Conker, 39
Coot, 15, 16, 30, 174, 191
Coppicing, 44
Cord-grass, Common, 96
Cork, 45
Cormorant, 23, 31
Corn-cockle, 94
Cornflower, 95
Cotoneaster, 104
Cow Parsley, 71, 82, 92
Cowslip, 78, 125
Crake, Spotted, 191
Cranesbill, Bloody, 71
Crayfish, 187
Creeping Jenny, 81
Cricket, 134, 144, 154
   Bush, 134
   House, 138, 159
   Mole, 146
   Oak bush, 159
   Short-winged Conehead, 124
   Speckled bush, 101, 159
   Water, 143, 190
Crocus, Autumn, 78
Crossbill, 9, 18, 56
Crow, 6, 7, 9, 15, 21, 31
Crowfoot, Water, 79, 129, 168

Cuckoo, 29
Cuckoo Flower, 95, 125
Cuckoo Spit, 113, 139
Curlew, 6, 7, 8, 22, 31
Cyclops, 187
Cypress, Lawson, 40, 60

Dace, 183
Daffodil, Wild, 78
Dahlia, 107
Daisy, 74, 89, 92, 106
   Michaelmas, 104, 111, 150
Damselfly, 142, 143, 164, 176
   Banded agrion, 142, 190
   Common, 156
   Common blue, 143
   Large red, 156
Dandelion, 75, 82, 88, 109, 151
Daphnia, 187
Deer, 55, 56, 57
Dipper, 25, 174
Dock, Curled, 109
Dog Rose, 67, 78, 82, 83, 94
Dog's Mercury, 74, 84
Dove,
   Collared, 15, 30
   Rock, 21
Dragonfly, 136, 142, 149, 154, 176, 178, 179
   Broad-bodied darter, 156
   Common hawker, 156
   Emperor, 131, 135, 190
   Larva, 166
   Southern Aeshna, 120
Duck, 16-17, 173
   Tufted, 17, 30, 172
Duckweed, 79, 168
   Ivy, 171
Dunlin, 22
Dunnock, 11, 15, 29

Eagle, Golden, 24
Earthworm, 57, 59, 102
   Brandling, 101
Earwig, 112, 134, 136, 138, 158
Eel, 183
Elm, 43, 44, 49, 62
   Elver, 183
Enchanter's Nightshade, 78
Eyes, 132, 144

Fat Hen, 127
Feathers, 8, 173
Feelers, 145
Feltwort, Autumn, 78
Fern, 109
   Broad Buckler, 56
   Maidenhair
   Spleenwort, 109
Fertilization, 47, 72
Feverfew, 92, 106
Fig, 63
Fir, 48, 51, 60
Fish, 182-183, 188
Flag, Yellow, 121
Flax, Blue, 95

Flea, 148
   Cat, 159
   Water, 166, 171, 187
Fleabane, 77, 90
Flight, 6
Flower map, 69
Flowers, 36, 39, 46
Flowers, pressing, 76
Fly, 136, 146, 147, 158
   Alder, 135, 143, 158, 178, 190
   Bee-fly, 126, 134, 158
   Blackfly, 126, 158
   Blowfly, see Bluebottle
   Bluebottle, 137, 144, 149
   Caddis, 135, 143, 155, 178-179, 190
   Cranefly, 103, 126, 134, 139, 158
   Drone-fly, 150, 178, 190
   Flesh, 158
   Greenbottle, 126
   Greenfly, 112, 113, 140, 148, 149
   Horse, 134, 148
   House, 134, 135, 147, 149
   Hover, 100, 113, 134, 143, 149, 151, 158
   Robber, 128, 149, 158
   Sawfly, 54, 135, 159
   Scorpion, 126, 135, 158
   Snake, 135, 158
   Snipe, 138
   St Mark's, 158
   Whitefly, 126, 158
Fly Agaric, 56
Fly Catcher,
   Pied, 18
   Spotted, 119
Food webs, 102
Footprint cast, 9
Forestry, 51
Forget-me-Not,
   Alpine, 91
   Water, 81, 169
Forsythia, 42
Fossil fuels, 167
Fox, 56, 123
Foxglove, 66, 71, 74, 82, 113, 150
Fritillary, 69, 107
Frog, 166, 184, 186
   Breeding, 184
   Common, 100, 121, 184, 189
   Edible, 184, 189
   European Tree, 189
   Painted, 189
   Parsley, 189
Frogbit, 79, 129, 168, 171
Froghopper, 113, 134, 139, 158
Frogspawn, 120, 184, 186
Fruit, 36, 39, 46, 48-49, 72
Fulmar, 23
Fumitory, 94
Fungus, 54-55, 104, 109
   Bracket, 121

Fungus (cont.)
Fairy-ring Toadstool, 109
Honey, 54
Poor Man's Beefsteak, 57
Purple Stereum, 109
White Pine Blister Rust, 54

Galls, 54, 55, 155
Gannet, 23
Garlic, Triangular-stalked, 128
Gean, 61
Geranium, 151
Girdle scar, 36, 37, 52
Glow-worm, 122, 156
Gnat, 137, 142, 143
Goldcrest, 18, 28, 56
Golden Eagle, 24
Goldeneye, 17
Golden Rain, 63
Golden Rod, 89, 106, 151
Goldfinch, 10, 29, 119
Goldfish, 120
Goosander, 173
Goose, 6, 172, 173
Brent, 22
Greylag, 173, 174
Gnat, 179
Gorse, 90, 93, 125
Grass, 96, 151
Arrow Grass, Sea, 86
Cocksfoot, 96
Cordgrass, Common, 96
Cotton-grass, 97
Couch Grass, 86, 107
Fescue, 96, 97
Giant Fescue, 97
Goosegrass, 108
Italian Rye, 96
Marram, 96
Meadow Fescue, 96
Meadow Grass, Annual, 107
Quaking, 97
Reed, 96
Reed Fescue, 96
Rye, 107
Sand Couch, 96
Timothy, 96
Grasshopper, 134, 136, 144, 146, 154
Common Field, 125, 134
Common Green, 159
Meadow, 139
Grayling, 183
Grebe,
Great Crested, 16, 30, 173, 174, 191
Little, 175
Greenfinch, 7, 11, 15, 29, 118
Greenhouse effect, 56
Groundsel, 93
Grouse, 24, 25, 56
Gudgeon, 182
Guillemot, 23
Gull, 17

Gull (cont.)
Black-headed, 7, 9, 20, 30, 191
Herring, 30

Habitat, 100, 107, 124
Hardwood, 38, 53
Harebell, 71, 91, 95, 125
Harvestman, 126
Hawfinch, 9, 18
Hawkweed, Mouse-Ear, 71
Hazel, 39
Heartsease, 85
Heartwood, 37, 52
Heath, 125
Heather, 90, 91, 125
Hedgehog, 57, 101, 104, 122
Helleborine, 74, 85
Hemlock, Western, 48, 60
Herb, 106
Herb Robert, 67, 83
Heron, 6, 9, 15, 166
Grey, 7, 17, 31, 175, 191
Hogweed, 92, 150
Holly, 37, 40, 61
Sea, 86, 95
Honeydew, 112
Honeysuckle, 82, 83, 122, 123, 151
Hornbeam, 62
Hornet, 126, 139, 159
Horsetail, Water, 188
Humus, 56

Ice Plant, 110, 111
Insects, 47, 54, 160, 161, 170, 176-177, 178-179
Antenna, 176
Aquarium, 177
Egg, 178
Flying, 177
Larva, 177, 178
Nymph, 177, 178
Pupa, 179
Iris, Yellow, 79, 170
Ivy, 57, 104

Jackdaw, 8, 31
Jay, 5, 8, 18
Juniper, 48

Kale, Sea, 87
Kestrel, 20, 29
Kingfisher, 15, 17, 29, 172, 175

Laburnum, 63
Lacewing, 135, 137
Common golden eye, 141
Green, 135, 139, 158
Ladybird, 154
10-spot, 141
14-spot, 124
22-spot, 156
Seven-spot, 125, 130, 149, 156
Two-spot, 101, 134, 156
Lady's Mantle, Alpine, 91
Lampern, 188

Lamprey, Brook, 188
Lapwing, 15, 30
Larch,
European, 39, 46, 48, 60
Japanese, 60
Larkspur, Field, 95
Larva, 103, 134, 136-137, 139, 141, 142-143, 154, 155, 177, 178
Lavender, Sea, 86, 95
Lawn, 106
Leafhopper, 158
Potato, 126
Leatherjacket, 103
Leaves, 36, 37, 38, 40-41, 54, 59, 70, 71
Leech, Horse, 187
Lichen, 56
Lily-of-the-valley, 106
Lily,
Tiger, 150
Water, 79, 93, 120, 170, 171, 188
Lime, Common, 38, 40, 43, 44, 62
Linnet, 29
Loach, 188
Locust Tree, 63
Loosestrife, 78, 79, 94
Louse, Book, 159

Magnolia, 43
Maggot, Rat-tailed, 178, 190
Magpie, 6, 8, 21, 31
Maidenhair Tree, 41
Mallard, 15, 16, 17, 30, 172, 175, 191
Mallow, 76, 78
Mammals, 180-181
Mandible, 149
Maple, 38, 40, 63
Marestail, 169
Marigold, 106
Bur, 79
Marsh, 66, 80, 93, 120, 169
Martin,
House, 13, 15, 21, 28, 119
Pine, 56
Sand, 15, 28, 174
Mayfly, 135, 142, 176, 190
Green drake, 159
Nymph, 164
Meadow Pipit, 24
Meadowsweet, 128, 169
Melilot, White, 92
Mezereon, 107
Midge, 143
Migration, 26-27
Milfoil,
Spiked Water, 79
Water, 168, 170
Milkwort, Common, 95
Millipede, 59, 114, 132
Pill, 114
Spotted Snake, 114
Miner, Leaf, 54, 148
Mink, European, 181

Minnow, 182, 183
Mint, Water, 170
Mirid Bug, Green, 149
Mistletoe, 57
Mite,
Red Velvet, 126
Soil, 102
Water, 187
Mole, 102, 103
Monkey Flower, 93
Moor, 125
Moorhen, 15, 16, 17, 30, 172, 191
Chick, 165
Mosquito, 134, 148, 149, 190
Moss, 57, 90, 104, 109
Bog, 90
Silky Wall Feather, 109
Moth, 103, 110, 111, 121, 123, 136, 150-151, 154, 157
Angle shades, 157
Blood vein, 157
Brimstone, 157
Brown China mark, 142, 143
Buff Tip, 126, 148, 157
Burnished Brass, 123, 157
Common swift, 141
Dark arches, 139
Dot, 101, 103, 157
Drinker, 125, 139, 157
Elephant Hawk, 123, 127
Emperor, 125, 145
Engrailed, 138
Eyed Hawk, 100, 157
Five-spot burnet, 135
Forester, 130
Garden tiger, 138
Ghost swift, 157
Goat, 140
Green oak-roller, 141
Grey dagger, 148
Hawk, 147, 151
Heart and Dart, 123
Herald, 138, 157
Lackey, 110, 157
Large yellow underwing, 138
Leopard, 140
Looper, 135
Magpie, 127, 148, 157
Maiden's blush, 140
Mottled umber, 140
Oak beauty, 140
Oak Eggar, 125
Pale tussock, 157
Poplar Hawk, 111, 157
Puss, 138, 148, 157
Red-green carpet, 140
Scalloped oak, 157
Silver-Y, 123, 157
Six-spot burnet, 131, 157
Small magpie, 157
Swallow-tailed, 126
Turnip, 139

Moth (cont.)
Vapourer, 126, 157
Woolly Bear, 111
Yellowtail, 139, 148, 157
Moulting, birds, 17
Mouse, 101, 122
Muskrat, 181
Mussel, Swan, 187

Nectar, 36, 74, 101, 104, 110, 113, 150-151, 153
Guides, 74
Nesting box, 12-13
Nests, 14-15, 23
Nettle, 108, 151
Red Dead, 108
Stinging, 82, 83, 107
White Dead, 92
Newts, 184-185, 186, 189
Alpine, 189
Common or Smooth, 100, 120, 185
Great Crested, 165, 189
Palmate, 189
Nightingale, 15, 18
Nightjar, 19
Nightshade, Enchanter's, 78
Nuthatch, 2, 5, 9, 15, 19, 28, 57, 118
Nuts, 49
Nymph, 136, 142, 154

Oak, 38, 39, 51, 54, 55, 57, 84
Common, 140-141
Cork, 45
English or Pedunculate, 38, 40, 44, 45, 62
Holm, 61
Red, 41
Turkey, 43, 62
Oat, Wild, 97
Olive, 61
Ophion, Yellow, 139, 159
Orange, 50, 61
Orchid,
Early Marsh, 188
Early Purple, 85
Marsh, 81
Military, 69
Osprey, 191
Otter, 181
Ouzel, Ring, 25
Ovary, 46, 47, 49, 68, 72, 170
Ovule, 46, 47, 48, 49, 72
Owl, 9
Barn, 30
Eagle, 19
Little, 19
Long-eared, 19, 56
Pygmy, 19
Scops, 19
Short-eared, 24
Tawny, 18, 19, 57, 122
Oxygen, 37, 166
Oystercatcher, 8, 22

Palm trees, 39, 52
Pansy, 15, 88, 113

Pea, Sea, 87
Pennycress, Field, 92
Pennywort, Wall, 89
Perch, 166, 182
Perforate St John's Wort, 93
Petals, 68, 70, 71
Pheasant, 15, 31, 57, 125
Pheasant's Eye, 94
Phloem, 37, 45, 52
Pied Fly Catcher, 18
Pigeon, 21
Pimpernel,
Scarlet, 71
Yellow, 78
Pine,
Corsican, 40, 60
Scots, 37, 39, 44, 45, 48, 60
Stone, 48
Pink, Sea, 124
Pike, 182
Pintail, 17, 173
Pistil, 72, 73
Plane, London, 38, 43, 49, 63
Plantain,
Floating Water, 128
Greater, 106
Ribwort, 88, 127
Sea, 86
Water, 169
Plantation, 51
Plover,
Golden, 25
Little Ringed, 175
Plywood, 53
Pochard, 175
Policeman's Helmet, 75, 79, 94
Pollarding, 44
Pollen, 36, 46, 47, 72, 74, 112, 150-151, 153, 170
Pollination, 46, 47, 72, 75
Pollution, 167
Pond, 120-121, 164-165, 167, 168-169, 182
Food chains, 166
Pondskater, 120, 165
Pond survey, 164-165
Pondweed, 166, 168, 171, 188
Poplar, 38, 40, 41, 43, 44, 62
Poppy,
Common, 72, 73, 106
Yellow Horned, 87, 93
Primrose, 57, 71, 84, 124
Evening, 89
Proboscis, 110
Ptarmigan, 25
Puffin, 23
Pupa, 103, 110, 179
Purslane, Sea, 86

Rabbit, 55, 57, 125
Ragwort, 86, 89
Rail, Water, 191
Rat, Brown, 180
Tracks, 181
Rattle, Yellow, 80, 93
Raven, 25

Razorbill, 23
Redshank, 173
Redstart, 124
   Black, 20
Redwing, 27
Redwood, Dawn, 41
Reeds, 96, 168
Rest-Harrow, 94
Rhizome, 169, 170, 171
Roach, 188
Robin, 7, 11, 15, 29, 118
Rocket, Sea, 75, 86, 92
Rockrose, Common, 93
Rock Sea Spurrey, 87
Roller, Leaf, 54
Rook, 15, 31, 57
Roots, 54, 108, 109
Rose, 107
   Burnet, 124
   Dog, 67, 78, 82, 83, 94
Rowan, 41, 49, 63
Rudd, 182
Rushes, 97
   Club-rush, Common,
   188
   Compact, 97, 170
   Flowering, 79
   Soft, 97, 169
   Spike-rush,
   Common, 97

Salmon, 183
Sandpiper, Common,
173
Sap, 37, 45, 52
Sapwood, 37, 52
Sawbill, 16
Saxifrage, 91
Scale Insects, 54
Scorpion,
   False, 126
   Water, 143, 176, 177,
   178, 190
Seablite, Shrubby, 87
Sedges, 97, 169
Seedling, 36, 37, 50, 51
Seeds, 36, 39, 46, 48-49,
50, 51, 108, 170
Sepal, 46, 68, 70, 71, 72
Shag, 23
Sheep's Bit, 90
Shelduck, 22
Shepherd's Purse, 88
Shield Bug, 126, 134,
158
   Curled, 188

Shield Bug (cont.)
   Green, 134
   Hawthorn, 158, 168,
   171
   Perfoliate, 188
   Pied, 158
Shoveler, 16, 172
Shrew,
   Common, 57, 123
   Water, 165, 180
Shrike,
   Great Grey, 25
   Redbacked, 25
Shrimps, 166
   Freshwater, 187
Silverfish, 139, 159
Silverweed, 93
Siskin, 2-3
Skylark, 20, 29
Slow Worm, 105, 127
Slug, 132
   Black, 56
   Garden, 115
   Great Grey, 115
   Large Black, 127
   Netted, 127
   Shelled, 102
Snail, 102, 114-115, 132
   Brown-lipped, 101,
   115
   Garden, 114
   Great Pond, 120, 165,
   187
   Ramshorn, 120, 187
   Strawberry, 127
Snake,
   Adder, 125
   Grass, 185
   Tesselated, 189
   Viperine, 189
Snipe, 191
Snowdrop, 78
Soapwort, 78, 94
Softwood, 38, 53
Soil, 102-103
Solomon's Seal, 85
Sorrel, Wood, 85
Sparrow,
   House, 11, 12, 29, 118
   Tree, 12, 29
Sparrowhawk, 6, 8
Speedwell, 67
   Creeping, 95
   Germander, 85
Spider, 59, 116-117,
160-161

Spider (cont.)
   Babies, 161
   Cocoon, 161
   Crab, 117
   Dysdera, 126
   Eggs, 161
   Garden, 116, 117, 160
   House, 116
   Hunting, 117, 161
   Money, 116
   Nursery tent, 117,
   161
   Wall, 116
   Water, 161, 165, 187
   Wolf, 117
   Zebra, 117
Spider web, 116, 117,
160-161
   Hammock, 160
   Orb, 160
   Sheet, 160
Spike-rush, Common, 97
Spore, 54, 55
Springtail, 147, 176
   Water, 159
Spurge, Petty, 127
Squirrel, 55
   Grey, 56, 121
   Red, 56, 121
Stamen, 46, 68, 72, 73,
   150, 170
Starling, 11, 21, 27, 28,
   119
Star-of-Bethlehem, 92
Stick Insect, Water, 177,
   190
Stickleback, 165, 168,
   177
   Three-spined, 183
Stigma, 46, 47, 68, 72,
   150
Stitchwort, Greater, 78,
   83, 92
Stock, Night Scented,
   123
Stonechat, 3, 15
Stonecrop, White, 92
Stonefly, 159, 190
Stork, White, 27
Strawberry, Wild, 83
Sundew, 91, 171
Swallow, 15, 17, 21, 26,
   28, 119, 168, 191
Swan,
   Bewick's, 31
   Mute, 17, 31, 174

Swan (cont.)
   Whooper, 31
Sweet William, 151
Swift, 20, 28, 119, 172
Sycamore, 36, 38, 39,
   43, 50, 63

Tadpole, 120, 143, 166,
   168, 177, 184, 185
Teal, 162, 191
Teasel, Common, 82, 95
Tern, 6
   Arctic, 26
   Common, 22, 23
   Sandwich, 8
Thistle, 151
   Creeping, 127
   Marsh, 80
   Prickly Sow, 88
Thorax, 132
Thrift, 87
Thrip, Onion, 159
Thrush,
   Mistle, 11, 15, 28, 119
   Song, 9, 11, 14, 15, 28,
   102, 104, 115
Thyme, 151
Tit, 15
   Blue, 2, 11, 12, 28,
   57, 119
   Coal, 11, 18, 28
   Great, 8, 9, 28, 118
   Long-tailed, 15, 20, 28
Toadflax,
   Common, 89
   Ivy-leaved, 88, 127
Toads, 184-185, 186,
189
   Common, 57, 105,
   122, 185, 189
   Fire-bellied, 189
   Green, 189
   Natterjack, 189
   Spadefoot, 189
   Yellow-bellied, 189
Toadspawn, 120, 185
Toadstool, 109, 121
   Fairy-ring, 109
Tortoise, European
   Pond, 189
Touch-me-not, 171
Treecreeper, 7, 28,
56, 118
Trefoil, Bird's-foot, 83,
86, 106, 107
tree survey, 58-59

Trout, 183
Tulip Tree, 39, 63
Turnstone, 7
Twigs, 41, 42-43, 52

Underwater viewer, 179

Valerian, 123
   Common, 81
   Red, 94
Vegetable patch, 107,
   126
Vetch, 91,93, 95
Violet,
   Common Dog, 85
   Marsh, 95
   Sweet, 78
Voles,
   Field, 55
   Tracks, 181
   Water, 180, 181

Waders, 22
Wagtail,
   Blue Headed, 191
   Grey, 7, 191
   Pied, 29, 118, 191
   White, 29, 191
   Yellow, 124, 191
Wallflower, 87, 88, 111,
   151
Walnut, 43, 49, 63
Warbler,
   Garden, 18
   Reed, 174
   Willow, 4, 27
Wasp, 104, 112, 113,
   135, 138, 146, 147,
   149, 150, 159
   Common, 112, 159
   Digger, 126
   Gall, 54, 141, 159
   Giant wood, 148
   Mournful, 104
   Red-banded sand, 149
   Sand, 124, 159
   Tree, 132
   Wall Mason, 100, 138
Water Boatman, 121,
   142, 146, 158, 176,
   177, 190
   Lesser, 143, 177, 190
Watercress, 169
Water Measurer,
   142, 176, 190

Water Plants, 168-169,
   170-171
Water Soldier, 79, 129
Waterweed,
   Canadian, 120
Weasel, 125
Weeds, 88, 106, 107, 108
Weevil, 140
   Nettle, 156
   Nut, 54, 140, 148
   Pine, 54
Wheatear, 25
Whitebeam, 43, 62
Whitefly, 126, 158
Wigeon, 17, 172
Willow, 42, 43, 46, 49
   Crack, 40, 47
   Pussy or Goat, 61
   Weeping, 38, 44, 61
Willowherb,
   Great, 170
   Great Hairy, 79, 94
   Rosebay, 70, 75, 89,
   108
Wing-cases, 134
Wings, 8, 134-135, 146
Winkle, Freshwater,
   187
Wireworm, 103, 139
Wood, 53, 54
Woodcock, 19
Woodland, 124
Woodlouse, 59, 101,
   113, 115, 132
Woodpecker, 6, 8, 9, 15
   Black, 19
   Great spotted, 29, 56,
   100
   Green, 4, 19, 29, 57,
   118
   Lesser spotted, 19
Woodpigeon, 15, 30
Woodruff, Sweet, 84
Worm, 57, 59, 101, 102,
   103, 139, 166, 187
Woundwort, Hedge, 94
Wormery, 102
Wren, 15, 28, 104, 118

Yarrow, 92, 127
Yellowhammer, 29
Yew, 38, 46, 48, 60

Zones, Water, 168-169

Illustrated by: Mike Atkinson, Dave Ashby, Graham Austin, John Barber, Amanda Barlow, David Baxter, Andrew Beckett, Joyce Bee, Stephen Bennett, Roland Berry, Isabel Bowring, Hilary Burn, Liz Butler, Lynn Chadwick, Patrick Cox, Christine Darter, Michelle Emblem, Don Forrest, John Francis, Victoria Gordon, Edwina Hannam, Tim Hayward, Christine Howes, Chris Howell-Jones, David Hurrell, Ian Jackson, Roger Kent, Colin King, Deborah King, Jonathan Langley, Richard Lewington, Ken Lilly, Josephine Martin, Malcolm Mcgregor, Doreen McGuinness, Richard Millington, Robert Morton, David Nash, Barbara Nicholson, David Palmer, Julie Piper, Gillian Platt (The Garden Studio), Charles Raymond (Virgil Pomfret Agency), Barry Raynor, Phillip Richardson, Jim Robins, Michèlle Ross, Gwen Simpson, Annabel Spenceley, Peter Stebbing, Joyce Tuhill, David Watson, Phil Weare, Adrian Williams, Roy Wiltshire, John Yates